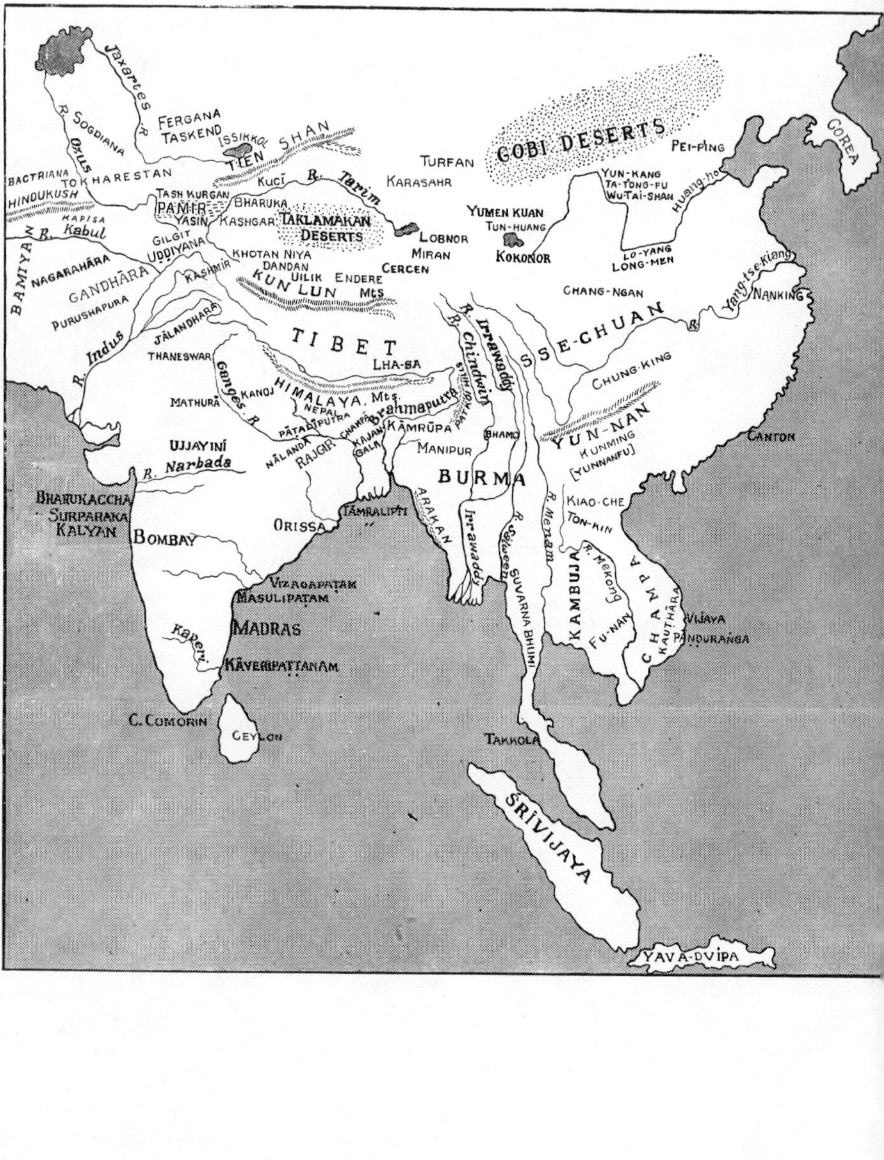
Jaxartes R.
R. Oxus
SOGDIANA
FERGANA
TASKEND
ISSIKKOL
TIEN SHAN
GOBI DESERTS
PEI-PING
COREA
TURFAN
BACTRIANA
TOKHARESTAN
HINDUKUSH
KUCI
R. Tarim
KARASAHR
YUN-KANG
TA-TONG-FU
WU-TAI-SHAN
Huang-ho
TASH KURGAN
PAMIR
BHARUKA
YASIN
KASHGAR
TAKLAMAKAN DESERTS
YUMEN KUAN
TUN-HUANG
KAPISA
R. Kabul
GILGIT
UDDIYANA
LOBNOR
MIRAN
KOKONOR
LO-YANG
LONG-MEN
BAMIYAN
NAGARAHĀRA
KHOTAN NIYA
DANDAN
UILIK
ENDERE
CERCEN
GANDHĀRA
KASHMIR
KUN LUN Mts
CHANG-NGAN
Yang-tse-Kiang
NANKING
PURUSHAPURA
JĀLANDHARA
TIBET
SSE-CHUAN
R. Indus
THANESWAR
LHA-SA
R. Chindwin
R. Irrawaddy
CHUNG-KING
Ganges R.
KANOJ
HIMALAYA. Mts.
MATHURĀ
NEPAL
Brahmaputra
PĀTALIPUTRA
CHAMPĀ
KĀMRŪPA
BHAMO
YUN-NAN
CANTON
UJJAYINĪ
NĀLANDĀ
RAJGIR
KAJANGALA
MANIPUR
KUNMING
[YUNNANFU]
R. Narbada
BURMA
BHARUKACCHA
SURPARAKA
KALYAN
BOMBAY
ORISSA
TĀMRALIPTI
ARAKAN
Irrawaddy
R. Salween
R. Menam
KIAO-CHE
TON-KIN
KAMBUJA
R. Mekong
CHAMPA
KAUTHĀRA
VIJAYA
PĀNDURANGA
VIZAGAPATAM
MASULIPATAM
MADRAS
Kaveri
KĀVERIPATTANAM
SUVARNA BHUMI
FU-NAN
C. COMORIN
CEYLON
TAKKOLA
ŚRĪVIJAYA
YAVA-DVĪPA

INDIA AND CHINA

A THOUSAND YEARS OF CULTURAL RELATIONS

By

PRABODH CHANDRA BAGCHI
M. A., Dr. ès-lettres (Paris), F. A. S. B.
Director of Research Studies, Visva-Bharati, Santiniketan

SECOND EDITION
REVISED AND ENLARGED

GREENWOOD PRESS, PUBLISHERS
WESTPORT, CONNECTICUT

Originally published in 1951
by Philosophical Library, Inc., New York

Reprinted with the permission
of Philosophical Library

First Greenwood Reprinting 1971

Library of Congress Catalogue Card Number 71-136053

SBN 8371-5203-8

Printed in the United States of America

To

FRIENDS IN CHINA

"To show that we are not forgetful.

The road is long, so do not mind the smallness of the present.

We wish you may accept it."

「示不空心
路遠莫怪其少
願領」

PREFACE TO THE FIRST EDITION

The accidents of the war have brought together the two peoples who had almost forgotten their common past. The roads connecting their countries had lost themselves in the desert sands or in tropical forests, uncared for; the footprints of the ancient messengers had been effaced by the ravages of time and the old literature had become a sealed book. The history of the cultural collaboration of the two peoples has to be unfolded by the historians and archæologists. Yet, the theme has more than a mere historical interest. The great Song philosopher Chu-hi said : "The act is past, the ancestor is no more, but life and gratitude remain." Perhaps we are not yet fully aware of the magnitude of this gratitude which we should feel for our ancestors who had sacrificed themselves for the selfless work of building up a common civilization for the two largest agglomerations of people in Asia. The accounts of their efforts may be an inspiration to us, their descendants, in the twilight of a new age.

An outline of those accounts will be found in this small book. The materials are too scrappy to allow a more connected treatment. I have, however, tried to make it as free from academic discussions as possible and it is for the reader to judge if I have been able to make it interesting enough. It has not been possible for me to attach illustrations to the chapter on Art but I have referred to only such relics of art as are illustrated in the standard works on the art of China and Central Asia.

I have presented this little book to our friends in China as a token of our gratefulness for what we owe to them. In this I have been led by the same sentiments that were expressed almost thirteen hundred years ago by a Buddhist scholar of Bodhgaya in a letter written by him to the famous Chinese pilgrim Hiuan-tsang. A translation of this letter will be found on pp. 81-2 of this book.

I have to thank Mr. S. F. Che, the Director of the China Press Ltd., without whose kind help this book would not have come out in this form.

P. C. BAGCHI

PREFACE TO THE SECOND EDITION

As the first edition was soon exhausted it was necessary to bring out a new edition. My absence from India for the last two years and other preoccupations did not permit me to carry out all the improvements that I wanted. I have, however, corrected some mistakes in the old edition and added a new chapter to the book.

P. C. B.

Note : *The method of transcription of the Chinese names followed in this book is the French method with such modifications as :* ch *for* tch, u *for* ou, sh *for* ch, *etc.*

CONTENTS

CHRONOLOGICAL TABLE

Ancient Empires :

Ts'in 221-206 B. C.
Former Han 206. B. C. -24 A. D.
Latter Han 25-220

Period of Three Kingdoms :

Shu Han	221-264
Wei	220-265
Wu	220-280
Western Tsin	265-316
Eastern Tsin	317-420
Former Leang	317-376
Former Ts'in	350-394
Latter Ts'in	384-417
Western Ts'in	385-431
Northern Leang	386-439

Dynasties of North and South :

1.	**North :**	Wei Toba	381-534
		Ts'i	550-557
		Chou	557-581
2.	**South :**	Song	420-478
		Ts'i	479-501
		Leang	502-556
		Ch'en	557-589

United Empires :

Sui	589-618
T'ang	618-907
Song	960-1279
Yuan (Mongol)	1280-1368

CHAPTER I

ROUTES TO CHINA AND THE FIRST CONTACT

HISTORICAL BACKGROUND

The ancient world was not so large as we are often used to think. Since Alexander led his campaigns in the east, the line of demarcation between the west and the east gradually disappeared. Communication by sea and by land became brisk and regular. Exchange in trade and commerce brought about the prosperity of the two worlds. Exchange in culture contributed to the growth of their respective civilizations.

India did not play a mean part in this great exchange. The natural barriers of India were insurmountable only in appearance. The mountain ranges in the north neither effectively checked any outside infiltration nor hampered the expansion of the Indian civilization to the outside world. The Indian Ocean was navigated at an early date and hence it was easy for the Indian traders and missionaries to proceed unhindered to the Far Eastern countries across the seas. This slow and steady expansion of the Indian civilization in different directions over the Asiatic continent brought India closer to countries which were widely separated from it by geography. Thus at a particular stage the history of India became inseparable from the history of the rest of Asia.

We have to go back to the time of the great Maurya Emperor Aśoka in order to trace the origin of this grand effort made by India. The empire which Aśoka governed had reached the natural frontiers of India. He was a devoted follower of the Buddhist religion, of which the fundamental doctrine had an international appeal. It was therefore quite natural for him to look across the frontiers and to try to bring the innumerable foreign people under the influence of the religion which he himself followed and admired.

We know on undisputed authority that Aśoka sent emissaries on a mission of religious conquest (*dharma-vijaya*) not only to the frontier countries but also to such distant kingdoms as Syria, Egypt, Macedonia, etc. Conversion of Ceylon to Buddhism is also ascribed to him. He had sent a prince and princess of his own family to Ceylon on the same sacred mission. A similar mission was also sent to Nepal and probably another across the ocean to the Land of Gold (*Suvarṇabhūmi*) which was the name given by the Indians to the Malay Peninsula and the neighbouring islands.

Although it is not known what immediate success these missions attained, one thing remains certain. It led to the foundation of a closer relation between the Greeks and the Indians over the north-western frontier of India. After the disintegration of the Aśokan empire the Greeks, who had settled in Bactria, began to take an active interest in Indian politics. India was invaded by the Greeks under Demetrios and Menander. A Greek kingdom was established in the Punjab by them in the second century before Christ.

Thus the Bactrian Greeks, who had come up to India shortly after the downfall of the Aśokan empire, not only adopted Indian culture, but also had a special contribution to make to its development in the course of barely two centuries. But they had a still greater contribution to make towards its expansion. They carried the tale of Indian wisdom and prosperity across the frontiers to the barbarian hordes of the Central Asian steppes on the one hand, and to the Græco-Roman world in the west on the other.

The first to be attracted to India were the Śakas or the

Scythians. They were settled in the Oxus valley which was previously in the hands of the Greeks. They were ousted from that region in the second century B. C. by the nomadic hordes of a people who are known in history as Yue-che, a name by which the ancient Chinese called them. They were previously settled near the Chinese frontier but they were soon driven out of this region by other barbarians. They migrated to the west and compelled the Śakas to leave the Oxus valley to them and to go in search for a new land to settle down. The Śakas went to the south. As the Northern Punjab was then in the hands of the Greeks they entered India by a different route, took possession of the lower Indus valley and then spread to Western India. They also, like the Greeks, adopted the Indian civilization and before long they became great protagonists of Indian culture, both in India and abroad.

The Yue-ches had set up a powerful kingdom in the Oxus valley. A branch of this people named 'Kushan' rose to power in the first century B. C. Taking advantage of the weakness of the Greek kingdom in north-western India, the Kushans soon entered the country and in the course of a century founded one of the mightiest empires which extended from the Oxus valley up to Bengal in the east. It included the whole of Northern India, Afghanistan, Bactria, and probably also Khotan. The Yue-ches like all other nomads were quick in adopting foreign cultures. They had accepted the Iranian culture in the Oxus valley, and had begun to show sympathy towards the Buddhist faith. They had also been in contact with the Græco-Roman culture which the Iranians and the Indian Greeks carried to them. After their conquest of India they became great patrons of Indian culture and religion and specially of Buddhism.

The empire of the Yue-ches thus established contact with four great civilizations prevalent in Asia—the Chinese, the

Persian, the Roman and the Indian. They played an international role which is best symbolized by the adoption by King Kanishka, the greatest of the Kushans, of the four titles—the Son of Heavens (*Devaputra*), the King of Kings (*Shaonana shao*), Kaisara (Cæsar) and Mahārāja—which signified the imperial dignity in the four countries, China, Persia, Roman Empire and India respectively. The Kushans began to play a great part in the dissemination of Indian culture abroad since the beginning of the Christian era. Thus in less than three centuries the policy of cultural internationalism which Aśoka had so successfully inaugurated reached its culmination, and in spite of political accidents brought countries within a cultural association of which the guiding genius was India.

While these new political movements were establishing links since the time of Aśoka between India and the neighbouring kingdoms to the north of the Hindukush and in Central Asia, China was independently led to a policy which ultimately resulted in the opening of her doors to the foreign nations. In the beginning of the third century B. C., when India was a united Empire under the Mauryas, China was still divided among feudal chiefs. A centra authority existed but that was more or less in name. The chief of one of these principalities, called Ts'in, successfully destroyed a number of feudal states and established a central government which, in a short time, united the whole of China under one empire. Towards the close of the third century (202 B. C.) a new dynasty of rulers named Han came into power. The Han rulers followed the same policy of maintaining the integrity of the newly founded Chinese Empire. They were soon faced with new problems in regard to its security.

The western marches of the Chinese Empire were at this period in the hands of the barbarian Ḥiung-nu (Hun) hordes who were the hereditary enemies of China. The northern frontiers of the Empire had already been secured against their attacks by raising the famous Great Wall as early as 244 B. C.; China was now to be protected against their attacks from the west. For this purpose the Han Emperor thought of seeking alliances with people living further to the west such as the Yue-ches, the Sogdians, the Tokharians and others. Thus alone could he bring pressure on the Huns from both sides.

A certain Chang K'ien was accordingly entrusted with the mission in 138 B. C. to proceed as far as the Oxus valley where the Yue-che capital was then situated. But as soon as Chang K'ien crossed the Chinese frontier he was taken prisoner by the Huns and kept in confinement. In order to win their confidence Chang K'ien married and settled down among the Huns. After ten years of stay with them, it became possible for him to elude their vigilance and take the route for the west. He proceeded as far as Bactriana. His negotiations with the Yue-ches, however, did not yield any immediate result. He returned to China in 126 B. C.

Although his mission was not successful Chang K'ien's expedition had a considerable effect in opening up to China for the first time an entirely new world. The report which he submitted to the Emperor contained precise information on western countries such as Ta-yuan (Ferganah), Ngan-si (Parthia), Ta-hia (Bactriana), etc. He made another important discovery: while he was in Bactriana he found to his great surprise that bamboo and cotton stuff from the south-western provinces of China were being sold in the local market. These, he heard, had been brought by Indian caravans through Northern India and Afghanistan.

Chang K'ien's report impressed the Chinese Emperor on the necessity of opening up routes to the western countries and to India. The Huns were soon ousted from the western frontiers of China and their territory was annexed to the Empire. The routes leading towards the west through Central Asia were thus opened. Embassies began to be sent at regular intervals to the countries to the west and friendly relations were established with Ferganah. In order to secure the routes for trade and commerce against all aggression, the Chinese Government undertook a number of military operations in Central Asia. By the first century A.D. many of the small kingdoms in this region accepted the suzerainty of the Emperor of China. As soon as safe passage through Central Asia was assured, traders from all directions began to pour into the Chinese Empire and the missionaries as well as cultural emissaries followed suit. It is in this period that we get the first historical reference to the arrival of the Buddhist missionaries from India at the Chinese court.

The story of the first contact between India and China is mixed up with legend. We are told that Buddhist missionaries from India made their first appearance in the Chinese capital as early as 217 B. C. under the Ts'in dynasty. But this story has no historical confirmation and has been discarded as a pious legend forged in later times when Buddhism had been well established in China. We are informed by a quasi-historical account that a golden statue of the Buddha was taken by a Chinese general in 121 B. C. from the Hun country where he had led a military expedition. It is not probable however that Buddhism had reached the Chinese capital before the end of the first century B. C. It is known on undisputed authority that in the year 2 B. C. Buddhist texts and images were first presented to the Chinese court by the Yue-che rulers. Buddhist missionaries however did not arrive in China before the year A. D. 65.

The story of the arrival of the first Buddhist missionaries is again mixed up with a legend. It is said that the Emperor Ming of the Han dynasty saw a golden man in a dream.

On learning from his courtiers that it was the Buddha, he sent in A. D. 65 ambassadors to the west to invite Buddhist missionaries to China. The ambassadors brought with them two Buddhist monks, both of whom were Indian, named Dharmarakṣa and Kāśyapa Mātaṅga. The two missionaries had with them a white horse laden with sacred texts and relics. The first Buddhist monastery built for them in the capital at the Imperial order came to be known as *Po-ma-sse* (The White Horse Monastery) in memory of the horse. The two monks are said to have lived in China for the rest of their lives, translating Buddhist texts into Chinese and preaching Buddhism among the people. A number of translations is attributed to them. Only one of them has come down to us. It is entitled "The Sūtra of the Forty-two Sections", a catechism of the Buddhist religion such as would be useful to the first preachers of the law. It contains explanations of terms relating to the Buddhist order and gives the rules of initiation, ordination, etc. to guide the conduct of monks.

This is the story of the first official relation between China and India by the Central Asian route. South China however seems to have come into contact with India a little earlier and in an independent way. We have already discussed Chang K'ien's reference to India's trade with South-western China through Assam and Burma as early as the second century B. C. The Mahābhārata, the Great Epic of India, which substantially is a compilation of about the same period, refers to China as *Cīna*. This is a Sanskrit adaptation of the name "Ts'in" that was given to China under the Ts'in dynasty. An eminent Sinologist has pointed out the possibility of the migration of Indian stories to China at an early date. Traces of them are found in the writings of a Chinese author named Huai-nan-tseu also known as Prince Liu Ngan who lived in the second century B.C. The author speaks of the great Yū who "while going to the country of the naked people left his clothes before entering it and put them on when coming out, thus showing that wisdom can adapt itself to circumstances." The story is reminiscent of a Buddhist legend which tells us that the Bodhisattva did a similar thing while going to trade with the country of the naked people. The story migrated to China either from India directly or through the intermediary of some bordering people. Besides, there is evidence to show that Buddhist missionaries were already active in South China by the middle of the first century A.D. Buddhists were received in the South by Prince Ying of Ch'u in A. D. 65. The Emperor Ming's dream only symbolizes the first official recognition of the introduction of Buddhism in China.

Thus Buddhism brought the two countries, China and India, together. The Buddhist missionaries of India were the most active agents in uniting the two people by cultural ties which in spite of the disappearance of the old religious beliefs still remain unbroken. A brisk trade continued to exist between the two countries from very early times, but its history is still in the dark. The Sino-Indian relations from the first to the eleventh century primarily centre round this powerful religion which for nearly one thousand years inspired the diverse races of almost the whole of Asia. It was through this religion that the greatest cultural exchange took place between the Asiatic races during the first millennium of the Christian era. The routes of communication between India and China, although essentially trade-routes, thus appear to us as Buddhist routes through which culture in all its aspects flowed from one country into the other.

OVERLAND ROUTES—CENTRAL ASIA

The principal overland route opened since the Han times passed through Central Asia. This region has been aptly called "Ser-India" as it had drawn mainly upon India and China in order to build up a civilization of which the relics now remain buried under the sand dunes of the desert. It has also been described as the "Innermost Heart of Asia" because through the ages it has received the currents of life and civilization from different quarters, the north and the south, the east and the west. It has also served as an intermediary through which different cross currents passed and gave shape to new cultures.

The region is bounded on the north by the T'ien-shan or "Celestial Mountains" and separated on the south from Tibet by the K'un-lun ranges. On the east it is bounded by the Nan-shan which is an extension of the K'un-lun and from which some of the biggest rivers of China take their rise. On the west the Pamirs, called by the Chinese geographers Ts'ong-ling or "Onion Ranges" and known to the classical writers as Imaos, connect the T'ien-shan and the Hindukush.

From these mountains spring important rivers which flow towards the Taklamakan Deserts, gradually dry up and ultimately lose themselves in the sands. The Kashgar Daria rises from the T'ien-shan and the Yarkand Daria from the Pamirs. They are very powerful at their source, but as they flow on they gradually diminish in volume due to evaporation in the proximity of the moving sands. It is along the basin of these rivers that flourishing colonies had been established in ancient times by people coming from various directions.

It was during the Kushan period that Buddhism was first taken to these countries. Colonizers from Kashmir and North-Western India must have proceeded to the region of Khotan and Kashgar in the same period and set up small colonies with kings who claimed descent from Indian royal families. Thus in the first and second centuries A. D. when Buddhist monks began to take the route for China they had to pass through countries and peoples which were bound to give them a warm reception. For about one thousand years this Central Asian route remained the most important avenue of the traders and the missionaries from the west to China as well as from China to the west. Hence, this intervening region between India and China was for all practical purposes a Ser-Indian world.

The route which started from North-Western India proceeded along the valley of the Kabul river, passed by Hidda and Nagarahāra (Jelalabad) and reached Bamiyan before crossing the Hindukush. Bamiyan is a valley surrounded on all sides by the snowy cliffs of the Hindukush and commands one of the most important passes which connect the Kabul region with Balkh. Bamiyan is mentioned in the old Chinese records as Fan-yen-na. It had grown very early into an important centre of Buddhist culture and was a halting place for the Indian monks travelling to Central Asia and China. It was also the prosperous and populous seat of a government and attracted traders and pilgrims from all quarters. A Buddhist tradition runs that when Kapilavastu, the birthplace of the Buddha, was destroyed by the king of the neighbouring kingdom of Kosala, four princes of the Śākya family were compelled to leave their country for having opposed the attack. One of them was received by the people of Bamiyan as their king and Hiuan-tsang in the middle of the seventh century still pretended to have seen a descendant of the Śākya family on the throne of Bamiyan. How far this story is true, we do not know. It is however certain that Bamiyan had risen to be a great centre of Buddhism in the early centuries of the Christian era. It continued to be so till the eighth century.

A number of grottos in the hills around Bamiyan had been converted into Buddhist temples of the type of Ajanta and served as quiet shelters for those monks who wanted to pass their days in study and meditation. Colossal images of the Buddha had been carved out from the side of the hills to arouse pious admiration in the hearts of all passers-by. Manuscripts of Buddhist texts which have been discovered in these grottos are written in Indian scripts of the Kushan and the Gupta periods.

Further to the north of this region beyond the hills the route brought the travellers to Bactriana (modern Balkh) which the ancient Chinese called Fo-ho, and the Indians Bālhika. Though Iranian in its substratum, the local culture of Bactriana had successively come under the influence of the Hellenic and Indian civilizations from very early times. Buddhism was introduced there in the first century B. C. or a little earlier. The sovereignty of the country changed hands many a time—from the Greeks to the Śakas, from the Śakas to the Yue-ches and from the Yue-ches to the Hephthalite Huns. But the people remained faithful to the Buddhist religion till the seventh century A.D. Hiuan-tsang tells us in the seventh century that the great Buddhist establishment of Balkh, the *Navasaṅghārāma*, was the only institution to the north of the Hindukush where there was a continuous succession of masters who were commentators of the canon. The monastery was destroyed towards the end of the same century by the Muslim invaders; and its chief priests,* converted to Islam, were taken to the court of the Caliph. Albiruni informs us that it was they who inaugurated the study of Indian astronomy and mathematics at Baghdad.

Bactriana was the meeting place of two different roads leading to Central Asia and China. One passed northwards and proceeded through ancient Sogdiana. It then crossed the Jaxartes, passed by Tashkend, went westwards through

*The famous Barmak family of the Abbaside Court, described in Arabic accounts as formerly hereditary chief priests of the fire temple of *Nawbahar* (=*Nava Vihāra*).

the passes of the T'ien-shan and at last reached Uch-Turfan. The other, which was shorter and more frequented by the Buddhist missionaries travelling to China, passed through the country of the Tokharians, whom the Chinese called T'u-ho-lo, near Badakhshan, and over the difficult passes of the Pamirs reached the plain at Kashgar. Another and shorter route joined Kashgar with the upper valley of the Indus. It passed through the Gilgit and the Yasin valleys up to Tash-kurghan, where it joined the other route proceeding towards Kashgar.

Kashgar was thus an important stage in the journey to China. To the early Chinese geographers the country was known as Shu-le but later on it came to be known as Kie-sha. After the tiresome journey through the hills and the ascent of the steep cliffs of which the danger often discouraged the travellers, the hospitable monasteries of Kashgar were of great relief to the Buddhist missionaries. By the middle of the seventh century Kashgar and Yarkand abounded in hundreds of Buddhist monasteries.

From Kashgar again two different routes went up to the frontier of China, one along the southern fringes of the Tarim basin, and the other along the north. A number of prosperous states had grown up along the southern route. Kashgar, Yarkand, Khotan, Niya and a number of colonies, now forgotten, which existed near the sites of Dandan Uilik, Endere and Miran, played for centuries an important role in the trade and cultural relations between China and the western countries. All this region primarily constituted an Iranian zone, but it had received from very early times a deep Buddhistic influence. Evidence of the early existence of some Indian colonies in this region has been discovered by archæologists.

Amongst the ancient kingdoms on the southern route, Khotan figures most prominently in the ancient records. It was known to the ancient Chinese writers as Yü-t'ien. Buddhist traditions would have us believe that Khotan was colonized by Indians from North-Western India in the time of Aśoka. A son of Aśoka, Kunāla, was the Viceroy at Taxila. As he was the eldest prince he was destined to succeed to the throne. This prospect was not relished by his step-mother and he was blinded through her machinations. Kunāla's courtiers and followers, infuriated by this inhuman act of the queen, left the country with the blinded prince, went to Khotan and set him up as the king of the newly founded kingdom. We know that there was an intimate relation between North-Western India and Khotan in the Kushan period. Ancient documents coming from the Khotan region show the early existence of a ruling dynasty of Indian origin. State documents written in an Indian dialect have also been discovered from this region.

In the Buddhist world too, ancient Khotan played a very important part. The premier Buddhist establishment of Khotan was the Gomatī-vihāra. It was one of the biggest institutions of Buddhist learning in Central Asia. There was a time when the Chinese pilgrims instead of coming up to India stopped in Khotan for their special studies in Buddhism. This was because it was possible for them to get the help of capable Indian scholars who had settled there. It was then that Khotan, not satisfied with the task of mere transmission of the Buddhist lore, also tried to contribute to its development. Texts which received a canonical importance were composed by the teachers of the Gomatī monastery.

The countries lying along the northern route from Kashgar to the Chinese frontier were no less important in the history of Ser-India. They played an equally important part in the dissemination of Indian culture in Central Asia and China. Po-lu-kia or Bharuka near Uch-Turfan, K'iu-tse (also Kiu-yi) or Kucī, i.e. modern Kuchar, Yen-k'i or Agni, i.e. Karasahr, and Kao-ch'ang, i.e. Turfan had their distinctive contribution to make to the spread of Indian culture to China.

The people and the language of the northern countries were different from those of the south, but it was again the Buddhist civilization which bound them together. Kucī was the most important amongst the northern countries and played the same role as that of Khotan in the diffusion of Buddhism. The Chinese historians took notice of the country for over one thousand years and recognized its greatness in the political and cultural history of Central Asia. China had often been in conflict with Kucī and brought her under submission, but she was quick in re-asserting her independence at the earliest opportunity.

The ancient rulers of Kucī bore Indian names such as Suvarṇapuṣpa, Haradeva, Suvarṇadeva, etc. The Kuchean language was an independent branch of the Indo-European family of languages. It had however received a deep Sanskritic influence through Buddhism. The Chinese pilgrims who visited the country from time to time tell us that the Buddhist monks of Kucī knew Sanskrit and could speak it. Fragments of Sanskrit manuscripts and Kuchean-Sanskrit bilingual documents discovered from the Kucī region tell the same tale. The script used in Kucī and the adjacent countries was, like the script used in Khotan, a variety of the Indian script.

Kucī was not merely a seat of Buddhist studies but also a centre of Buddhist propaganda. The Buddhist teachers of this country who went to China took a leading part in spreading the Buddhist lore in China during the third, fourth and fifth centuries. The grottos in the hills, in the neighbourhood of Kuchar, were places for retirement for the Buddhist monks who wanted to spend their life in quiet study and practice of meditation. They served the same purpose as the caves of Ajanta and Bamiyan.

The next stage on the northern route was Agnideśa (Karasahr). By culture, race and language, ancient Karasahr was linked up with Kucī. It followed the Buddhist religion as fervently as its sister state. The remains of literature and art that have been discovered in this region clearly show that Karasahr also played a very active part in the spread of the Buddhist culture to China. Turfan situated on the northern route, further towards the east, was more within the Chinese sphere of activity and served only as an inevitable stage in the journey to the frontier of the Chinese Empire. It had received currents of the hybrid civilization of Central Asia and had also preserved relics of it but it had not played the same role as that of Kucī and Karasahr in the spread of the Buddhist culture in China.

The two routes coming from the south and the north of the Tarim desert met on the Chinese frontier at a place called Yu-men-kuan or the "Jade Gate". Not far from it, at a place called Tun-huang, was once situated one of the biggest establishments of Buddhist learning. In the hills near Tun-huang a large number of grottos was constructed between the fifth and the eighth centuries A.D. for the use of the Buddhist monks proceeding to China. These grottos were called by the Chinese Ts'ien-fo-tong or "the Caves of the Thousand Buddhas". These caves were the meeting place of the Buddhist scholars coming from various western countries and for this reason they soon developed into a prominent Buddhist institution. Buddhist monks from Persia, Bactria, India, Sogdiana, Khotan, Kucī and other countries used to assemble here before proceeding to the Chinese capital with their burden of manuscripts. They held religious discussions and even translated the sacred texts into Chinese before passing them on to Buddhist institutions in China.

Tun-huang played a great role in the history of China's relations with the west. Situated as it was on the cross-road of the two principal highways leading to the undefined west, from the first century of the Christian era it became a meeting place of the Chinese with the foreigners. Already in the middle of the second century the Buddhist pilgrims found a place of shelter there on their way towards the capital. In the third century we hear of Indian families having settled there. The grottos of the thousand Buddhas began to be scooped out in the hills from the fifth century. These grottos, which had long fallen into oblivion, cherished silently for about a thousand years a wonderful library of the ancient times. The very large number of manuscripts which it contained and which have since been discovered by archaeologists shows that Tun-huang had also risen to be an active centre of learning. The diversity of languages and scripts in which these manuscripts are written, Chinese, Sanskrit, Tibetan, Syriac, Khotanese, etc., proves that Tun-huang was really a great meeting place of China and the west.

OVERLAND ROUTES—TIBET AND SOUTH-WEST CHINA

There were two other overland routes from India to China in ancient times. As they were more difficult of access than the Central Asian routes, and as they passed through uncivilized countries and barren tracts of land, they were not in common use. One of these passed through Assam, upper Burma and Yunnan, and the other through Nepal and Tibet. These routes by their very nature were difficult and discouraging to the travellers. The unhealthy condition of the countries through which they passed, scarcity of food and drink, and, above all, insecurity for the fact that the countries were inhabited by barbarians who had no respect for religion and culture, contributed to their inaccessibility.

We have seen from the report of Chang K'ien that

commodities of South-West China were being carried by Indian caravans through Northern India as far as Bactriana as early as the second century B. C. We also know on the authority of the classical writers that Chinese merchandise used to be taken through Eastern India to the Gangetic valley for export by the sea in the first century A. D. It is also likely that the Buddhist monks had carried Buddhism to South China by the Assam-Burma route in the early centuries of the Christian era.

The Assam-Burma route to China started from Pāṭalīputra (Patna) which was the ancient capital of India, passed by Champā (Bhagalpur), Kajaṅgala (Rajmahal) and Puṇḍravardhana (North Bengal) and proceeded up to Kāmarūpa (Gauhati) in Assam. From Assam the routes to Burma were three in early times as now : one by the valley of the Brahmaputra up to the Patkoi range and then through its passes up to Upper Burma; the second through Manipur up to the Chindwin valley; and the third through Arakan up to the Irrawaddy valley. All these routes met on the frontier of Burma near Bhamo and then proceeded over the mountains and across the river valleys to Yunnanfu, i.e. Kunming, which was the chief city of the southern province of China.

Though Hiuan-tsang had no personal knowledge of this route, still he has carefully recorded what information he could gather about it in Eastern India. "To the east of Kāmarūpa," he says, "the country is a series of hills and hillocks without any principal city, and it reached to the south-west barbarians of China; hence the inhabitants were akin to the *Man* and the *Lao*." The pilgrim learnt from the people of Kāmarūpa that the south-west borders of Sse-chuan were distant by two months' journey, "but the mountains were hard to pass, there were pestilential vapours and poisonous snakes and herbs." When the king of Kāmarūpa, Bhāskaravarman, met the pilgrim, he enquired from the latter about a song which had come from China and was very popular in Assam in that period: "At present in various states of India a song has been heard from some time called the music of the conquests of Ts'in-wang of Mahācīna." Bhāskaravarman, king of Kāmarūpa, related to Hiuan-tsang that he had heard of the prince of Ts'in of Mahācīna who had brought that country out of anarchy and ruin into prosperity and made it supreme over distant regions to which his good influence extended. "All his subjects", the king continued, "having their moral and material wants cared for by this ruler, sing the song of Ts'in-wang's conquests and this fine song has long been known there (in Kāmarūpa)." The song referred to was the song of the victory of the Prince of Ts'in, the second son of the T'ang Emperor Kao-tsu, over the rebels in A. D. 619. The account shows that a Chinese musical piece which was composed after A. D. 619 had been carried to Eastern India where it had attained a popularity already before A. D. 638 when Hiuan-tsang visited the country. This further shows that notwithstanding the difficulties in communication the intercourse between Eastern India and South-Western China was very close and intimate.

The route through Tibet was opened in the second quarter of the seventh century when the first king of the united Tibetan states, Srong-btsan Sgam-po, was converted to Buddhism and allied himself with China and Nepal by marrying a princess from each of the two countries. From this period Indian and Chinese missionaries began to pour into Tibet. They slowly contributed to the growth of the Buddhist civilization of Tibet, and in fact for many centuries it has been the only civilization of the country. A friendly Tibet also helped in the passage of the Buddhist missionaries from India to China and the Chinese pilgrims from China to India. In fact, throughout the latter half of the seventh century, a large number of Chinese monks travelled to India through Tibet.

No detailed description of the Tibetan route has come down to us. A Chinese pilgrim named Hiuan-chao who came to India in A. D. 627 by this route has left a short description of his travels. On leaving the frontiers of China he crossed the desert, passed by the Iron Gates (Darbend), traversed the country of T'u-ho-lo (Tokharestan), passed through the country of the barbarians (Hu) and at last reached T'u-fan (Tibet). Here he met the Chinese queen of King Srong-btsan Sgam-po and according to her orders he had a safe conduct through Tibet up to Jālandhara in the Punjab. This was certainly not the usual route. Hiuan-chao must have gone as far as Badakshan and then retraced his steps eastwards up to Kashgar and Khotan. He entered Tibet from the north-west. From the Tibetan capital also he did not take the usual route to India through Nepal but traversed the central steppes and entered India by the Shipki pass which is not far from Simla. The Tibetan route could not be followed by the Chinese pilgrims in the eighth and the ninth centuries on account of strained political relations between those countries. Towards the end of the tenth century a Chinese traveller named Ki-ye seems to have followed this route on his way back to China from India. He passed through Nepal and a place which he names Mo-yu-li (probably Mayurato in Tibet) and visited the temple of San-yue (Samye in Lhasa). Under the Mongols regular friendly relations between China and Tibet were restored, and along with Lamaistic Buddhism elements of Indian culture were taken to China in this period. It was in this period that the Tibetan Buddhist scholars trained under Indian teachers began to take a leading part in the Buddhist world.

SEA ROUTES—INDO-CHINA AND INSULINDIA

While the Indian traders were thus leading their caravans over the mountains and across the deserts towards

Central Asia and China, and the Buddhist missionaries were slowly plodding along their tracks converting new people and new countries to Buddhism, Indian sailors were also exploring the sea along the coast line towards the Far-Eastern countries. Maritime people in the coastal region of India were acquainted with crude means of navigation from prehistoric times. With the Aryanization of India the art of navigation developed slowly and steadily. Indian merchants and political adventurers had learnt to take advantage of this traffic by sea a few centuries before the Christian era. The story of the Buddhist mission sent to Suvarṇabhūmi by Aśoka does not seem to belong to the domain of fiction.

Suvarṇabhūmi or the "Land of Gold", as the name indicates, was a sort of 'El Dorado' for the Indian sailors. It seems to have been a general designation for the entire insular and peninsular portions of the Far East on the Bay of Bengal. Greek writers like the author of the *Periplus of the Erythraean Sea* and the famous Alexandrian geographer Ptolemy knew about the 'Chryse' island and the 'Chryse' peninsula. They also knew in the first and the second centuries of the Christian era that it was possible to reach that land by sailing along the coast and that the land of Thinae (China) was not far from there. Speaking about China, Ptolemy mentions its important sea-port of Kattigara, a name still unidentified, which was situated on the Tonkinese coast and was the destination of sailors bound for China.

Names like Indo-China, Further India, Insulindia, Indonesia, etc. which are applied to various parts of the Far Eastern region are as significant as the name of Ser-India. This region is geographically an extension of India and in fact Ptolemy includes it in the region which he calls "Trans-Gangetic India". Aryan culture was carried there from North India in the same slow and natural process in which it was carried to other parts of India. Thus Indo-China became from ancient times a sort of buffer state between the two worlds, China and India, and along with the slow expansion of the Aryan culture from India there also took place a regular infiltration of the Chinese culture from the north.

During the first few centuries of the Christian era a number of kingdoms had been founded in the Far East by the Indian colonizers. The principal among them were Fu-nan, Champā and Śrīvijaya. Fu-nan is the name by which the Chinese knew it. The original name of the country cannot now be traced. It included parts of Cambodia and Siam. The foundation of this kingdom goes back to the first century A.D. The Chinese historians have told the story of its first colonization by an Indian. "The original ruler of Fu-nan", the tradition says, "was a woman named Ye-liu. There was a foreigner named Huen-tien (Kauṇḍinya) who practised a mystic cult. He was given in dream a bow and an arrow and received an order for embarking on a junk of commerce and to take to sea. He discovered the bow in a temple and decided to follow the merchants across the sea. He reached Fu-nan and subjugated the country and married the ruling queen. The earlier rulers of Fu-nan were descendants of this Hindu."

The kingdom of Fu-nan was the nucleus round whieh was built in the sixth century, the powerful kingdom of Kambuja (Cambodia) by fresh immigrants from India. Kambuja in the heyday of its power included the whole of modern Cambodia and Siam and portions of the adjacent states. It played the most important role in the political and cultural history of the Far East till the twelfth century A. D. Brahmanism was the established religion of the country. Buddhism was also introduced at a later period. The Indian alphabet was adapted to the Cambodian language. Sanskrit was much cultivated. The epigraphic records in Sanskrit show that the Sanskrit of the country had attained a high degree of refinement. The Cambodian court was in constant communication with China, beginning from the third century A. D. A number of Buddhist missionaries was sent to China from this country in the sixth century. Thus it is quite evident that Cambodia played a very important part in the history of Sino-Indian relations.

As early as the second century A. D. the Indian colonizers had reached the coast of Annam either through Cambodia or directly by the sea. The first Hindu kingdom to be founded in Annam was Champā. Unlike the colonizers of Kambuja the men of Champā depended more on the sea for their communication with other kingdoms and made the ports on the Annamese coast accessible to the sea traffic. Champā was thus an important stage in the sea route connecting India and China.

In its most prosperous days, the boundary of Champā reached on the north the confines of the great Chinese Empire of which Tonkin was then a province. Champā was thus in direct contact with China both by land and by sea. The Indian colonizers of the country had brought with them the Hindu religion and Sanskrit culture. For nearly ten centuries the kingdom of Champā remained faithful to the Indian traditions. Sanskrit was adopted as the language of culture and all the epigraphic records are written in this language. Hinduism was the established religion of the kings and the people. Numerous temples built on the rocks and cliffs along the Annamese coast overlooking the sea still bear testimony to the prosperity which Hinduism enjoyed for long centuries. Buddhism also had its followers in Champā. We are told by the Chinese historians that in the beginning of the seventh century after a military expedition in Champā the Chinese returned with a rich booty which contained amongst other things 1350 Buddhist manuscripts in 564 bands, all of which were written in a script of Indian origin.

A Chinese Buddhist scholar named Yen-tsong was entrusted with the work of translating these works into Chinese. A number of ports had come into existence on the Annamese coast such as Pāṇḍuraṅga (Phanrang), Vijaya (Bindinh), Kauṭhāra (Nhatrang), etc. They were important stages in the coastal traffic towards China.

In the ocean south of the Malay Peninsula two names, Yavadvīpa and Śrīvijaya, stand out very prominently in this period. The former is the same as Java while Śrīvijaya, which is a less definite geographical denomination, is identified with the eastern coast of Sumatra. Śrīvijaya, in its most flourishing days, included not only Java but also the Malay Peninsula and its adjoining islands. Yavadvīpa (Ye-tiao) is mentioned by the Chinese annalists as early as the beginning of the second century A. D. Ptolemy refers to it in the same period under the name Ibadiu and includes it in the trans-Gangetic division of India. Indian colonizers seem to have reached the islands earlier than this period and founded a Hindu kingdom there. While in the beginning of the fifth century Fa-hien was passing through Java on his way back from India, the island was a strong centre of the Hindu religion and culture. Buddhism was introduced for the first time, probably in the beginning of the sixth century, by Indian monks travelling to China by the sea routes. Henceforth Java and the neighbouring islands became important halting places for the Indian travellers going to China.

From the seventh century the name of Java recedes into the background and the name of Śrīvijaya emerges out as the name of a powerful empire which included the entire insular portion and a considerable part of the peninsula adjoining it. The Chinese writers mention it in the earlier period as She-li-fo-she and in the later period, from the end of the tenth century, as San-fo-ts'i. The Empire of Śrīvijaya played as great a role as Kambuja in the history of Indian colonization of the Far East up to the thirteenth century, when the centre of political power was shifted to Java.

Śrīvijaya entertained close relations with India on the one hand and with the Chinese court on the other. The famous Chinese pilgrim Yi-tsing who came to India in the second half of the seventh century found it useful to halt at Śrīvijaya for six months on his way to India. While returning from India he stayed at Śrīvijaya for four years. He returned to China in 689 to come back soon to Śrīvijaya to make another long sojourn. From his account it appears that Śrīvijaya was in this period not only a great centre of Buddhist studies but also of Sanskrit learning. "In the fortified city of Śrīvijaya," he says, "Buddhist priests number more than 1000 whose minds are bent on learning and good practices. They investigate and study all subjects that exist just as in the middle kingdom (Madhyadeśa, India); the rules and ceremonies are not at all different. If a Chinese priest wants to go to the west in order to hear (the lectures) and read (the original) he had better stay here one or two years and practise the proper rules and then proceed to Central India." This shows what great importance was attached to Śrīvijaya as an advanced outpost of Indian culture towards the east.

Sanskrit was the language of Śrīvijaya culture. All old epigraphic records were written in Sanskrit. Both Hinduism and Buddhism were followed by the kings and their subjects. Indian literature was held in esteem and studied. Indian manners and customs were held in regard and followed. With such affiliation it was easy for the missionaries of Śrīvijaya to transmit, quite faithfully, elements of Indian culture to the neighbouring countries as well as to China.

Thus, for over one thousand years, the entire Indo-Chinese peninsula and the islands of the Indian archipelago were for all practical purposes a Greater India. Indian colonizers had set up flourishing kingdoms. Indian culture permeated the people of the country. Regular lines of communication by sea connected these kingdoms with India on the one hand and with China on the other. With the progress in navigation, these sea routes proved more useful for trade and commerce between the two countries. Even for pilgrims, who were not interested in the Buddhist institutions in Central Asia, this route was shorter as well as less arduous to follow. In fact, from the latter half of the seventh century when China lost its hold on Central Asia, the sea route remained the only line of communication between China and India.

The important ports on the western coast of India kept up this line of communication by sea. Bharukaccha (Broach), Śūrpāraka (Sopara), Kalyāṇa, etc. are not mere names. Although they have long ceased to play any part in the seaborne trade of India, constant references to them in old literature in connexion with voyages undertaken by the Indian merchants show what important role they played in ancient times. Bharukaccha, which is mentioned by the classical writers under the name Barygaza, was the main western gateway of Northern India. All trade routes from the north and the north-west converged on Ujjain which for long centuries was the chief city of Western India. Commodities from Ujjain were taken to Bharukaccha for export to foreign countries. Merchandise from Afghanistan, Central Asia and also China were carried to Bharukaccha by the same route. Śūrpāraka and Kalyāṇa were known to the classical writers as Sopara and Calliena. They served as active ports of the western part of the Deccan.

On the Bay of Bengal was situated a large number of ports amongst which two at least attract our attention from early times. They were Kāveripaṭṭanam (Puhar) at the mouth of the Cauvery and Tāmralipti (Tamluk) at the mouth of the Ganges. Both were known to the Greek sailors under the names Khaberos and Tamalitis. The former was the biggest emporium of the southern countries and an active port for trade with the Far East. Tāmralipti monopolized the trade of Eastern India and played a unique part in the economic history of Bengal up to the seventeenth century.

These were the important ports of embarkation for the Far East. In the beginning of the fifth century A. D. when Fa-hien was returning to China he preferred the sea route to the land route. Starting from Pāṭalīputra (Patna) Fa-hien followed the course of the Ganges and descending eastwards he found on the southern bank of the river the great kingdom of Champā (Bhagalpur). "Continuing his journey eastwards he came to the country of Tāmralipti, the capital of which bore the same name and was a great port. He embarked there on a large merchant vessel and went floating over the sea to the south-west. It was the beginning of winter and the wind was favourable. After sailing day and night for 14 days he reached the country of Ceylon. Sailing from Ceylon he reached in 90 days Yavadvīpa (Java) where Brahmanical religion was flourishing. The ship took a course to the north-east from Java intending to reach Canton. The wind of stormy sea drifted them far away. More than seventy days passed and the provisions and water were nearly exhausted. They used salt water for cooking and carefully shared the fresh water. The merchants took counsel and found out that they had taken a wrong course. After twelve days' sailing they reached Shantung."

The merchants in earlier times were probably not in the habit of undertaking such long voyages as from Ceylon direct to Java. They followed a surer and safer route along the coast of the bay and discovered a port on the Malay Peninsula whence they could proceed overland to Siam and Cambodia. This was the port of Takkola of which the earliest mention is found in the geography of Ptolemy. Takkola which has long since disappeared was situated near the Isthmus of Kra. The first colonizers of the Malay Peninsula and Cambodia must have followed this route.

With greater acquaintance with the conditions in the Far East, the Indian sailors were soon in a position to sail round the peninsula and go up to Tonkin. A number of ports on the Malay Peninsula, and Pāṇḍuraṅga, Vijayapura and Kauṭhāra on the Annamese coast gradually rose into prominence as important ports of disembarkation for the colonies.

This sea route at first terminated at Tonkin (Kiao-che) which was the principal port of China on this side and all ships coming from India and the islands of the South Sea used to unload there. The Central Government of China soon found it inconvenient as Tonkin was a protectorate and not an integral part of the Empire. Henceforth trade with Tonkin was discouraged and foreign ships were compelled to sail up to Canton. This gradually contributed to the growth of Canton as the chief southern port of China. As such from the seventh century it became the most important landing place of Buddhist missionaries from India and the South Sea islands.

CHAPTER II

BUDDHIST MISSIONARIES OF INDIA TO CHINA

To a Buddhist monk the present life is nothing but a part of an almost endless journey which terminates only when he attains the perfect spiritual knowledge after having passed through long cycles of troubles and sufferings. The goal is hard and difficult to attain. It depends on how he undertakes the journey and how he performs it. Once he takes the plunge he can ill afford to live a quiet and settled life. His wandering life must be a life of charity and sacrifice, his conduct must be scrupulously pure and he must have infinite patience to march forward with energy and confidence. Such an arduous life of sacrifice and industry alone can lead much earlier to the end of the journey which may otherwise be interminable. So once he has renounced the world and taken such a vow nothing can thwart him from his determination, much less the hills, the deserts or the seas, in a journey which he undertakes to carry the message of love (*maitrī*) that Buddha had delivered to him for the suffering mankind.

Such was the ideal which inspired these Indian monks who served as the torch-bearers of Indian civilization to Central Asia and China. Unfortunately the ancient records of India are silent about them. The Chinese historians have handed down to us information of these noble sons of India who through their selfless work had built up a common civilization for nearly three quarters of the Asian continent.

These missionaries of India, in the course of their journey over hills and deserts, subjected themselves to a hardship and suffering which cannot fail to move us even after the lapse of so many centuries. It had been possible for them to make such great sacrifices as they had confidence in the greatness of their mission.

We have already met with the first Indian missionaries Dharmarakṣa and Kāśyapa Mātaṅga who went to China in the third quarter of the first century. We are told that they had succeeded in getting together a number of admirers and followers in the newly founded White Horse Monastery in the Chinese capital. The Chinese nobles began to show an interest in the newly arrived missionaries and in their religion, though they did not go to the extent of adopting this new faith and giving it an official recognition. It seems that their interest was more or less intellectual and political. Buddhism had already been established in some parts of Central Asia and they knew well that any sympathy shown towards it would greatly facilitate commercial and political relations between China and the foreign countries.

BUDDHIST SCHOLARS FROM CENTRAL ASIA

Encouraged by the reception given to their religion by the Chinese officials the Buddhist missionaries began to pour into China from the Western countries. The lead in this direction was given by different foreign people living in Central Asia such as the Parthians, the Yue-che, the Sogdians, the Kucheans, the Khotanese, etc. In the first period of Sino-Indian relations these were the people who acted as intermediaries, and their missionaries contributed the most to the establishment of Buddhism in China. Their interpretation of Buddhism created in China a great interest in Indian culture and aroused in the heart of the Chinese people a sympathy for it which ultimately led to the foundation of a direct contact between China and India.

We know that following the downfall of the Hellenistic and the Śaka powers in India, the Parthians wrested a portion of North-Western India and founded a short-lived kingdom of their own. They are known in history as Indo-Parthians. Thus was contact established between India and the Parthian Empire. It is therefore quite conceivable that the Buddhist religion, while it was getting a foothold in Bactria and Sogdiana, had also penetrated into other parts of the Parthian Empire.

Towards the middle of the second century a Parthian prince, converted to Buddhism, appeared on the western frontier of China with a collection of Buddhist sacred texts. His name has been handed down by the Chinese historians as Ngan She-kao.* She-kao was a prince of true royal descent, probably a member of the tottering Arsacidan family. He abdicated the throne in favour of his uncle and was converted to Buddhism at an early age. It is not known if he had been to India. It is likely that he had spent some years in the study of Buddhism in some established centre of Buddhist learning. He was a profound scholar of Buddhism as is shown by the large number of texts translated by him into Chinese. On his arrival at the capital of China, he settled in the White Horse Monastery (Po-ma-sse) and passed the rest of his life there in translating Buddhist texts and preaching Buddhism. The school of translators founded by him was called by the Chinese "unrivalled". He exercised an abiding influence on his Chinese followers. Amongst the associates of She-kao are found not only a number of Parthian monks but also a few Sogdian monks.

Ancient Sogdiana roughly corresponded to modern Samarcand and Bokhara. The Sogdians were a branch of

*She-kao is the Chinese translation of a Buddhist name which means "the best in the world" (Lokottama). "Ngan" is the shortened form of Ngan-si (Ar-sak) which was used by the Chinese as common designation of the Parthians. Arsak was the name of the ruling dynasty (Arsacides) and hence it was adopted as the name of the country by the Chinese.

the ancient Iranian people and occupied the entire cultivable zone between the mountains and the steppes to the north of the T'ien-shan range. They had gradually advanced towards Eastern Turkestan and established numerous settlements in different parts of Central Asia towards the beginning of the Christian era. Buddhism was introduced amongst them very early, most probably from Bactriana. Archæological explorations in Central Asia have brought to light the remains of a Sogdian Buddhist literature. The Sogdian monks had also been to China and contributed their mite to the spread of Buddhism in that country. The names of a number of Sogdian translators of Buddhist texts into Chinese have come down to us. The most important among them is the name of K'ang Seng-hui. Seng-hui is the translation of a Buddhist name, Saṅghabhadra.*

Seng-hui was born of Sogdian parents in Tonkin. His parents were at first settled in India and it was from there that they migrated to Tonkin. He was born in the first quarter of the third century. On the death of his father he became a Buddhist monk, went to Nanking, built a monastery and founded a Buddhist school there. He was the first monk to carry on Buddhist propaganda in a systematic way in South China.

The foundation of the Kushan Empire led to the establishment of Yue-che supremacy not only in India and Bactriana but also in some parts of Central Asia, most probably along its southern route. Small settlements of the Yue-che were in evidence in different places from the frontier of India up to the Chinese borderland. Buddhism attained almost the status of a state religion in the time of Kanishka. The encouragement which he gave to the Buddhist teachers renders

*K'ang is the abbreviation of K'ang-kiu, the name under which the Chinese knew Sogdiana. "K'ang-" was used with the names of the Sogdians to show their nationality.

it probable that he also took a personal interest in the propagation of Buddhism outside his Empire. The first two Buddhist missionaries who had gone to China in the first century A. D. were found in the Yue-che country when the Chinese envoy came to invite them to China. Even earlier, it was from the Yue-che court that a certain number of Buddhist texts had been presented for the first time to the Emperor of China.

A number of Buddhist missionaries of the Yue-che nationality went to China in the second and third centuries A.D.* Amongst the Yue-che missionaries who had been to China we come across a great personality. This is Dharmarakṣa, better known by his Chinese name Fa-hu (Protector of Law), who went to China in the middle of the third century. He was born of Yue-che parents long settled at Tun-huang on the frontiers of China. He was educated at Tun-huang under Indian teachers and travelled with them in various parts of Central Asia and had undoubtedly visited some countries on the frontiers of India. He knew, we are told, thirty-six different languages including Sanskrit and Chinese. His knowledge of Buddhism was profound as is shown by the large number of texts translated by him into Chinese. He went to the capital of China where he passed the whole of his active career in propagating Buddhism and translating Sanskrit texts into Chinese.

The Kuchean monks also played a considerable role in the propagation of Buddhism during the first few centuries of the Christian era. The kingdom of Kucī, we have seen, was the most important centre of Buddhist activities in the northern part of Central Asia. A number of Kuchean monks

*Their nationality is indicated by the ancient Chinese writers by prefixing to their names the word "Che" which is an abbreviation of "Yue-che".

had been to China in this period.* The Kuchean missionaries began to take a leading part in the interpretation of Indian Buddhism to the Chinese from the fourth century. It began with the great Kumārajīva who was taken to China as a prisoner by a Chinese general at the conclusion of a military expedition against Kucī.

The father of Kumārajīva was an Indian named Kumārāyaṇa. The family from which he sprung fulfilled by hereditary rights the ministerial function of an Indian state. For reasons unknown to us he abdicated his rights in favour of his relatives and left the country. After a difficult journey over the Pamirs he reached Kucī where he was warmly received by the king. He soon rose to the position of the Rājaguru—"the preceptor of the king". It was then that Jīvā, a princess of the royal family of Kucī, fell in love with Kumārāyaṇa. They were ultimately married. The issue of this union was Kumārajīva. Soon after his birth, Jīvā embraced Buddhism and became a nun. After Kumārajīva had received some elementary education at Kucī his mother left for Kashmir with him to give him further education. Kumārajīva was only nine years of age at that time.

At Kashmir Kumārajīva studied Buddhist literature and philosophy under a teacher named Bandhudatta. In the course of a few years he attained great proficiency in different branches of Buddhist studies. He at last returned to Kucī with his mother after visiting various centres of Buddhist learning in Central Asia. By then he had attained an eminence which attracted Buddhists from all parts of Eastern Turkestan—Khotan, Kashgar, Yarkand, etc.

Kumārajīva was not however allowed to live peacefully

*Their nationality is distinguished by the use of the word "Po" which is always prefixed to their names by the Chinese writers. The word means "White" and it was used by the Chinese writers to designate the Kucheans probably because the latter were a white race.

at Kucī for a long time. Owing to a rupture of political relations with China a vast expeditionary force was sent against Kucī. The city was reduced to submission after a stubborn fight and Kumārajīva, whose name was already known in China, was taken as a prisoner to China in 383. He was compelled to stay at Leang-chou with the local Governor till 401 when at the special request of the Emperor he was sent to the capital.

He was in China till his death in 413. He was responsible for starting a new epoch in the transmission of Buddhism to China. The translations of Buddhist texts by earlier missionaries were not satisfactory because none of the previous translators had a deep knowledge of the Buddhist philosophy. Kumārajīva's acquaintance with various schools of Buddhist philosophy enabled him to render the sense of religious texts more clearly and precisely. He had also a great command not only of Sanskrit but also of Chinese. Hence his translations of Buddhist texts show remarkable improvement on the works of earlier missionaries.

He had also won an unparalleled reputation in China as the most efficient interpreter of Buddhism. Scholars from various parts of China came to him and many became his disciples. The human side of his character is also not wholly unknown to us. At the time of his death he is reported to have warned his disciples not to take his life as ideal. "Accept my work," he said, "but do not take my life to be ideal. The lotus grows from the mud. Love the lotus and not the mud." Kumārajīva symbolizes the spirit of cultural collaboration between Central Asia and India and the joint effort made by the Buddhist scholars of these countries for the dissemination of Indian culture in China.

From the beginning of the third century to about the end of the sixth, for nearly three hundred years, the political history of China was disturbed by the encroachment of foreign invaders, internecine quarrels and rise of small short-lived dynasties. But the cultural life of the country was unshaken. In all spheres of national life there was a pulsation which led to great creations specially in the field of art. Buddhism was also greatly benefited by the general interest shown by the educated people in art, religion and literature. Some of the best Chinese intellects spoke and wrote in defence of Buddhism. The Buddhists in China were no longer satisfied with the teachings of Buddhist missionaries of foreign extraction. They were anxious to come in touch with India directly. Buddhist scholars in India did not fail to take advantage of this situation and hundreds of them went to China either by the overland route or by sea, carrying with them collections of the Buddhist texts not available in China. The biographies of leading Indian personalities who went to China have been preserved in Chinese history. They reveal to us the ideal followed by Buddhist scholars and the work of immense importance that they did in China.

SCHOLARS FROM KASHMIR

Kashmir takes the leading part in the transmission of Buddhist traditions directly to China. The number of Buddhist scholars who went to China from Kashmir in this period is larger than that of those who went from other parts of India. Kashmir was the most flourishing centre of Buddhist learning in India in this period. It was the centre of the most powerful Buddhist sect of Northern India, the Sarvāstivāda. The impetus which the Kushan Emperors gave to Buddhism led to the prosperity of Buddhism in Kashmir. We have seen that Kashmir also attracted scholars from outside. It was to Kashmir that Kumārajīva was brought from distant Kucī for higher education in the Buddhist lore.

One of the first Kashmirian scholars to go to China was

Saṅghabhūti. He reached the northern capital in 381. It is not known if he remained in China till the end of his life. His activities can be traced up to the year A. D. 384. He was welcomed by some of the leading Buddhist personalities of China and it was at their request that he translated a number of texts into Chinese. The most important of these works was an extensive commentary on the disciplinary code (Vinaya-piṭaka) of the Sarvāstivāda school.

While Saṅghabhūti was still working in China another scholar of a more outstanding genius arrived in the Chinese capital from Kashmir. This was Gautama Saṅghadeva who came to Ch'ang-ngan in 384. His Chinese biographers tell us that he was a scholar of profound knowledge and a born teacher. He had specialized in the metaphysical literature (Abhidharma) of Buddhism. He remained in the north a few years revising the earlier translations and explaining the texts to his Chinese friends. He utilized his stay in acquiring a knowledge of the Chinese language. In 391 Saṅghadeva went to South China where a strong Buddhist school had been founded by the Sogdian monk Seng-hui, whom we have already mentioned. He was at this time invited to a new Buddhist institution at Lu-shan that had been founded by a Chinese Buddhist scholar named Hui-yuan who played a great role in the co-ordination of Buddhist studies in China. Saṅghadeva translated a few Sanskrit texts during his stay at Lu-shan. He then went to Nanking in 397 where he made a deep impression on the official circle. One of the high functionaries of the state had a monastery built for him. It was here that he translated a number of important Buddhist texts with the assistance of his Chinese friends and Kashmirian followers. Saṅghadeva probably stayed in China till his death.

Two other Kashmirian scholars, Puṇyatrāta and his pupil Dharmayaśas have their names associated with the

Chinese translations of a number of important texts belonging to the Sarvāstivāda school. It is not clear if both of them came together to China. Puṇyatrāta was a collaborator of Kumārajīva in China but the name of Dharmayaśas is not mentioned in that connexion. The Chinese biographers tell us that Dharmayaśas had come in contact with Puṇyatrāta in Kashmir at the age of 14. He studied the sacred texts under the latter's direction and soon attained a great proficiency in the Buddhist lore. He left the country at the age of thirty and having travelled in various countries in Central Asia reached China in the period 397-401. He was in China till the period 424-453 and passed several years also in the south. He translated a number of works in collaboration with his compatriots. After completing his work he returned to Central Asia. It is likely that he had gone back to Kashmir. About Puṇyatrāta information is very meagre. It is said that he came to China towards the end of the fourth or the beginning of the next century and worked in A. D. 404 as a collaborator of Kumārajīva. It is not unlikely that he was in Kucī when Kumārajīva was taken to China and that he followed the latter to China in order to help him in the work of translation.

Relations between Kucī and Kashmir were very close in this period. They centred round the personality of Kumārajīva whose association with the Kashmirian scholars must have been very intimate. Apart from his Kashmirian collaborators in China we know that other noted scholars from Kashmir had also been attracted to Kucī. Among those who had been thus attracted to Kucī the name of Buddhayaśas stands as the foremost. Chinese biographers have left a complete account of his activities in Central Asia. This clearly brings out the great international role that Indian scholars were playing in this period.

Buddhayaśas was born in Kashmir in a Brahmanical

family. We are told that his father was no believer in Buddhism. On one occasion he assaulted a Buddhist monk. Retribution came in the form of paralysis of the hands. In order to expiate his sin he invited the monk he had assaulted, honoured him and gave him his son Yaśa who was only 13 years old at that time. Yaśa became a monk and followed his teacher to distant countries taking instruction in the sacred lore. He completed his study at the age of twenty-seven when he became a full-fledged monk. He then left Kashmir for foreign countries and first came to Sha-le (Kashgar). The king of the country had then invited three thousand Buddhist monks on a religious occasion. Yaśa was among them. His appearance and manners were so striking that the king was very much impressed and invited him to live in the palace. At this time Kumārajīva came to Kashgar on his way to Kucī and met Yaśa. Kumārajīva passed some time there studying the sacred texts with Yaśa and then returned to Kucī. Kucī was then being invaded by the Chinese army. The king of Kucī asked the king of Kashgar for help. The latter left the young prince in charge of Yaśa and started for Kucī with his army. But it was too late. Kucī had been already reduced to submission before the help could reach it. Kumārajīva was taken to China as a prisoner. Yaśa, we are told, was much upset when this news was brought to him by the king of Kashgar.

Yaśa remained at Kashgar ten years more and then went to Kucī. From Kucī he wrote a letter to Kumārajīva expressing his desire to join him in the Chinese capital. After a year's stay at Kucī, Yaśa left for China and was able to join Kumārajīva at Ch'ang-ngan through the intervention of the Emperor. He worked there with Kumārajīva for some time and himself translated a few works into Chinese. After Kumārajīva's death he returned to Kashmir. The biographer tells us that he was a man of strong character and refused on all occasions the presents offered by the Emperor on the ground that Buddhist monks had no right to accept such presents.

In this period we hear of another Kashmirian scholar who was closely associated with Kumārajīva. This was Vimalākṣa who had first gone to Kucī and worked with Kumārajīva, and then when Kumārajīva was taken to China he also left for the same destination. He was in Ch'ang-ngan from A. D. 406 to 413 working with Kumārajīva. He translated a number of works himself and also explained the translations made by Kumārajīva to Chinese scholars. After Kumārajīva's death in 413 he went to South China where he passed the rest of his life preaching Buddhism and explaining the Buddhist texts.

A number of Kashmirian monks had come to South China in this period by the sea route. One of them was Buddhajīva who reached Nanking in A. D. 423. He was a collaborator of Fa-hien. The latter had come back to China after a long tour in India and brought a number of important Sanskrit manuscripts from India. Some of them were translated by Buddhajīva. He probably remained in China till his death.

A greater personality was Guṇavarman who reached Nanking a few years later by the sea route after visiting Java. Guṇavarman, we are told, was a prince of the royal family of Kashmir. His grandfather Haribhadra was banished from the country on account of his oppressive rule. His father Saṅghānanda also had to pass his life in retirement in the hills and the marshy lands. It is likely that Guṇavarman left the house at the age of twenty and began to live as a Buddhist monk. He soon mastered the Buddhist canon in all its nine sections, studied the four āgamas and learnt to recite thousands of verses. After a few years' study he attained the position of the "master of the law". When he was thirty years of age the king of Kashmir died without issue. After long deliberation the ministers came to Guṇavarman and invited him to ascend the throne and give up his monastic robe. But he rejected the offer and with the permission of his teachers retired to the forest far away from human habitation.

After some time he went to Ceylon and was warmly received by the Buddhists there. He spent some time there preaching Buddhism and helping the local teachers to improve their customs. He then went to Java. Buddhism was also flourishing in that island. The king received him well and invited him to stay in the island. All members of the royal family were converted by him to the Buddhist religion. At this time the name of Guṇavarman reached all the neighbouring islands and he was invited from all quarters. Some Buddhist monks of Nanking who had heard about the high qualities of Guṇavarman made representations to the Emperor and prayed that he might be invited to come to China. A number of Chinese monks were accordingly sent to Java to request Guṇavarman to go to Nanking. After passing a few years in different places on the way, Guṇavarman reached Nanking in A. D. 431. The Emperor himself went out to receive the distinguished monk. He was accommodated in the monastery of Jetavana which was so called after the famous monastery of that name in India. He died the same year in the monastery in which he lived. It was however a year of intense activity as he has left no less than eleven works, translations from Sanskrit texts into Chinese.

At Nanking, in the Jetavana monastery, Guṇavarman probably saw another Kashmirian scholar and worked with him. The name of the latter is Dharmamitra. He was a famous teacher of the doctrine of meditation (*dhyāna*) and introduced a number of works on meditation in China. He had at first gone to Kucī. The officials of that country would not allow him to go to China. He had therefore to leave the country secretly. He then went to Tun-huang where he founded a vihāra and planted more than one thousand trees. He went in 424 to South China where he remained till his death in 442. He used to live a quiet life teaching the sacred texts to his disciples. Up to 433 he was at Nanking in the Jetavana monastery and probably met Guṇavarman there in the year 431.

Chinese historians have preserved these few names from amongst a host of other scholars who had gone to China from Kashmir in this period. But they are enough to show that Kashmir was playing a preponderating role in the transmission of the Buddhist learning to China. This was not without reason. In all likelihood, Kashmir was the chief centre of Buddhist and Sanskrit learning from about the beginning of the Christian era to the fifth century when Nālandā began to attract Buddhist scholars for the first time. India was again connected with Central Asia and China through Kashmir and this contributed to the greatness and importance of that kingdom in the history of Buddhist propaganda.

SCHOLARS FROM OTHER PARTS OF INDIA

But other parts of India were also conscious of this great movement which was slowly and steadily bringing the two great countries of Asia together. Many Buddhist scholars from other parts of India as well went to China in this period and the names of some of them stand out prominent in the accounts of the Chinese historians.

A number of Indian scholars went to China from Central India (Madhyadeśa). The Chinese writers after the ancient Buddhists used to call the whole of North India from the Punjab up to Bihar by this name. This is why it is difficult to know precisely from which part of this region Buddhist scholars went to China. Nālandā had not yet grown into an important institution. Ayodhyā (Oudh) and Pāṭalīputra (Patna) were the two metropolitan cities in this period and both of them were old centres of Buddhist learning. It is likely that the Buddhist monks living in the monasteries of these two cities had knowledge of the hazardous journey undertaken by Kashmirian monks and were inspired by their example.

Dharmakṣema was a Central Indian monk. He studied in his young days the Hīnayāna Buddhism but later on was attracted by the Mahāyāna which was gaining ground in this period. He came to learn that Kashmir was a great centre of Buddhist learning. So he went to Kashmir but the local Buddhists were still averse to Mahāyāna. Dharmakṣema did not have great success there with his new doctrine. He went to Kucī and from Kucī to the western province of China which was then an independent principality. The local chief detained him and he was thus forced to settle down in that place. He worked incessantly from A. D. 414 to 432 and translated a number of works. He then asked for permission from the local chief to return to India in order to bring back the remaining portions of a work which he had translated into Chinese. The permission was refused lest he might go to other Chinese kingdoms with which the local chief was on unfriendly terms. Like a true Buddhist monk he was not to be cowed by official threats. He defied the order and started on his journey in 433 to be murdered in cold blood in the sands of the desert by the envoys of the oppressive ruler. Gautama Prajñārucī, a Buddhist scholar of Benares, came to China in A. D. 516 by the overland route and settled in North China. He remained in China till A. D. 543 working on the Buddhist texts in different places. Many of the books translated by him have come down to us.

Another scholar of note, Guṇabhadra, came to China in the same period, by the sea route and worked in South China.

He was born in a Brahmanical family in Central India. He at first learnt all the Brahmanical lore, but he had leanings towards Buddhism. In spite of the objections of his guardians he secretly joined the Buddhist order and studied the Buddhist literature with capable teachers. He then went to Ceylon and from Ceylon took the sea route to the east, reaching Canton in A. D. 435. He was then sent to the Southern capital, Nanking, where he was accommodated in the Jetavana-vihāra. Guṇabhadra remained at Nanking till his death in A. D. 468 and witnessed a great political upheaval in 453-454. His work was not affected by the political troubles and he continued to receive the patronage of the new rulers. A large number of translations made by him has come down to us.

Among those who worked in North China in this period we get the names of three monks of Eastern India. By Eastern India the Chinese writers meant specially Bengal and Kāmarūpa (Assam). The names of the monks who went from these countries to China were Jñānabhadra, Jinayaśas and Yaśogupta. But unfortunately the biographical notices on them are too meagre. All of them worked in North China during the latter half of the sixth century A. D.

Upaśūnya and Paramārtha were two scholars of Western India who had been to China in this period. Both of them were from Ujjayinī (Ujjain) which was in that period a great centre of Sanskrit learning. It is not known by which way Upaśūnya reached China. It is probable that he went by the sea route as Nanking was the place where he settled down. He worked there during the latter half of the sixth century. Paramārtha who came to China in the same period was also known as Guṇaratna. He was well trained in all the branches of Buddhist literature. After completing his education he went to North India, where he settled most probably at Pāṭalīputra. At that time a Chinese mission had come to

Magadha and requested the king to send a Buddhist scholar of repute to China. In pursuance of this request Paramārtha was sent to that country. He travelled by the sea route most probably in the company of the Chinese envoys and reached China in A. D. 546. He had taken with him a large collection of Buddhist texts. At the request of the Emperor he began to translate them. He worked without interruption till 557 when political troubles upset all his plans. He was obliged for some time to travel from place to place. He also tried to leave the country and go over to the South Sea Islands. He got the opportunity of sailing on a south-bound vessel but unfavourable winds obliged him to come back to Canton. He passed the last few years of his life in retirement and died in A. D. 569. In spite of the troubled time he had in China he worked tremendously and has left us translations of about 70 different works.

Among those who went to China from the North-Western parts of India in this period three names stand out as prominent. These are Buddhabhadra, Vimokṣasena and Jinagupta. Buddhabhadra was born at Nagarahāra. He claimed direct descent from Amṛtodana, the uncle of Buddha. Left an orphan at an early age, he was admitted to the Buddhist order, completed his studies at the age of seventeen, and went to Kashmir. At that time Che-yen who was travelling in India with Fa-hien came to Kashmir and requested the Buddhist community there to send to China a scholar of repute. The choice fell on Buddhabhadra. Buddhabhadra was searching for such an opportunity. He at once started for China with Che-yen. They travelled on foot for three years. They did not travel by the Central Asian route but altogether by a new route. They went to Tonkin on foot evidently through Burma, and from there by boat to China. As soon as he heard that Kumārajīva had come to China and was then working at Ch'ang-ngan, he immediately started for

Ch'ang-ngan to meet him. They were probably old acquaintances in Kashmir. Kumārajīva admitted the superiority of Buddhabhadra and used to consult the latter so long as he was at Ch'ang-ngan.

Buddhabhadra, we are informed, was a Buddhist teacher of independent spirit. This is why he never thought of paying respects to the Emperor as was the custom in those days. He however established close contact with the Chinese Buddhist teachers. At the request of Hui-yuan he went to the famous institution of Lu-shan in the south. Through the intervention of Hui-yuan the Emperor sent a formal request to Buddhabhadra to go to the capital and translate Buddhist texts there. Buddhabhadra accepted this invitation and went to Nanking in 421 where he remained till his death in 429. He translated there a number of important works which still bear testimony to his profound erudition.

Vimokṣasena was also a prince of the Śākya family which had gone to Uḍḍiyāna (Swat valley). The story runs that Kapilavastu, the land of the Śākyas, was invaded by King Virūḍhaka of Kośala and razed to the ground. As the true law of Buddha demanded, the members of the Śākya clan decided not to fight. But four princes of the family did not follow the advice of the Buddha and resisted the enemy. They were subsequently forced to leave the country. Two of these princes went to the north-west, one became king at Uḍḍiyāna and the other at Bamiyan. Vimokṣasena was a descendant of the former and Buddhabhadra, who we have seen was born at Nagarahāra (Jelalabad), was probably a descendant of the latter. Vimokṣasena was probably educated in Kashmir and specialized in the Abhidharma or the metaphysical literature of Buddhism. He was in North China in 541 when he translated a number of works into Chinese. Nothing more is known about him in the meagre biographical notices.

Jinagupta was born in Gandhāra and lived at Puruṣapura

(Peshawar) which was still a metropolitan city in that period. His father was a Government official. Jinagupta joined the Buddhist order at an early age with the permission of his parents, retired to the monastery named Mahāvana-vihāra and studied with reputed teachers different branches of the sacred lore. At the age of 27 he decided to travel in foreign lands in the company of his teachers. The route passed through Kapiśā where they stopped for about a year. Then, after crossing the snowy mountains, they came to the country governed in that period by the Hephthalite Huns. They then passed through Tash Kurghan and ultimately reached Khotan. They did not stay in Khotan long but followed the southern route towards China. They reached Kan-su in 557.

Jinagupta and his teachers Jñānabhadra and Jinayaśas reached Ch'ang-ngan in 559. A monastery was built for them by special orders of the Emperor. The three teachers translated a number of texts into Chinese but unfortunately they were not able to complete their work. Political trouble broke out in 572. This obliged them to leave the country and take the route for India. They first came to the country of the Turks in Central Asia where they had to stop at the request of the Turkish chief. Jinagupta's teachers died there and he was left alone. He however stayed among the Turks till 581 preaching Buddhism and probably initiating the local scholars into the work of translation of the sacred texts.

Political order was restored in China under the Sui dynasty in 581. Jinagupta was then invited to go back to China which he readily did. He returned to China in 585 to direct the work of translation once again. He died in China at an advanced age in A. D. 600.

Jinagupta had the good fortune to assist in bringing about a renaissance of the study of Buddhism in China.

Buddhism in China had been passing through different vicissitudes since the first quarter of the third century. The rise of the Sui dynasty to power brought about a political unity in the country and once again quiet was restored which was not to be disturbed for over two centuries. Jinagupta returned to China after this to reorganize the activities of the Buddhist monks and scholars.

Other Indian scholars followed suit. The most noted amongst them was Dharmagupta. He was born in the Lāṭa country (Kathiawar) and at the age of 23 went to Kānyakubja (Kanoj) where he resided in a monastery named Kaumudi-saṅghārāma and studied Buddhist literature under the guidance of able teachers. He received the ordination at the age of 25. He then went to the Ṭakka country (Northern Punjab) where he stayed for some time in the royal monastery named Devavihāra. It was here that he heard about the flourishing state of Buddhism in China most probably from some Chinese visitors and decided to go to China.

He therefore started on his difficult mission and proceeding westward first came to the country of Kapiśā. He stayed at Kapiśā for two years. It was the meeting place of the caravans of merchants coming from countries to the north of the Himalayas. Dharmagupta gathered from these merchants further information on China. He then crossed the mountains on foot, passed through the countries of Tukhāra, Badakshan, Wakhan and at last reached Tash Kurghan. He passed about a year at this latter place and then went to Kashgar. He passed two years in the royal monastery of Kashgar and then took the northern route through Central Asia. This road took him to Kucī where also he had to pass two years with the Buddhist scholars of the locality. All the places through which he passed were flourishing centres of Buddhism in this period and everywhere there were scholars eager to turn to advantage the visits of Indian

Pandits whenever they chanced to meet them. This was apparently the reason for which Dharmagupta like his compatriots had to pass a considerable time at each of the important places on the route to China. The king of Kucī wanted to keep Dharmagupta at his capital, but the latter, anxious to reach China, left Kucī without the knowledge of the king. His route lay through Agnideśa (Karasahr), Turfan and Hami. All these places were important centres of Buddhism on the northern route and so Dharmagupta had to pass a year or two at each of these places. He reached Ch'ang-ngan in 590 after a fateful march through the desert.

He stayed in Ch'ang-ngan for a few years and then accompanied the Emperor to Lo-yang where the capital was transferred. He died there in A. D. 619. He translated a number of important works into Chinese and helped a good deal in the revival of Buddhist literary tradition in China. He is reported to have compiled a book on the countries visited by him. This book is now lost; but if it is ever re-discovered from any inaccessible corner of China, it will be a great thing. It dealt with things which used to be invariably neglected by ancient Indian writers. It had ten sections named as follows: (1) produce, (2) climate, (3) houses and mode of habitation, (4) government, (5) rites and customs, (6) food and drink, (7) dress, (8) education, (9) wealth and commercial commodities, (10) mountains, rivers, kingdoms, cities and celebrities. Even the keenest Chinese observers like Hiuan-tsang failed to notice so many things about the Central Asian countries.

INDIAN SCHOLARS OF THE T'ANG PERIOD

Political power in China passed almost quietly into the hands of the T'ang dynasty in 618. This dynasty held the throne till the beginning of the tenth century and they had undisputed sway over the whole of China for about two centuries. This was the most glorious period of the history of China in all respects. Buddhism was in a flourishing condition in spite of the most vehement attacks from the orthodox section of the Chinese literati. Both political and cultural relations with India were the closest in this period. Thousands of Indians were found in the metropolitan cities of China; of them many were merchants, many probably ordinary visitors, and a considerable number were Buddhist monks and scholars.

The famous institution of Nālandā had come into exis tence in Bihar in the fifth century, and under the patronage of the Gupta Emperors it soon rose to be the greatest centre of Buddhist learning. Scholars from far and near began to come to Nālandā and students flocked round them in large numbers to receive the most efficient instruction in the Buddhist lore then possible in India. This great institution, from the beginning of the seventh century, began to play the same role in Buddhist propagandism in China as Kashmir in the earlier period. Throughout the T'ang period and later, Nālandā attracted hosts of Chinese visitors more than any other place in India, and the Indian Buddhist scholars, from whichever part of India they might have come, deemed their education incomplete without having passed some time at Nālandā.

One of the most noted scholars of Nālandā, Prabhākaramitra, was the first to go to China in the T'ang period. He was born in a royal family of Central India. He left home at the age of ten and took up religious studies under able teachers. He made so much progress in the course of a few years that he could recite a hundred thousand verses of the Mahāyāna sūtras. He was then given ordination and he took up the study of the Buddhist discipline. He was however of a contemplative temperament, and took to meditation under the direction of great teachers. He settled in the monastery of Nālandā, studied the philosophical texts with the greatest Buddhist teacher of the age named Śīla-bhadra, and was then appointed a professor of the Buddhist metaphysics (Abhidharma) at Nālandā. He had soon a number of brilliant disciplies who afterwards became famous professors at Nālandā.

Prabhākara had a great desire to travel in foreign lands. He heard that Northern Barbarians (Tibetans?) had not yet been converted to Buddhism. He therefore started for the north with ten disciples. Travelling towards the north by stages he reached the headquarters of the chief of the Western Turks. He taught the Buddhist law to him and the latter began to take great interest in this foreign religion. On the invitation of the Chinese ambassador at the Turkish court in 626, Prabhākara decided to go to China. But the Turkish chief would not allow him to go away. Afterwards, at the request of the Chinese Emperor, Prabhākara was permitted to start for China. He reached the capital towards the end of the year 627 and settled in a monastery allotted to him there. The Emperor was very much attracted by the intelligence and scholarship of Prabhākara and requested the latter to translate some texts into Chinese. Prabhākara translated a number of works into Chinese which have come down to us. The Confucian literati however could not tolerate the respect and admiration which the Emperor showed towards Prabhākara. They began to carry on a vehement propaganda against him and this had its desired effect. The Emperor soon ceased to take any interest in him. Prabhākara had no more enthusiasm for work and died broken-hearted in 633.

But the Imperial policy in regard to Buddhism soon changed. In order to cultivate better relations with the Central Asian kingdoms and with India it was found necessary to give some patronage to Buddhism. This alone could favourably impress the western countries towards China. The changed policy was to the great benefit of those Indian scholars who went to China later.

Among those who came later one of the most noted was Bodhiruci. He was a Buddhist monk of Southern India. He left home at the age of twelve and at first joined a Brahmanical school. Here he specialized in the Brahmanical philosophy and sciences such as the Sāṅkhya, the phonetics, astrology, mathematics, medicine, etc. Final examination of such scholars in ancient times consisted of public discussions with scholars of other schools. While carrying on such a discussion with a Buddhist elder named Yaśaghoṣa, Bodhiruci was greatly impressed by the superiority of the Buddhist teacher. He therefore adopted the Buddhist faith and began to study the Buddhist literature.

A Chinese envoy, who had most probably come to the Chālukya court in A. D. 692 requested Bodhiruci to go to China. Bodhiruci readily accepted the invitation and reached China by the sea route in 693. The very same year Bodhiruci commenced the work of translation. The Buddhist monk Brahma, the ambassador of the king of Central India, who was then in China took part in the interpretation of the Sanskrit texts. Another Indian monk named Canda and a Brāhmaṇa who had come from North-West India translated the words. The Chinese monk Hui-che verified the translation. Chu-yi and others took down the translation, Sse-hiuan and others put it in good style and Yuan-ts'ie and others controlled the meaning. Thus a full-fledged board was set up to help Bodhiruci in his work.

Bodhiruci came to the capital (Ch'ang-ngan) in 706 with the Emperor. He stayed in the monastery of Si-chong-fu where he translated one of the most extensive works of Mahāyāna—the *Ratnakūta*. Hiuan-tsang had brought the manuscript from India and commenced the translation. But he died before the work could advance far enough. Bodhiruci commenced his work in 706 and completed it in 713. The Chinese biographer tells us that the Emperor was present when the translation was finished and took down notes with his own hand. It was a unique occasion on which all the chief functionaries and the queens and other women of the palace were present. The board set up to help Bodhiruci consisted of Indians as well as Chinese scholars. Among the Indians who assisted, there were Īśvara, a chief of Eastern India who was then in the Chinese court, Dharma, a Buddhist monk of India, and Prajñāgupta of South India.

Bodhiruci translated in all 53 volumes of sacred texts. The translation of the *Ratnakūṭa* was his last work. After the completion of this work he passed most of his time in meditation. In 724 he accompanied the Emperor to Lo-yang. He died there in A. D. 727. The biographer tells us that he had at this time attained the incredible age of 156! We are further told that on seeing that his end was approaching he told his disciples: "My body is getting weaker like the drops of water which gradually evaporate. Although I have lived long I feel that my end is approaching. So long I have been taking food in order to remove my weakness. Now that I have reached the end, what is the good of prolonging my life?" So saying he took to fasting which lasted for 55 days. He then asked his disciples to leave him alone—"I need an atmosphere of tranquillity. Don't make any noise." He then quietly passed away surrounded by his disciples, friends and admirers.

Another great Buddhist scholar who went to China in this period was Śubhākarasiṁha. He claimed descent from Amṛtodana, the uncle of Buddha Śākyamuni. He was at first in the monastery of Nālandā where he studied different branches of the Buddhist literature. He was anxious to preach the law in foreign countries and so undertook the hazardous journey to China. He first went to the country of the Eastern barbarians (the Turks?). Subsequently a request was sent to him from China to go to that country. He accepted the invitation and reached Ch'ang-ngan in 716 with a large collection of Sanskrit manuscripts which he presented to the Emperor. He then went to Lo-yang with the Emperor. He was evidently in the party of Bodhiruci who also accompanied the Emperor to Lo-yang in the same year. Śubhākara translated a few works and died there in 735 at the age of 99. His reputation as a teacher was very great in China, where he introduced a special form of Buddhist mysticism.

The last great Indian teachers to go to China were Vajrabodhi and his disciple Amoghavajra. Both of them were regarded as great personalities at home and in China. Vajrabodhi was the third son of Īśānavarman, a king of Central India. He left home at the age of ten and joined the Nālandā institution for studies. He was at Nālandā for five years and then passed four years in Western India most probably at Valabhī, which was then an important centre of Buddhist learning. He came back to Nālandā to continue his studies for a further period of six years. He then went to South India and passed some time at Kañcī as the teacher of the Pallava king Narasiṁha Potavarman. He next went to Ceylon and from there accompanied a mission sent by the king of Ceylon to the Emperor of China for presenting to the Emperor a copy of the *Mahāprajñāpāramitā-sūtra*, and other precious objects. He reached Canton in A.D. 720. He made a number of disciples, the most famous of them being the Indian Amoghavajra. Vajrabodhi translated a number of mystic Buddhist works between 723 and 730. The propagation of his mystic doctrines was entirely successful. Many studied them in the two capitals. Neither the Buddhist laymen nor the monks escaped the influence of the new doctrines. Vajrabodhi died at Lo-yang in A. D. 732.

Vajrabodhi's principal disciple Amoghavajra was better known in China under his Chinese name Pu-k'ong. He was born in a Brahmanical family settled in Ceylon. He was converted to Buddhism by Vajrabodhi at the age of fifteen and was initiated by the latter into the mystic practices of Buddhism. He was at Lo-yang with his teacher from 724 to 731 when he was asked by the latter to go back to India to make a collection of Buddhist texts. Vajrabodhi died in 732 and that delayed the proposed departure of Amoghavajra for some time. He left China in 736 and after a difficult sea voyage reached Ceylon. He passed three years in the Danta-vihāra (Ceylon) studying the mystic doctrines of five different schools. It was at this time that he was entrusted by the king of Ceylon with a mission to carry presents of Buddhist texts to the Emperor of China. Amoghavajra returned to China with this mission in 746. Since then till his death in 774 he remained in China working incessantly for the propagation of mystic Buddhism. He translated a large number of works of this school and initiated the Chinese disciples to the mystic practices. He wrote to the Emperor in 771 a few years before his death—"From my childhood I followed my teacher Vajrabodhi for 14 years (719-732) and was initiated by him in the practice of Yoga. I then went to India and made a collection of 500 texts which I brought back to China. I returned to China in 746. Since then up till now I have translated 77 texts consisting of 120 chapters."

These were the most eminent of the Indian scholars who went to China in the T'ang period for the propagation of Buddhism and Buddhist literature. There were many others who were less important but worked none the less to the same end. Biographical notices on them are very meagre and in many cases only names have come down to us. Eminent Indian teachers residing outside India in Khotan, Java and other places also went to China in this period to collaborate in the stupendous work that was being done for the preservation and propagation of the sacred texts of Buddhism.

THE LAST INDIAN MISSIONARIES

The latter part of the T'ang rule was disturbed. Relations between China and India by the overland route had ceased. Intercourse by the sea route was also restricted. The best period of Sino-Indian relations was practically over. There was an attempt by the rulers of the Song dynasty who followed the T'ang to revive the Buddhist traditions of earlier times, and some activity from the end of the tenth century to the beginning of the eleventh is to be noticed. But it was the last flicker of a lamp that was soon going out.

Buddhism, although on its last legs in India, was still alive. Nālandā, although no longer in its former splendour, was still a centre, if not of first rate scholars, at least of innumerable pious monks. A number of these monks went to China in the Song period to keep up the old tradition. In 972 the Indian monks K'o-che, Fa-k'ien, Chen-li and Su-ko-t'o accompanied by forty other monks of Western India came to Ch'ang-ngan. In 973 the Emperor received a monk of Nālandā named Fa-t'ien (Dharmadeva) and showered great honours on him. Fa-t'ien was the greatest translator of this period and translated a very large number of Sanskrit texts into Chinese. He died in China in 1001. A prince of Western India named Mañjuśrī came to the Chinese capital in 971. A monk from the same part of India named Ki-sang came to the capital in 977 and translated a number of works into Chinese. In the same period T'ien-si-tsai, a native of Kashmir, She-hu, a native of Uḍḍiyāna (Swat), and Hu-lo, a monk of Central India, came to the capital. The first two translated a large number of works into Chinese. In 982 the Emperor appointed a board of translators at the head of which were placed the three Indian scholars Fa-t'ien (Dharmadeva), T'ien-si-tsai and She-hu. It was probably due to their activity that the Chinese Buddhist collection was enriched by 201 volumes between 982 and 1011. Numerous Sanskrit manuscripts were being brought to China by the Indians coming to China and the Chinese pilgrims returning to their country. Many of these texts could not be translated for want of good Indian translators. Probably some of these Sanskrit manuscripts will be one day discovered from the now inaccessible monasteries of China.

Notices of a number of Indians who came to China in this period have been preserved in the Chinese Buddhist Encyclopædia, but detailed information on them is not given. These were: Yong-she who came between 984 and 987, Pu-t'o-k'i-ti (Buddhakīrti) a monk of Nālandā who came in 989, Kia-lo-shen-ti (Kālaśānti? Śāntikara) who came from Central India in 995, Ni-wei-ni of Central India and Fo-hu (Buddharakṣa) of Western India both of whom came in 999, Fa-hu (Dharmarakṣa) of Western India and Kie-hien of Northern India who came in 1004, Mu-lo-she-ki of Kashmir and Ta-mo-po of Western India in 1005, Chong-to of Western India and Kio-kie of Central India in 1010, Che-hien of Western India, T'ien-kio of Uḍḍiyāna, Miao-to of Ceylon, T'ong-shou of Central India, P'u-tsi of Varendra in Bengal and many others in 1016. The Chinese chronicler tells us that there were never so many Indian monks in the Chinese court as then. The last of the Indians to come to China were Ngai-hien-che, Sin-hu and their companions from Western India in 1024, five monks including Fa-ki-siang in 1027 and Shan-ch'eng and eight others in 1036.*

*The names of the Indian monks are here given in their Chinese forms. Some of them are transcriptions of Indian names and some are translations but the original names cannot be restored with any amount of certainty. In some cases the Indian monks seem to have adopted pure Chinese names.

After 1036, the Chinese chronicles have nothing more to report on the arrival of the Indians to the Chinese court. The glorious days of Buddhism were over. Buddhism was in a tottering condition in the land of its birth through the increasing encroachment of Brahmanism. India was divided into small states of which the rulers had no longer any interest in the great Buddhist institutions which had played so important a part in the intellectual and religious history not only of India but of practically the whole of Eastern Asia. The internal forces of the Buddhist religion were on the wane. Personal mysticism had weakened the community, and the brethren, no longer bound by any unbreakable tie, were incapable of deciding greater issues. The internationalism of Buddhism had lost its *raison-d'être* with the decline of Buddhism. The forces that had brought India closer to China and other countries of Asia were no longer operative.

CHAPTER III

ANCIENT CHINESE PILGRIMS TO INDIA

We have seen that China came into contact with India as early as the first century B. C., but we do not hear of any Chinese visitor to India till about the end of the fourth century A.D. Hiuan-tsang tells us the story of the Chinese Princes who were sent to India as hostages to the Kushan Emperor, Kanishka, after his victory in a war against the Chinese in Central Asia. Certain territories were allocated to them in the Northern Punjab which came to be known as *Cīna-bhūkti* or "China-allotment". Hiuan-tsang visited this place in the seventh century. It is now identified with a village named Chiniyari near Amritsar. The Chinese Princes used to pass the winter in the Punjab and the summer in Khotan. We are further told that these Princes were responsible for introducing in India two fruits, the 'peach' and the 'pear' till then unknown in India. For this reason they came to be known respectively as '*cīnāni*' and '*cīnarājaputra*'. We do not know how far this story is authentic. It is certain that there was some conflict between the Kushans and the Chinese in Central Asia, but its history is still shrouded in mist.

The Chinese traders from South-Western China and Central Asia must have been visiting India periodically since the days of Chang K'ien and they were responsible for introducing many things into India the history of which is still to be unfolded. Chinese silk, which is mentioned in the early Sanskrit works as *cīnāṁśuka*, was one of the most prized commodities. The Chinese merchants also introduced amongst many other things vermilion and articles made of Chinese bamboo. Vermilion bears a Chinese name in

Sanskrit. *Sindūra* seems to have been derived from *ts'in-t'ung* or 'China red'. Another name for vermilion in Sanskrit is *nāgarakta* or 'dragon's blood'. Such a legendary story of the origin of vermilion must have been told by merchants from the land of the fabulous dragon. For bamboos growing in the hills there is a Chinese name in Sanskrit—*kīcaka* derived from Chinese *kī-chok*. Many a word for commercial products brought to India from outside bears the hidden history of Chinese traders who had once led their caravans through the dangerous hilly tracts of Burma and Assam and across the deserts of Central Asia to Upper India.

While these merchants were plodding towards India by difficult routes the Chinese intelligentsia were still indifferent in regard to India. The lack of interest on their part during the first period of Sino-Indian relations is easy to understand. Buddhism had been carried to China from Central Asia. This region was still looked upon by the Chinese as a "country of the barbarians". The first missionaries of Buddhism had also gone to China from the same region. No direct contact had been made between the Chinese and the Indian intelligentsia. Hence genuine interest in Buddhism and Indian culture was still lacking in China. This is clearly stated in a memorial which one of the Confucian opponents of Buddhism submitted to the Chinese Emperor in the sixth century. He wrote: "Buddhism infiltrated into China from the Tarim under a strange and barbarous form. As such it was then less dangerous. But since the Han period the Indian texts began to be translated into Chinese. Their publicity began to affect the faith of the princes adversely."

Isolated attempts were made in the third century by some Chinese Buddhist monks to come to India either with the purpose of learning Buddhism at first hand or to pay respect to the places hallowed by the memory of the Buddha. One sure case has been recorded in the ancient annals and that is of a Chinese monk named Chu She-hing. He was converted to Buddhism at an early age. He studied the sacred texts at first at Lo-yang, most probably in the famous institution of Po-ma-sse. Anxious to carry on his studies under more competent teachers, he decided to leave for India. He started in A. D. 260 and after visiting different countries in Central Asia came to Khotan. Khotan had then regular communications with Kashmir and hence it was possible for Chu She-hing to find not only competent Indian teachers there but also Sanskrit texts. So he did not come up to India but passed the rest of his life at Khotan. It was from Khotan that he sent a collection of Sanskrit manuscripts to China through some of his disciples.

But some of the Chinese monks must have come to India in the third century. It is reported by Yi-tsing in the seventh century that twenty Chinese monks had come to India in the middle of the third century by the Yunnan-Burma overland route on pilgrimage. A monastery was specially built for the use of these monks near Bodhgayā by king Śrī-Gupta, an ancestor of the Gupta Emperors. The monastery was known as *Cīna Saṅghārāma* and the Chinese visitors to India in the seventh century professed to have visited the ruins of that old institution dedicated to the use of their compatriots.

From the end of the fourth century the Chinese Buddhists began to take a keener interest in India and Indian culture. A great Chinese scholar named Tao-ngan was directly responsible for creating this interest in Indian culture. He was born in a Chinese family which was famous for its studies in the Chinese classics and its adherence to Confucianism. Tao-ngan, however, had a leaning towards Buddhism and got himself initiated to the Buddhist religion at an early age. He studied the Buddhist literature under very competent teachers at Lo-yang and soon attained a unique place in the

Buddhist community in China. He brought together a number of the best Chinese intellects, gave them a perfect training in Buddhism and sent them to different parts of the country in order to preach the religion according to the strict laws of Buddhist discipline. He was himself a great Buddhist scholar and a rigorous critic. He was the first to examine critically the ancient Chinese translations of Buddhist texts and to compile a series of commentaries in order to bring out the inner meaning of the Buddhist doctrines. The earlier translations, we are told, were sometimes inaccurate and it was he who obviated the difficulties in understanding the deeper sense of those texts by his lifelong work.

Tao-ngan was thus responsible for awakening a new spirit in China in the understanding of the Buddhist culture. He was the first to invite to China a number of Indian scholars, then found in Central Asia, and also to compile a book on India in order to encourage the Chinese monks to go to India and learn Buddhism at first hand. As his disciples were found in all parts of China he exercised through them a great influence on the Chinese Buddhist communities all over the country.

THE AGE OF FA-HIEN

Tao-ngan's efforts were not in vain. Soon after his death in A. D. 385, there appeared in China a number of Chinese Buddhist scholars and monks ready to undertake the difficult journey to India for the cause of the religion which they had learnt to admire.

The first among these enterprising monks was Fa-hien, who started on his journey in 399 with the avowed intention of collecting books of Buddhist discipline in India to remove the imperfections from which it was then suffering in China. In this he got the assistance of four other Chinese monks named Hui-king, Tao-king, Hui-ying and Hui-wei, who all accompanied him. When they had come up to the frontiers of China they met another party of monks which had independently started for India on a similar mission. This party consisted of Che-yen, Hui-kien, Seng-shao, Pao-yun and Seng-king. The two parties henceforth proceeded in pleasant association on their journey through Central Asia. They received official help for their journey at Tun-huang.

Fa-hien and his companions followed the northern route up to Agnideśa (Karasahr), and then proceeding right across the desert they came to Khotan. The difficulties which they encountered in crossing the rivers and the deserts and the sufferings they endured were, we are told, unparalleled in human experience. From Khotan their route lay through the hills to Karghalik and Tash-kurghan and then along difficult valleys and mountain passes to Kashmir and the neighbouring countries.

During his travels in Northern India, Fa-hien visited almost all the principal centres of Buddhism as well as places of pilgrimage. The places which thus attracted him were: Uḍḍiyāna (Swat valley), Suvāstu (Swat), Gandhāra (Peshawar), Takṣaśilā (Taxila), Nagara (Jelalabad), Mathurā, Kānyakubja (Kanauj), and such places in Eastern India as were hallowed by the memory of the Buddha—Kośala (Oudh), Śrāvastī, Kapilavastu, Vaiśāli, and Magadha (Bihar). In the country of Magadha he visited the capital city, Pāṭalīputra (Patna), Rājagṛha (Rajgīr), Gayā and Benares. While at Pāṭalīputra, Fa-hien studied the laws of Buddhist discipline (*Vinaya*) and collected a manuscript of one of the principal codes of such discipline—the *Mahāsāṅghika-vinaya*. The last places to be visited by him were Champā (Bhagalpur) and Tāmralipti, the famous port of Bengal. He passed two years in the monastery at Tāmralipti copying the Buddhist texts and drawing pictures of images.

From Tāmralipti he embarked on a large merchant vessel and went floating over the sea to the south-west. After fourteen days' sailing he reached Ceylon. Fa-hien passed two years in the monasteries of Ceylon, listening to the lectures of eminent teachers and copying manuscripts of sacred texts. He then took passage on a large merchantman and started for China. Fa-hien has given us a vivid description of his perilous voyage. The stormy sea, a leakage in their ship and other difficulties hampered his journey and he arrived at Java after being ninety days on the sea. Java was not yet a centre of Buddhism and the dominant religion of the land was Brahmanism. Therefore Fa-hien's stay in Java was not long. He again embarked on a merchantman bound for the Chinese ports. This time also the voyage was a difficult one. Fa-hien was on the point of being left in the sea but was saved by a passenger favourably disposed towards him. Fa-hien says : "After more than a month, when the night drum had sounded the second watch, they encountered a black wind and tempestuous rain, which threw the merchants and passengers into consternation. Fa-hien again with all his heart directed his thoughts to Kuan-she-yin and the monkish community of the land of Han, and through their dread and mysterious protection, was preserved to day-break. After day-break, the Brahmans deliberated together and said—'It is having this Śramaṇa on board which has occasioned our misfortune and brought us this great and bitter suffering. Let us land the Bhikṣu and place him on some island-shore. We must not for the sake of one man allow ourselves to be exposed to such imminent peril.' " This could not be done on account of the intervention of an influential passenger of the ship. The ship, however, was led astray by tempestuous wind and Fa-hien had to land in Shan-tung far away from his destination.

Fa-hien had started on his journey in A. D. 399 and

returned to China in A. D. 414. The route he had travelled, if not quite untrodden before, was till then unfamiliar to the Chinese, and the journey involved hardships which were serious enough to have discouraged any other traveller. But the great ideal before him supplied the spiritual force that was needed for the fulfilment of his religious mission. He has expressed it himself in moving language: "When I look back on what I have gone through, my heart is involuntarily moved, and the perspiration flows forth. That I encountered danger and trod the most perilous places, without thinking of or sparing myself, was because I had a definite aim, and thought of nothing but to do my best in my simplicity and straightforwardness. Thus it was that I exposed my life where death seemed inevitable, if I might accomplish but a thousandth part of what I hoped." This great ideal inspired all Chinese pilgrims who proceeded to India in later times.

The account which Fa-hien has left of his travels in Central Asia and India is a valuable record of Buddhism. He was not interested in any other thing except the Buddhist institutions and the sacred literature of Buddhism, specially its code of discipline which was till then not available in China. He knew Sanskrit and evidently that was the language which was his medium of communication with the Buddhist scholars of India. That his knowledge of this language was very deep is proved by his voluminous translation of the disciplinary code of one of the principal Buddhist schools known as Mahāsāṅghika. India in this period was known in China as the Country of Buddha (Fo-kuo) and hence the account of his journey is entitled *Fo-kuo-ki* or "the Record of the Country of Buddha".

Among the companions of Fa-hien only one, Pao-yun, has left his trace in the Chinese annals. We know that Pao-yun undertook the journey independently and started from China a little earlier, in 397. He met Fa-hien and his party on their way to Central Asia. He accompanied Fa-hien throughout the long journey. While in India Pao-yun studied Sanskrit and on his return to China translated a number of Buddhist texts. He also compiled an account of his travels entitled *Ki yu li wai kuo chuan*, but this account has now been lost.

Soon after the departure of Pao-yun and Fa-hien for India, another enterprising Chinese monk named Che-mong started from Ch'ang-ngan on a journey to India (A. D. 404). His party consisted of fourteen other Chinese monks. In Central Asia he visited Shen-shen (near Lob-nor), Kiu-tse (Kucī) and Yu-t'ien (Khotan). From Khotan Che-mong and his companions went south-west and after a difficult journey over the Pamirs at last reached Bolor near Kashmir. The ascent of the Pamirs was so difficult that nine of his companions did not continue their journey and went back to China. An Indian monk who was probably acting as guide died of fatigue. But nothing could discourage Che-mong. He continued his journey with only four companions left to him, crossed the Indus and went to Kashmir. He then visited the principal places of Buddhist interest in North India such as Kapilavastu and Kusumapura (another name of Pāṭalīputra, ancient Patna), and made a collection of Buddhist texts. He returned to China in 424 by the same route by which he had come to India. Three out of his four companions died on the way. In 439 he composed a detailed account of his travels in Central Asia and India but it has been lost.

In 420 another Chinese monk Fa-yong started for India with 25 Chinese monks. The route followed by him was the northern overland route of Central Asia which passed by Turfan, Kuchar and Kashgar, and then over the Pamirs and along the Gilgit valley went up to Kashmir. Fa-yong, we are told, passed more than a year in Kashmir to study the Sanskrit language and the Buddhist texts. He then resumed his journey and went to all the important places in Northern India as far as Bengal and then returned to China by the sea route. Details of his journey in India are lacking as the memoir which he had written on it is now lost.

Of the other Chinese visitors to India in this period the names of Tao-pu, Fa-sheng, Fa-wei, Tao-yo and Tao-t'ai have come to us. Tao-pu was ordered by an Imperial decree to proceed to India in search of Buddhist texts. Ten scribes also were sent with him in order to help him to make copies of the texts. Tao-pu started by the sea route but through an unfortunate ship-wreck he died before he could reach his destination. Fa-sheng lived in the same period as Tao-pu. We are told that he also had been to Buddhist countries in the west and compiled a memoir on his journey. As this memoir is now lost it is difficult to ascertain if he had come up to India. Of other monks we know definitely that only Tao-yo had really come to India some time between 424 and 451. He had come as far as Sāṅkāśya, a place near modern Thaneswar. He had also written an account of his journey, but it has been lost.

None of the Chinese monks who came to India after Fa-hien, attained the latter's reputation. But they were all inspired by that same noble ideal as that of Fa-hien. They did not come to India for sight-seeing. Their sole aim was to learn Buddhism at first hand and to take back home as many authentic Buddhist texts as possible. The acquisition of merit by visiting the sacred places of Buddhism in India was also an ulterior motive. The journey which they undertook, as we have seen, was not an easy one. Many had died on the way unable to stand the fatigue, many had gone back home from the midway unable to continue the arduous march to the land of the Buddha but still some had defied all the obstacles on the way and reached their destination. Most of them had undertaken their journey without any official backing.

The work of these first travellers was not in vain. They succeeded in impressing the Emperors of China on the necessity of sending Buddhist scholars to India. Towards the beginning of the sixth century (518) an Empress of the Wei dynasty sent an official mission to India to offer presents to the Buddhist sanctuaries and bring back Buddhist texts from India. The official envoy was one Song-yun. A Buddhist monk named Hui-sheng was asked to accompany him. Song-yun and his companions followed the southern route of Central Asia—Shen-shen (near Lob-nor), Tso-mo (Chalmadana, modern Cherchen) and Khotan. From Khotan they went to Karghalik, Wakhan and Chitral. They then followed the valleys of Yasin and Gilgit and ultimately reached Bolor to the north-west of Kashmir. The visit of Song-yun was restricted to north-western India, specially to Uḍḍiyāna (the Swat valley) and Gandhāra (the region of Peshawar). Song-yun returned to China in 522 and compiled an account of his journey which is now lost.

PILGRIMS OF THE T'ANG PERIOD—HIUAN-TSANG

No activities of Chinese pilgrims are to be heard of for nearly three quarters of a century. The Wei rulers who were great patrons of Buddhism lost their power in 535 and the interest of the new rulers in Buddhism was not so great. We no longer hear of any official attempt to send Buddhist scholars to India. Information is also lacking on the individual attempts made by the Chinese monks to maintain the relations already established between the two countries for nearly a hundred years. We have seen that the Indian monks were coming to China in this period as usual, but their reception at the court was not so warm as before.

The period of inactivity did not however continue long. Towards the end of the century (586) far-reaching political changes took place in China. A new dynasty called the Sui brought about the political unity of the country which had been disturbed for about four centuries. The Sui dynasty was shortlived. But during their short rule they made attempts to resume relations with India. The Emperor Yang of the Sui dynasty (605-616) sent a mission to Central Asia and India. The mission was entrusted to Wei-tsie and Tu Hing-man. We are told that they went to India by the overland route and visited, besides various kingdoms in Central Asia, a number of places in India such as Kashmir, Rajgīr, etc. Unfortunately the account of their journey is lost.

The great T'ang dynasty succeeded the Sui in 618. They consolidated still further the central political authority. With them started a new epoch in all spheres of the national life of China. Buddhism also profited by this all-round renaissance. In no period of the history of China did so many Chinese monks and official missions come to India as in the seventh century. There was fervent desire in the heart of the Chinese Buddhists to go to India and to study Buddhism and the Buddhist texts in the University of Nālandā which was then the premier Buddhist institution in India. They also made it a point to search for Sanskrit manuscripts in India and to take back home, not only large collections of texts relating to Buddhism but also images and other relics. They were also interested in other branches of Indian thought such as Brahmanical philosophy, mathematics, astronomy, medicine, etc. The T'ang Emperors made it a point to encourage the monks to undertake such journeys and granted them all possible facilities.

The person who played the greatest role in the history of Sino-Indian cultural relations, not only during the T'ang period, but in all times, was Hiuan-tsang. He was eminently successful in drawing the attention of the rulers to the great contribution made by the Chinese travellers towards a perfect understanding between the Chinese and the Indians. His ancestors belonged to the ancient Chinese nobility. His father was a learned, widely esteemed person and an orthodox Confucian. He was the youngest of four sons, and was born in 600. He received from his father along with his brothers a good education in the old system. He was, we are told, a precocious child and showed cleverness and wisdom in his early years. As a Confucian he studied the classics on filial piety and also other canonical works of the same school. As one of his elder brothers joined the Buddhist order he also resolved to become a Buddhist monk. He was ordained at the age of 20 and travelled for some time within the country, visiting the various Buddhist institutions. He studied the Buddhist literature under the guidance of eminent monks and soon won a reputation throughout the country as a learned and eloquent monk.

Hiuan-tsang longed to come to India in order to visit sacred places and to make a deeper study of the Buddhist literature. He was dissatisfied with the existing Chinese translations of the Buddhist texts. He was however obliged to leave the country in secret. On account of the strained relations of China with Central Asia in this period, Chinese subjects were not allowed to leave the country without official permission. As Hiuan-tsang was extremely keen upon coming to India he did not like to take the risk of an official refusal to give him the necessary permit.

Hiuan-tsang started on his journey in A. D. 629. From Ch'ang-ngan he passed through Leang-chou, Kan-chou and Tun-huang. He then crossed the desert and followed the northern route. He first came to Kao-ch'ang (Turfan). Here he was induced by the king of Turfan to take a new route along the northern foot-hills of the T'ien-shan ranges which passed through the country of the Western Turks who were allies of the king of Turfan. The Western Turks were in this period masters of the entire region from the Jaxartes to the Indus. With the help placed at the disposal of the pilgrim by the king of Turfan he proceeded westwards, passed through A-ki-ni (Agnideśa—Karasahr), Kiu-che (Kuchar), Po-lu-kia (Bharuka—Yaka-Aryk) and then crossing the T'ien-shan reached the headquarters of the Turkish chiefs near Tokmak.

An Indian scholar of Nālandā named Prabhākaramitra had been to this camp of the Turkish chief a few years earlier on his way to China and made the latter interested in Buddhism. This was the reason why Hiuan-tsang also got a warm reception at the Turkish court and was granted further facilities to proceed to India. With the Turkish help the pilgrim passed through Sogdiana and Tokharestan and at last reached Kunduz, the capital of the latter country. From Kunduz his route lay through Balkh, Bamiyan, and Kapiśā (Kabul region) towards India.

Hiuan-tsang was in India for about 16 years. He visited almost all the principal kingdoms of Northern and Southern India and collected information on such distant parts of the country as Nepal, Ceylon, Further India, etc., which he had not visited himself. He made personal contacts with two powerful rulers of India—King Harsha of Kanauj and his ally king Bhāskaravarman of Kāmarūpa (Assam). He passed five years in the University of Nālandā and studied the most subtle philosophy of Buddhism, the Vijñānavada, with the greatest Buddhist teacher of the age, Śīlabhadra, who was the abbot of Nālandā. He established contacts with other rulers of India, particularly with the king of Kapiśā and also with the famous teachers in different parts of the country. On his way back to China he followed the southern route of Central Asia and passed through Kashgar, Khotan,

Chalmadana (Cherchen) and Shen-shen (near Lob-nor).

Hiuan-tsang returned to China in 645. While at Khotan he sent a memorial to the Emperor in justification of the long journey which he had undertaken without the permission of the Emperor. He said in this memorial: "If we admire the ancient masters for going afar in search of learning, how much more those who search into the secret traces of the profit-bringing religion of the Buddhas, and the marvellous words of the three piṭakas, able to liberate from the snares of the world? How can we dare to undervalue such labours, or not regard them with ardour? Now I, Hiuan-tsang, long since versed in the doctrine of Buddha, bequeathed by him in the Western world, the rules and precepts of which had reached the East in an imperfect form, always pondered on a plan for searching out the true learning, without any thought for personal safety. Accordingly, in the fourth month of the third year of the period cheng-kuan (630), braving dangers and obstacles, I secretly found my way to India. I traversed over vast plains of shifting sand, scaled precipitous mountain-crags clad with snow, found my way through the scarped passes of the iron gates, passed along by the tumultuous waves of the hot sea......Thus I have accomplished a journey of more than 50,000 li; yet, notwithstanding the thousand differences of customs and manners I have witnessed, the myriads of dangers I have encountered, by the goodness of Heaven I have returned without accident and now offer my homage with a body unimpaired, and a mind satisfied with the accomplishment of my vows. I have beheld the Gṛdhrakūṭa mountain, worshipped at the Bodhi tree: I have seen traces not seen before, heard sacred words not heard before, witnessed spiritual prodigies, exceeding all the wonders of nature, have borne testimony to the high qualities of our august Emperor, and won for him the high esteem and praise of the people."

The Emperor, we know, received the memorial with great consideration, sent a reply to it immediately, and ordered his officers at Khotan to render all help to the illustrious pilgrim. On his return the pilgrim received a great ovation. His biographer tells us: "Never in the history of China did a Buddhist monk receive such a joyous ovation as that with which our pilgrim was welcomed. The Emperor and his court, the officials and the merchants, and all the people made holiday. The streets were crowded with eager men and women who expressed their joy by gay banners and festive music. Nature too....sympathized with her children and bade the pilgrim welcome. Not with the thunders and lightnings did she greet him, but a solemn gladness filled the air and a happy flush was on the face of the sky. The pilgrim's old pine tree also by nods and waves whispered its glad recognition. This tree on which Hiuan-tsang patted a sad adieu when setting out, had, obedient to his request, bent his head westward and kept it so while the pilgrim travelled in that direction. But when his face was turned to the east and the homeward journey was begun the old pine tree true to its friend also turned and bowed with all its weight of leaves and branches towards the east."

The subsequent career of Hiuan-tsang was an equally busy one. He worked tremendously up to his death in 664, training a large number of disciples and translating the Buddhist texts which he had brought from India. His influence on the Chinese life was many-sided. He was one of the best scholars of the Buddhist philosophy and as such founded a school in China which carried on the study of this philosophy for many years. The famous account of his journey, the *Si-yu-ki* ("The Record of the Western Countries") inspired many new works on India and created an interest in Indian culture unprecedented in China. His relations with the Emperor were very cordial and it is probable that he was responsible for shaping the new imperial policy of establishing political contacts with the Indian rulers, a policy that was followed during the greater part of the T'ang period.

His personal relations with his Indian friends and specially with the scholars of Nālandā were very cordial. His attachment to his Guru Śīlabhadra and to his fellow students, specially Jñānabhadra, was also very great. His Indian friends reciprocated the same sentiments towards him. This is best shown by the incident which occurred at the time of his departure from Nālandā. On hearing that he had decided to go back to China, all the monks of the Nālandā monastery came to him in a body and begged him not to go back. They pointed out to him that India was the land of the Buddha and that China was not a holy land. They also said that the Buddha could never be born in China and the people there could not be meritorious. But Hiuan-tsang replied that the law of Buddha was designed for universal diffusion and that China could not be deprived of Buddha's favour. When all arguments were of no avail they carried the sad news to Śīlabhadra. Śīlabhadra then called for Hiuan-tsang and said: "Why, Sir, have you come to this resolution?" Hiuan-tsang replied: "This country is the place of Buddha's birth: it is impossible not to regard it with affection; only Hiuan-tsang's intention in coming hither was to inquire after the great law for the benefit of his fellow creatures....My visit here has been of the utmost profit. I desire now to go back and translate and explain to others what I have heard, so as to cause others also to be equally grateful to you." Śīlabhadra joyfully replied: "These are thoughts worthy of a great Bodhisattva; my heart anticipates your own wishes." He then arranged for the departure of the pilgrim. The separation must have been very painful to both the parties.

The personal contact of the pilgrim with Indian scholars

continued even after his return to China. The Chinese translations of three letters originally written in Sanskrit have been preserved in a solitary corner of Chinese Buddhist literature. They are examples of correspondence which passed between Hiuan-tsang and his Indian friends. The translations of these letters given in the Appendix will show in clear light what great friendship still existed between the pilgrim and Indian scholars even after the return of the pilgrim to China.

WANG HIUAN-TS'Ö

Soon after Hiuan-tsang's return, the Emperor sent in 643 an ambassador named Li Yi-piao to king Harsha of Kanauj. This was in return for a mission which king Harsha had sent to the Chinese Emperor, most probably at the instance of Hiuan-tsang, who was in the court of Harsha when it was despatched. Li Yi-piao was accompanied by another Chinese officer named Wang Hiuan-ts'ö. They reached Magadha after a journey of nine months. On the completion of their official mission they visited the Buddhist holy places such as Rajgīr, Gṛdhrakūṭa and Mahābodhi, and set up votive inscriptions in Chinese at Gṛdhrakūṭa and Bodhgayā. They returned to China in 647.

The same year (647) Wang Hiuan-ts'ö was entrusted with a second Chinese imperial mission to Magadha. On his arrival at the capital of Harsha he found that the latter had died and that his minister had usurped the throne. The usurper did not receive the Chinese ambassador well. His escorts were murdered and his treasures plundered. He alone saved his life by fleeing overnight to Nepal which was an ally of China in this period. The king of Tibet, Srong-bstan Sgam-po, had married a Chinese and a Nepalese princess and hence China, Tibet and Nepal, all the three countries, were bound by an alliance. Wang Hiuan-ts'ö now secured military help from Nepal and Tibet, marched on Magadha, defeated the usurper in battle and took him a prisoner to China.

Wang Hiuan-ts'ö was sent to India for the third time in 657 to take back home an Indian 'thaumaturge' (Tantrik?) who had been sent to China by some Indian prince at the request of the Chinese Emperor. The 'thaumaturge' who was a Brahmin professed that he was acquainted with the means of securing long life. He, however, failed to convince the Chinese Emperor about his ability. Wang Hiuan-ts'ö also carried presents from the Emperor to the Buddhist shrines in India. This time he went up to the Mahābodhi temple.

Wang Hiuan-ts'ö was sent to India for the fourth time in 664 with the purpose of bringing back a Chinese pilgrim named Hiuan-chao whom he had previously met in India. The ambassador came back to China with Hiuan-chao in a short time through Nepal and Tibet. He wrote an account of his different journeys to India but it now survives only in quotations found in other works. They give us a glimpse of his account which was probably as interesting and fascinating as the *Si-yu-ki*.

The Chinese texts have preserved the biographies of 60 Chinese monks who had been to India during the second half of the seventh century A. D. Among them are found some Corean and Central Asian monks who were educated in China and went to India from China. The example of Hiuan-tsang had aroused in their hearts a fervent longing to visit India. Some of them came by the overland route. Others came by the sea route as the overland communication had already begun to be interrupted by the Arab and Tibetan invaders. Some of these monks did not go back to their country but remained in India till their death, passing a quiet and retired life in the company of Indian monks in the monasteries of India. It was out of joy and not by compulsion that they had done so. We have seen that one of the most noted among them, Hiuan-chao, would not go back to China and had to be taken back by Wang Hiuan-ts'ö by special command of the Emperor.

Hiuan-chao was educated at the monastery of Ta-hing-sheng which was the place of Hiuan-tsang's residence. He might have seen the venerable old teacher and been inspired by his talks on India. He started for India some time after 650 by the Central Asian route. On his way he visited Sogdiana, Tokharestan and other countries and then passed through Tibet. But he entered India not by Nepal but by a completely new route—by the Shipki pass to Jālandhara. He visited different places in Northern India before he came to Magadha. He at last settled at Nālandā for the study of the Buddhist philosophy. Wang Hiuan-ts'ö met him in course of his third mission to India and on his return gave a good report about him to the Emperor.

On his return to China the Emperor gave him a long audience and heard from him the report on the foreign countries visited by him. Hiuan-chao did not stay long in China. He was soon ordered by the Emperor to escort a Brahmin who had come to the court from Kashmir. This time Hiuan-chao passed through Balkh, Kapiśā and Sind, at last reaching Lāṭa (Kathiawar) where he stayed for 4 years. He then went to South India where he collected different kinds of rare medicines for the Emperor. Before starting for China he went to Bodhgayā and Nālandā again, to pay his last homage to his teachers and friends. But it was impossible for him to return to China. Tibet had declared war on China and the Arabs blocked the land route of Central Asia. He passed the rest of his days quietly in a lonely monastery in Upper India.

YI-TSING

The last great Chinese pilgrim to come to India was Yi-tsing. Next to Hiuan-tsang he was the greatest Buddhist scholar in China. He joined the Buddhist church very early and already at the age of 15 began to entertain the idea of going to India. He used to admire the great perseverance of Fa-hien and the noble enthusiasm of Hiuan-tsang. But temperamentally he was unlike Hiuan-tsang. He had no interest in the philosophy of Buddhism and put greater emphasis on the observance of monastic discipline like Fa-hien.

His projected journey to India could not be undertaken before A. D. 671. He was then 37 years of age. He assembled a number of monks around him, but at the time of taking passage on a merchantman all his followers got frightened and went back; he alone continued his voyage. He did not go to India directly. He passed several years at Śrīvijaya (Sumatra) which had grown to be the most important centre of learning under the patronage of the Śailendra kings. He scrupulously studied the manners and customs of the Buddhists of this kingdom and one of his personal works, the *Nan hai ki kui nei fa ch'uan*, is a record of the Buddhist religion as practised in that region.

Yi-tsing then passed over to India. The places visited by him in India were: Tāmralipti, Rajgīr, Vaiśāli, Kuśinagara, Sarnath, Nālandā, etc. He spent ten years in Nālandā studying and making copies of Buddhist texts. When he returned to China in A. D. 695 he had with him a collection of 400 Sanskrit manuscripts. The most stupendous work of his busy life in China was the translation of the code of discipline of the Buddhist school called *Mūlasarvāstivāda*. He also compiled a short Sanskrit-Chinese dictionary for the use of the Chinese monks who desired to learn Sanskrit.

The last Chinese traveller to come to India in the T'ang

period was Wu-k'ong. When he left China in A. D. 751 he was still a layman. He was sent on an official mission to escort the Indian ambassador who had come to China from the kingdom of Kapiśā. He passed by Kuchar, Kashgar, Shignan in the Pamirs and Wakhan and reached the Indus by the route of Yasin and Gilgit valley. He first came to Uḍḍiyāna and Gandhāra which were under the kingdom of Kapiśā in this period. Here he was converted to Buddhism. He spent several years in Kashmir probably studying the Buddhist texts. He then visited the holy places in different parts of India before returning to China in A. D. 790. This time also he passed through Central Asia staying for some time in Kuchar. A short account of his travels has been preserved.

China also entertained political relations with different Indian kingdoms such as Ceylon, Baltistan, Kapiśā, Uḍḍiyāna, Gandhāra, Magadha, Kashmir, etc., for about a hundred years from A. D. 643 to 758. In order to maintain these relations a number of imperial envoys came to India in different periods but no systematic accounts of the journeys undertaken by them have come down to us.

PILGRIMS OF THE SONG PERIOD

Although the great period of Sino-Indian relations practically came to an end towards the middle of the 8th century, Chinese monks still continued to come to India at irregular intervals up to about the middle of the 11th century. The closing years of the T'ang period were quite barren. Political troubles had started within the country. Central Asia had passed out of the control of the Chinese central authority. The overland routes to India were all blocked.

A number of Chinese monks came to India between A. D. 950 and 1039. Their names have been preserved in the Buddhist Encyclopaedia, the *Fo-tsu-t'ong-ki,* but no detailed account of their travels is available. They came to India as mere pilgrims to the holy places. They had no further interest in India. The age of Hiuan-tsang and Yi-tsing was long over. The period of cultural collaboration between the two great countries had ended. But piety still moved the heart of many devout Buddhists of China. The number of those who came to India in this period was imposing. In A. D. 964, we are told, 300 Chinese monks started for India. They were abroad for 12 years. One of them, Ki-ye, has left a short account of his travel. In 966, 157 persons responded to an invitation from the Emperor to go to India to pay the Imperial homage to the holy places. Last of all one Huai-wen, who had already been to India on two previous occasions, came to India for the third time in 1031. He went back in the year 1039.

Five Chinese inscriptions set up at Bodhgayā by some of these travellers have been discovered. The first of these is attributed to a Chinese monk named Che-yi who came to India towards the end of the 10th century. He had engraved this inscription in order to keep a record of his pious act. The second is dated 1022. It was set up by a monk named K'o-yun. The third and the fourth are dated in the same year (A. D. 1022) and are due respectively to two Chinese monks named Yi-ts'ing and Shao-p'in. The fifth inscription dated A. D. 1033 is due to Huai-wen who came to India to erect two votive stūpas at Bodhgayā in the name of the Dowager Empress and the Emperor of China.

The last of these inscriptions set up by Huai-wen in A. D. 1033 stands as a sort of tombstone of about a millennium of close relationship that existed between the two largest agglomerations of races on earth and bear testimony to the splendid work of civilization which they achieved. It is also the last homage that United China paid to the genius of India in a moving language which the vagaries of nature could not stamp out even after nine centuries of devastation.

APPENDIX I

SOME LETTERS OF HIUAN-TSANG AND HIS INDIAN FRIENDS

Three letters which have been preserved in Hui-li's *Life of Hiuan-tsang* (Chinese text, chap. vii) were originally written by the pilgrim and his Indian friends in Sanskrit. Two of them, partially preserved in the Chinese Buddhist Encyclopaedia—*Fo-tsu-li tai t'ong tsai*—were translated by Chavannes in French (*Les Inscriptions Chinoises de Bodhgayā*, Revue de l'Histoire des Religions, 1896). Full translations of the three letters are given here as they throw considerable light on the personal ties that existed between Indian and foreign scholars at such an early period. Hiuan-tsang had two Sanskrit names. The Mahāyānists used to call him *Mahāyāna-deva* while the Hīnayānists called him *Mokṣadeva* or *Mokṣācārya*. It is under this latter name that he is addressed in the following letter.

(*i*)

LETTER OF PRAJNADEVA AND JNANAPRABHA TO HIUAN-TSANG

(*Life of Hiuan-tsang*, Nanking edition, III, chap. vii, pp. 15a-15b).

In the summer, 5th month of the year 652 A. D., the Venerable monks Che-kuang (Jñānaprabha), Hui-t'ien (Prajñādeva)* and others of the Mahābodhi-vihāra in Middle India sent a letter to the Master of the Law (*i.e.* Hiuan-tsang). Jñānaprabha was a great scholar of both the Hīnayāna and Mahāyāna literature, and of the literature of other religions such as the four Vedas, the five vidyās, etc. He was at the top of all disciples of the great teacher of law, Śīlabhadra.

* The restoration of the name of Prajñādeva is not very certain. Literally it means: "Mind-God"—*Matideva*—but the Chinese word Hui (in Hui-t'ien) is sometimes confused with another Hui which means "Prajñā".

He was honoured by all learners of the Five Indies. Prajñādeva was well acquainted and exercised in the literature of the eighteen schools of Hīnayāna. His knowledge and great virtue had won for him universal esteem. While in India Hiuan-tsang had occasion to defend the teachings of Mahāyāna against the attacks of the partisans of Hīnayāna but the courteous polemics had not at all diminished the esteem and sympathy which they had for him. So Prajñādeva sent with the Bhikṣu Dharma-vardhana (? Fa-chang)* of the same Vihāra a letter to Hiuan-tsang with the copy of a Stotra which he had composed and a pair of white cloths. The letter was the following :

"The Sthavira Prajñādeva who associates with men of great wisdom in the temple of Mahābodhi near the Vajrāsana of Lord Buddha sends this letter to Mokṣācārya of Mahācīna who knows well and has penetrated well into the Sūtras, Vinayas and the innumerable Śāstras. He humbly wishes that the latter may ever be free from illness and suffering.

I, Bhikṣu Prajñādeva, have now composed an eulogy on the great divine transformations of Buddha (Trikāya-stotra?) and also a 'Comparative estimate of the Sūtras, Śāstras, etc.' I hand them over to Bhikṣu Fa-chang who will carry them to you. Among us the Ācārya, the Venerable Bhadanta Jñānaprabha, possessed of numerous and limitless knowledge, joins me in enquiring about you. The Upāsakas, here, always offer their salutations to you. We all are sending you a pair of white cloths to show that we are not forgetful. The road is long. So do not mind the smallness of the present. We wish you may accept it. As regards the Sūtras and Śāstras which you may require, please send us a list. We will copy them and send them to you. This is, Mokṣācārya, all that we want to inform you. This is for

*Chinese Fa-chang literally means " Dharma-long". This may be restored as Dharma-vardhana.

conveying to you from a distance our loving thoughts."

(*ii*)

LETTER OF HIUAN-TSANG TO JÑĀNAPRABHA

Fa-chang (Dharma-vardhana ?) returned in the 2nd month, spring, of the 5th year yong-hoei (654). The following letter was written by Hiuan-tsang to Jñānaprabha, the same year and sent through Fa-chang:

"The Bhikṣu Hiuan-tsang of the country of the Great T'ang rulers humbly writes to the Master of Law, the teacher of Tripiṭaka, Bhadanta Jñānaprabha of Magadha in Middle India. I returned more than 10 years ago. The frontiers of the countries are far away from each other. I had no news from you. My anxiety went on increasing. By enquiring from Bhikṣu Fa-chang I learn that you are well. My eyes become bright and it seems I see your face. Pen cannot describe the joy I feel at the news. The climate now is becoming hot and I cannot say how it will be afterwards.*

I learnt from an ambassador who recently came back from India that the great teacher Śīlabhadra is no more in this world. On getting this news I was overwhelmed with sorrow that knew no bounds. Alas! the boat of this sea of suffering has foundered: the eye of men and gods has closed. How to express the sorrow that his disappearance causes us? ....In the past when the Great Buddha withdrew his light Kāśyapa continued his work and extended it; while Śāṇavāsa left this world Upagupta continued to give exposition of his beautiful law. Now that a general of the Law has returned to his true place let the masters of law in their turn perform their duties. I only wish that the pure explanations and the subtle discussions (of the law) may spread in vast waves like

*This is evidently a reference to the terribly hot summer of Northern India which must have been very trying for the pilgrim during his stay in India.

the waves of the four seas and that the holy knowledge may be eternal like the five mountains.

Among the Sūtras and Śāstras that I, Hiuan-tsang, had brought with me, I have already translated the *Yogācāra-bhūmi-Śāstra* and other works in all 30 volumes. The *Kośa* and the *Nyāyānusāra-śāstra** are not yet fully translated. They will certainly be completed this year.

At present the Devaputra (*i.e.* the Emperor) of the great T'ang dynasty through his personal holiness and by his numerous felicities guides the country and brings peace to the people. With the affection of a Cakravartī king and like a Dharmarāja, he helps the propagation of the law to far away places. In regard to the Sūtras and Śāstras translated we have obtained the favour of a preface from his divine pen. In regard to them the officers have received the order for circulating the texts in all the kingdoms. Even the neighbouring countries will receive all of them when the order is executed. Although we are near the end of the *kalpa* the shining glory of the law is still very sweet and perfect. It is not at all different from its manifestation in the Jetavana at Śrāvasti.

I should humbly like to let you know that while crossing the Indus I had lost a load of sacred texts. I now send you a list of those texts annexed to this letter. I request you to send them to me if you get the chance. I am sending some small articles as present. Please accept them. The road is long and it is not possible to send much. Do not disdain it.

With the salutations of Hiuan-tsang."

**Kośa* here refers to *Abhidharmakośa-vyākhyā* of Vasubandhu in 30 chapters (Nanjio 1267). The translation was commenced on 10th of the 5th month of 651 and completed on the 27th of the 7th month of 654. The other work is the *Nyāyānusāra-śāstra* of Saṅghabhadra (Nanjio 1265). Its translation was commenced on the 1st day of the first month of 653 and completed on the 10th day of the 7th month of 654. The date of the letter is the 2nd month of 654.

(*iii*)

LETTER OF HIUAN-TSANG TO PRAJÑĀDEVA

"The Bhikṣu Hiuan-tsang of the great T'ang country respectfully writes to the Master of Law, the teacher of Tripiṭaka, Prajñādeva of the Mahābodhivihāra : A long time has elapsed. There was no news from you and so I was greatly anxious. There was no means of calming the anxiety. When Bhikṣu Dharma-vardhana (Fa-chang?) came with your letter I came to learn that you are all well. This gave me great joy. I have received the pair of fine white cloths and the bundle of Stotras (sent by you). It is a great honour to me which I did not merit. I feel much ashamed. The weather is gradually becoming hot. I do not know what it will be afterwards and how you will keep.

You have reduced to nothingness the Śāstras of hundred schools and maintained the integrity of the Sūtras with its nine divisions (*navāṅga-buddhaśāsana*). You have raised the banner of the Right Law and led every one to the goal. You have beaten the drum of victory and defeated the opponents. Supreme in knowledge you have challenged all the kings. You must therefore feel very happy.

I, Hiuan-tsang, am a fool. I am also growing old and failing in strength. I remember your merits and respect you for your kindness. These thoughts tire me more. When I was in India I met you in the Assembly at Kānyakubja and discussed the Śāstras together before the kings and their numerous followers in order to settle the doctrinal issues. One party defended the Mahāyāna and the other defended the incomplete religion (lit. half religion, *i.e.* the Hīnayāna). During the debate the atmosphere sometimes grew very tense and sometimes very low. My only intention was to follow the logic and not to show any partiality. It is due to this that we were opposed to each other. When the meeting ended our mutual opposition also ended. Now the messenger has brought your letter and your apology.* Why do you keep it in mind? You are deeply learned, your style is lucid, your determination is strong, and your character is high. Even the waves of the Anavatapta lake cannot be compared to yours. The clearness of a *maṇi* cannot equal yours. You are a bright example to your disciples. I wish you had followed the good law (*i. e.* Mahāyāna) in your elucidation of the religion. When the logic is perfect speech reaches its limits. Nothing can surpass the Mahāyāna. I am sorry that you have not yet imbibed a deep faith in it. You prefer goat and deer to the white cow, and crystal to a *maṇi*. You possess brightness and great virtue. Why do you ignore it? Your body is brittle and short-lived like an earthen pot. You should decide to have faith in Alaṁkāra (? *Mahāyāna-sūtrālaṁkāra*) so that you may not have to regret before your death.

The messenger is now going back. I send you this advice which is an expression of my love for you. I am sending you a small thing as an expression of my gratefulness for your present. This cannot represent my deep respect for you. I hope you understand me. During my return while crossing the Indus I lost a load of the holy texts. I am sending you a list of them with this letter. I request you to send them to me.

With respects of Bhikṣu Hiuan-tsang."

*The apology referred to by Hiuan-tsang must have been contained in the "Comparative estimate of the Śāstras and Sūtras" mentioned in Prajñādeva's letter. It was evidently composed to answer some of the points raised by Hiuan-tsang.

APPENDIX II

CHINESE INSCRIPTIONS OF BODHGAYA

I

THE INSCRIPTION OF THE MONK CHE-YI *circa* A. D. 990

The monk Che-yi of the great Han country had first taken the vow to exhort three hundred thousand men to practise the conduct which assures a higher birth, to make a charity of three hundred thousand copies of *Shan Shen King* (Sūtra relating to the higher birth) and to recite it himself three hundred thousand times. Such a merit, as mentioned above, conduces to the birth in the inner Tuṣita (heaven). Now, arriving in Magadha, he has admired the Vajrāsana and has humbly met the abbot of Vijñānamātra (School). Kui-pao and a group of venerable monks had together taken the vow to go to be born in Tuṣita (heaven). Amongst the three hundred thousand persons Kui-pao is the first, Che-yi is the second, Kuang-fong the third and the others mentioned in order are Hui-yen, Ch'ong-ta, Ts'iuan-tsun, Yuan-chen, Yi-sien, Hui-siu, Che-yong, Fong-sheng, Ts'ing-yun, etc. They have together desired to pay homage to Maitreya, the compassionate and the honoured one, and have now engraved the images of seven Buddhas which they place on record.

II

THE INSCRIPTION OF THE MONK K'O-YUN DATED A. D. 1022

Memoir on the bodies (kāya) and the thrones of Buddha by monk, K'o-yun, a transmitter of the Sūtras and teacher of the Śāstras, a native of Si-ho of the great Song Empire.

K'o-yun left the Imperial territory and came to contemplate on the country of Buddha. When he saw the marvellous traces and the holy vestiges how could he help not becoming a respectful panegyrist of the gladdening excellence (of the Buddha)? K'o-yun exhausted all his remaining resources and at thirty steps to the north of the Bodhi tree he set up a beautiful stūpa in stone of the 1000 Buddhas. He erected a lasting monument on the spot where (the Maitreya Buddha) will take three steps. Although the height of his capacities was not enough to express his sentiments by writing, the benign work of the Law surpassed his respect to such an extent as to impose itself on his inner self. He tried to compose some lines in an undignified language to celebrate the unborn.

He admired the true face of the Master of Bodhi in these words :

Oh Great One, Thou hast compassion for the beings and Thou supportest the truth.

Even when Thou dost not manifest Thyself outside, the supernatural influence of Thine exists.

All the erroneous doctrines are unfolded and exposed in Thy presence—all that is activity and knowledge is Thine.

Old by two thousand years—Thy moon-like face keeps itself ever fresh.

He also made this eulogy :

The contemplation of four times eight (*i. e.* 32 auspicious signs of Buddha) is limitless—the multitude (of specialities) of Thy majestic face is beautiful and rare.

The height of Thy head is round like a piece of green jade; Thy eyes which are ocean-like (deep) have the appearance of blue lotuses.

Thy breast which bears the svastika sign looks like a mass of gold; Thy eye-brows look like the accumulation of clouds.

Admirable are Thy divine and extraordinary arms; Thy corporal substance is beyond the dust and smoke.

Having thus sung on the substance of the shadow (of Buddha) he undertook to celebrate the real bodies. The bodies of Buddha are three in number—he celebrated them one after another.

He praised the *Nirmāṇakāya* in these words:

The depth of compassion is the truth (that is told by) Thy moon-like face; on many occasions Thou hast saved men from the midst of fire.

For the children Thou hast bequeathed a means of curing. Thou hast made a rosary of pearls to maintain through it friendship and relationship.

The three vehicles have opened the path of Bodhi, the five doctrines have fought the darkness of dust.

The day when we become hateful and plunged in the passions, we do not see any more the body that is beyond the reach of human beings.

He praised the *Sambhogakāya* in these words :

Having completed ten thousand voyages in course of countless *kalpas*—he carries with him all beings beyond the gates of human affection.

The original dust is all washed and its uncleanliness removed; a harmony penetrates the mountains and the rivers.

Of all the Buddhas the body has no obstacle; all the hearts are baffled in attempts to reach it.

For good, is given up the ocean of the three worlds ; the essence of egoism is entirely destroyed.

He praised the *Dharmakāya* in these words :

The field of knowledge borders on the domain of the Law Dharmadhātu) ; subtle excellence penetrates all through the sands and the dusts.

He is powerful, without birth and death—mysterious and beyond the grasp of the cause and the effect.

He is always within the world but he is not of the world—even in his holy place he cannot be found at all.

When the expressions of my admiring heart were exhausted I met for the first time the pure and calm body.

The three bodies having been praised, it remained to praise the three thrones that belonged to them.

He praised the throne of *Nirmāṇakāya* in these words:

The five Indies possess his marvellous vestiges; he is born in the centre of the six directions.

Downwards he penetrated up to the foundation of the golden wheel—upwards he went far above the surface of the earth.

Dust and pain never reach him—how can water and fire, affect him?

Once he routed the army of Māra his lion-like roaring was calmed.

He praised the throne of *Sambhogakāya* in these words:

The throne is set up beyond the three worlds—its brightness reaches the world of the gods above.

The fire of the *kalpa* will always be hard to attain; how could the artists of this world imitate this model easily?

The fame of the Queen of Flowers is extraordinary and reaches far—the doctrine of the marvellous knowledge is powerful and glorious.

Like a jewel it enters the grains of the dust and the sand—endowed with a long life it enters all parts of the great void.

He praised the throne of the *Dharmakāya* in these words:

Without beginning, without birth, without end—his traces are universally beyond the influence of the past and the future.

Although immobile, it has within it five paths—although silent and calm, it absorbs the three calamities.

The *gāthās* of the *prajñā* spread secretly—the obstacles such as suffering and hatred are removed.

Even after passing through myriads of *kalpas* it remains in its heart free from the worldly dust.

I have selected those that appeared to me to be the best of my humble expressions and I have used them for praising the beautiful principle of the unborn.

I seem to be trying to measure the heavens with the eyes of a mosquito. How can I know the height! I have feebly expressed my sentiments of faith and admiration.

I now make use of the eulogy of the marvellous excellence of the three bodies and of the sculptures that I have executed of the extraordinary acts of the thousand Buddhas, in order to secure the prosperity of the glorious sovereign of my country and to win for him for many years a holy longevity.

The Emperor of the Great Song dynasty humbly wished that his destiny should be like the water of the celestial lake which is abundant and which neither diminishes nor increases, that his prosperity should be like the celestial peak of the mountain which is high and which always remains high and majestic. My sovereign desired also that in future in this country there should be somebody to occupy continuously the place of Śaṅkha—that in other regions there would be in the future generations a fame like that of Candrachattra—that if henceforth any one composes a eulogy of the marvellous traces and the holy vestiges, he should take care to write it and make a memoir of it.

Recorded in the month *yi-se*, of the year *jen-siu* of the period *t'ien-hi* (A. D. 1022) of the great Song dynasty.

III

THE INSCRIPTION OF THE MONK YI-TS'ING DATED A. D. 1022

The monk Yi-ts'ing and the disciple of the master Yi-lin of the Dhyāna court of the prosperous religion in the eastern capital of the great Song Empire acquit themselves of the charge of offering a kaṣāya, woven with golden threads, offered as a token of gratitude for the four acts of kindness and three indulgences. After having spread it and hung it on the throne of Buddha in India they set up a stūpa in stone. The 4th day of the 4th month of the 6th year *t'ien-hi* (A. D. 1022), the Upādhyāya Pien-cheng being the great master (of the ceremony).

IV

THE INSCRIPTION OF SHAO-P'IN DATED A. D. 1022

The monk Shao-p'in of the court of holiness flourishing in the eastern capital of the great Song Empire has brought a kaṣāya of golden threads—after having spread it and hung it on the throne of Buddha, he has set up a stūpa in stone. He has done it in recognition of the four acts of kindness and three indulgences. For this good work he hopes to be under the tree with dragon flowers. Written on the 4th day of the 4th month of the 6th year *t'ien-hi* (A. D. 1022).

V

THE INSCRIPTION OF HUAI-WEN DATED A. D. 1033

The erection of a stūpa in honour of the Emperor T'ai-tsong by the Emperor and the Dowager Empress of the great Song dynasty :

Of the great Song dynasty, the Emperor who is of saintly and pacific character, a wise warrior, good and intelligent, pious and virtuous, and the Dowager Empress who is in harmony with the original principle, who honours virtue and is good, who has a long life, does good to others and is saintly, have respectfully charged the monk Huai-wen with the task of going to the country of Magadha in order to erect a stūpa by the side of the Vajrāsana dedicated to T'ai-tsong, the Emperor who was perfectly good, in harmony with reason, divinely meritorious, saintly and virtuous, pacific and warrior, clear-minded and illustrious, endowed with wide intelligence and profoundly pious.

The Emperor T'ai-tsong humbly desired to go up to the abode of the devas, to receive personally from Buddha the account which confirms the scriptures, to attain the residence of the good saints for all times as his place of habitation, so that the worship of Śakra and Brahma might be his great recompense and the majestic and supernatural influence might raise his dynasty for ever to a higher position.

Written on the 19th day of the first month of the 12th year *ming-tao*, the year being marked by the signs *kui-yu* (A. D. 1033).

CHAPTER IV

BUDDHISM IN CHINA

The dream of the Emperor Ming-ti to which we have already referred is a pious fiction. The story was forged in later times in the Buddhist *milieu* in order to lend to the foreign religion a prestige which it did not enjoy in China in the period when it was first introduced. The Chinese mind was from early times much imbued with Confucian ideals. It was largely concerned with the maintenance of the social order which centred round the ancestors and the Emperors who were placed in charge of that society by Heaven. The Emperor was the Son of Heaven. Any form of belief which ran counter to this ideal and which dissuaded people from fulfilling their obligations towards neighbours, relatives, ancestors and the Emperors would be decried by the Chinese intelligentsia, more so if it were a foreign religion.

Buddhism was not likely to get a warm reception from the Chinese at the first stage. It was more or less considered as an object of curiosity, and if not respected was not at least looked down upon. The foreign missionaries had to work hard in order to create in China an interest in Buddhism. The first two missionaries, Kāśyapa Mātaṅga and Dharmarakṣa, we know, translated a number of works into Chinese in order to give the people a general idea of Buddhism. Their works contained a *resumé* of the legends of the birth and childhood of the Buddha, his predication, and the main principles of Buddhism. There was also a text on the principles of ascetic life for those who wanted to follow the way of spiritual perfection. Another, entitled the "Sūtra of 42 Sections", which has been preserved up till now, is clearly a catechism for the use of the missionaries intending to preach the Buddhist religion in foreign countries. Such judicious selections from the sacred collection were made in order to create an interest in the Buddhist faith among the Chinese.

Ngan She-kao and his colleagues translated in the 2nd and 3rd centuries such a large number of texts that their work did not fail to create that sympathy for Buddhism which was required for its propagation. One hundred and seventy-nine translations are ascribed to Ngan She-kao alone. Apart from the translations, the life which these Buddhist missionaries led in China must have impressed the Chinese very favourably and attracted them quickly to this foreign religion. Buddhism was then in its prime purity. The missionaries were inspired by a great ideal and it was for the sake of that ideal that they had made the hazardous journey across the deserts of Central Asia. This great ideal had induced them to live the pure ascetic life which orthodox principles of Buddhism demanded.

Their sacrifice was not in vain. Chinese scholars soon came forward to take up the pen in defence of Buddhism and in order to establish its greatness as a religion. The first of these writers was a certain Mou-tseu who lived towards the end of the 2nd century. Mou-tseu compares the Confucian tenets with Buddhism and says:

"Let us consider the traditions transmitted by the three dynasties and the doctrinal practices of the literati....benevolence, justice and purity are much esteemed. Your fellow-citizens transmit your acts and your fame reaches the other shores of the sea. Such is the line of conduct followed by the average literati but not appreciated by the people who have practised detachment. The Śramaṇas practise the 'way' and the 'virtue' and replace by them the pleasures of the world. They turn to purity and wisdom and avoid the pleasures of the family life. What can be more wonderful than this? What can be more remarkable than this?"

Mou-tseu was well versed in the Chinese classics. He had

a powerful style and the arguments put forward by him in favour of Buddhism seem convincing. People like him must have done a good deal in the spread of Buddhism in China. That is the reason why Buddhism after its first infiltration in China went on gradually flourishing. Missionaries far from being discouraged to undertake the journey to China along the hard and dangerous route of Central Asia were more and more attracted towards that country.

The members of the small dynasties then ruling over China were not quite unsympathetic towards Buddhism. We do not know what interest they were actually taking in the propagation of Buddhism. The Chinese accounts tell us that many of them were responsible for building Buddhist monasteries in various parts of China. We are told that during the rule of the Tsin dynasty Buddhism became a very important factor in Chinese life. The Emperor Wu (265-290) showed great interest in the Buddhist religion and a large number of monasteries was built in different parts of the country by his order. The Emperor Min (313-316) also had two monasteries built: these were the *T'ong hiu sse* and the *Po ma sse* at Ch'ang-ngan. We are further told that during the reign of these two monarchs about 180 religious establishments were founded in the two cities, Nanking and Ch'ang-ngan. The total number of Buddhist monks was 3700 in this period. The figure is quite modest and the account seems to be reliable.

In the succeeding period also Buddhism is said to have received the same patronage from the rulers of China. The Song rulers had their capital in the south and under their patronage Buddhism was flourishing in the south. The official account tells us that Yuan-ti (317-322) built two large monasteries at Nanking, the *Wa kuan sse* and the *Long kuan sse,* each of which used to accommodate one thousand monks. Ming-ti (322-325) built two monasteries, the *Ming hing sse* and *Tao ch'ang sse* and assembled there more than one hundred Buddhist scholars. Ch'eng-ti (326-342) built two monasteries, the *Chong hing sse* and *Lu ye sse*, each of which accommodated about one thousand monks. Kien Wen-ti (371-372) erected numerous statues for the worship of the Buddhists and founded monasteries for accommodating the monks. Hiao Wu-ti (373-396) founded the monasteries of *Huang t'ai sse* and *Pen ki sse* and Ngan-ti (397-417) the monastery of *Ta she sse*. During 104 years of their rule 17068 small and great Buddhist institutions were founded throughout the Empire and 263 volumes of sacred texts translated. We do not know how far the figure given for the institutions founded is correct. So far as the number of translations is concerned it is quite accurate.

BUDDHISM UNDER THE WEI DYNASTY

A definite pro-Buddhistic attitude was taken in this period by the rulers of the North. The Wei (Toba) dynasty was founded by the foreign barbarians of the North in 386 and they were in power till the middle of the sixth century. The Wei period was one of the greatest epochs in the history of Chinese Buddhist art. We shall discuss later on the Wei contribution to the development of art in China. In regard to Buddhism one of the founders of the Wei supremacy, She-hu, promulgated in 335 an edict of toleration in the following terms :

"Buddha is a god worshipped in the foreign countries. He may not be worthy of receiving offerings from the Emperors of China and from the Chinese. But I, who was born in the frontier province, have the good fortune to be a ruler of China. In regard to religious duties I must abide by the customs of my people. As Buddha is a foreign god it is in the fitness of things that I should worship him. It is a pity that the same old laws of ancient times should be followed even now. When a thing is found perfect and faultless why should they still stick to the customs of the ancient dynasties? My people are called barbarian. I grant them the privilege to worship Buddha and adopt the Buddhist faith if they like to do so."

Such was the policy adopted by the Wei rulers. It was bound to give a great impetus to the propagation of Buddhism throughout North China. The official account which is given of their patronage to Buddhism may be exaggerated but still it gives an idea of the prosperous condition of Buddhism. The account runs as follows:

"Wu-ti (386-407) founded 15 caityas and two monasteries, the *K'ai t'ai sse* and the *Ting kuo sse* and personally copied sacred texts. He also erected a thousand statues in gold and every month entertained 3000 Buddhist monks in a religious convocation. Ch'eng-ti (453-465) encouraged the study of Buddhism in various ways. During his reign the number of monks and nuns had risen to 30,000. Hien Wen-ti (465-476) built the monastery of *Chao yin sse* solely for the use of the monks of the contemplative school of Buddhism (dhyāna). Hiao Wen-ti (476-479) built the *Ngan yang sse* and took a personal interest in the Buddhist religion. The number of Buddhist monks and nuns rose up to 40,000 during his reign. Siuan Wu-ti (499-515) himself explained the Buddhist text entitled *Vimala-kīrti-nirdeśa* in his palace and founded four monasteries *P'u sse, T'ong sse, Ta sse* and *Ting sse* and constantly entertained 1000 monks. Hiao Ming-ti (515-528) founded at Ye the *Ta kio sse* and his successor built five monasteries and constructed ten thousand statues in stone. Wu-ti (532-534) built in Ch'ang-ngan the monastery of the *Che k'i sse* in order to accommodate 200 monks. Wen-ti (534-51) built the *Pan jo sse* to accommodate the poor and the old and himself recited the sacred texts. Thus during 170 years of the Wei rule 47 big monasteries were built in

Lo-yang, Ch'ang-ngan and Ye by Imperial orders. Grottos were excavated in the northern hills near Ta-t'ong over a distance of 30 li. The smaller princes built in this period 839 temples and the private families more than 30,000 such temples. The number of monks and nuns were in this period more than two millions."

Under the patronage of the Wei, Lo-yang and Ch'ang-ngan became the greatest centres of Buddhist activities in China. It was then that the famous Tao-ngan, about whom we have already spoken, lived and wrote. He was responsible for creating the same interest in the Buddhist learning as the rulers were doing in the field of Buddhist art. Tao-ngan's disciples had imbibed a deeper interest in Buddhism than before and went into the interior parts of the country to propagate the new faith. Tao-ngan was also instrumental in attracting great Indian personalities to China. All the great translators of Buddhist texts, Kumārajīva, Buddhayaśas, Puṇyatrāta, Bodhiruci, etc., were in China in this period. Their personal influence and their work went a long way in establishing Buddhism firmly in China.

The break-up of the Chinese Empire at the end of the Han dynasty in 220, the encroachment of foreign invaders sympathetic towards Buddhism, the weakening of the Chinese literati who usually hung upon a strong centralized Imperial power, etc. contributed to the great success of Buddhism in China. The lack of a religion in China strong enough to counteract the influence of Buddhism was also helpful to the spread of Buddhism in such a short period.

The common people had a real need of religion. Besides, a section of the Chinese people who were under the influence of Taoism was already mystically bent and when they discovered that there were elements of mysticism in Buddhism which were similar to the Taoistic principles they were drawn to it.

LU-SHAN SCHOOL

The first definite conquest of Buddhism was soon evident. The Chinese monks began to take up Buddhism seriously as the religion of their life. In this period an institution founded by a Chinese monk rose into importance in the south. It was to play a great role in the early history of Buddhism in China. This was the monastery of Lu-shan which was founded by Hui-yuan, a disciple of Tao-ngan. Hui-yuan was born in 334 at Lou-fan, modern Tai-chou in North Shan-si.

In his young days he was an ardent student of Confucianism and Taoism. He wanted to pursue these studies under more capable teachers who were then in the south. But political troubles which broke out about that time did not allow him to proceed to the south. He therefore stopped at Ch'ang-ngan and took up Buddhist studies in which he soon excelled. After leaving his teacher Tao-ngan, he first settled in *Shang ming sse* in King-chou.

In 381 he shifted to Lu-shan in Kiang-si. Lu-shan was a solitary mountain spot, picturesque and eminently suited as a place of retirement for the Buddhist monks. In 386 the Governor of the province built a temple for Hui-yuan at Lu-shan. Visitors soon flocked round the place and their number, we are told, attained the incredible figure of 3000. Hui-yuan had at this time 123 disciples. He selected 17 out of them and founded with them a school which he named the "School of White Lotus" (*Po lien shu*). Amongst these 17 elites there were two Indian scholars, Buddhayaśas of Kashmir and Buddhabhadra of the Śākya clan about both of whom we have already spoken.

The school founded by Hui-yuan introduced in China the cult of Amitābha, which plays even now the most important role in the Buddhism of the Far East. It was a new form of Buddhism about which we shall speak later on.

Hui-yuan was a great Sanskrit scholar, but did not translate any text into Chinese; he only compiled a series of commentaries and devoted the greater portion of his time to the work of organization. It was at his suggestion that the whole of the *Sarvāstivāda-vinaya* was translated into Chinese. As he was too old to go personally to see Kumārajīva in the north he sent a number of scholars to the latter to be trained, and also exchanged letters with him. He sent a batch of his disciples, Fa-tsing, Fa-ling and others to the desert and snowy mountains (Central Asia) in search of Sanskrit manuscripts. After several years they came back with Sanskrit texts which were later on translated into Chinese.

The Lu-shan school, far from being a transplanted Indian school of Buddhism, was a definite contribution of the Buddhists in China. Chinese scholars were trying to acquire there a more profound knowledge of Buddhism.

It is therefore clear that from the 5th century onwards Buddhism was no longer considered in China as a foreign religion which excited mere curiosity. It was a living force in the life of the Chinese people and was exercising a deep influence on the Chinese culture which manifested more in the field of art and literature.

TRANSFORMATION OF BUDDHISM IN INDIA

But Buddhism itself was undergoing a considerable change in the land of its birth. It was no longer that simple faith of Buddha Śākyamuni which was primarily concerned with the problem of individual suffering that is concomitant with our birth in this world of woes, with its causes and the means of uprooting them. It was no longer that positivist religious attitude that demanded a scrupulously pure life of strict asceticism which alone could enable a man to uproot the causes of suffering and attain the ideal state called Arhatship. It had become an infinitely more complex religion.

A new mental attitude had grown up according to which the historical Buddha had no great place in Buddhism. He was considered to be one of a series of ephemeral Buddhas, transitory emanations of the ultimate reality, henceforth named *Dharmakāya*. The earthly Buddhas taught the same old reality that was eternal, omnipresent and changeless. The earthly hierarchy consisted not only of the Buddhas but also of Bodhisattvas, who were potential Buddhas, Arhats, ordinary monks, etc. There were Bodhisattvas of a higher category such as Maitreya, Avalokiteśvara, Amitābha, etc., who were all god-like, full of great commiseration, ever ready to lead the faithful ones in distress to the peaceful abodes or heavens of which each of them was the sole master. It was no longer considered a fruitful end to practise the religion for one's own salvation only. A life of sacrifice for the good of the suffering mankind was the most ideal life and one initiated to such a life was a follower of the way of the Bodhisattvas (Bodhisattvayāna). This new attitude was called the Mahāyāna or the "Great Vehicle" and the earlier Buddhism in way of contradistinction came to be known as the Hīnayāna or the "Little Vehicle".

This Mahāyāna was capable of greater expansion. All kinds of kindred beliefs could be easily assimilated to it and that would mean only the creation of new Bodhisattvas. Thus Hindu gods like Nārāyaṇa, Viṣṇu, Śiva, etc., were all introduced in the Buddhist pantheon under new names. Even the Iranian god Mithra was given the place of a Bodhisattva under the name Amitābha—"the Bodhisattvas of infinite light". A large amount of theism was thus introduced in the originally atheistic Buddhism. Personal gods were fit for worship and realization. Contemplation was the very basis of realization. Contemplation also involved a series of spiritual exercises called Yoga. Hence Yoga found its place in the Buddhist religion of those days.

But this thought development did not in any way negative the original basic creed of Buddhism. The real Buddha was the Dharmakāya Buddha, the *tathatā* or the ultimate reality which could not be defined in words. The world of phenomena was still considered to be either transient or illusory and so also our individuality. The ultimate goal was the realization of this illusory character of our personal identity. That alone leads to the cessation of suffering and the ultimate attainment of the Dharmakāya or perfect beatitude. All the powerful Bodhisattvas, Maitreya, Amitābha, etc. show us the way to that goal.

Two important systems of philosophy were developing in this Mahāyāna school. One was the Mādhyamika founded by Nāgārjuna who lived in the first century A. D. and was a contemporary of Kanishka. The other system was the Yogācāra which was founded by two brothers named Asaṅga and Vasubandhu in the 4th century or a little later. Nāgārjuna's philosophy is called Śūnyavāda or "the philosophy of voidness" as its main teaching was that the world of phenomena is an illusion pure and simple. There is neither the subject nor the object. The notion of time was also illusory. According to the other system the world of phenomena was an illusion but a *mental* illusion, an illusion created by the mind (*citta, vijñāna*). Hence the system was also known as Vijñānavāda. Both the systems admitted the necessity of practising meditation for the realization of the truth that all was an illusion and that the ultimate reality was beyond the grasp of this illusion.

This new form of Buddhism both in its religious and philosophical aspects had been gaining ground in India from the Kushan times and was the predominant form of Buddhism all over India till the 7th century A. D. As a religion it had features which were capable of easily attracting all the foreigners who came in contact with India, the Iranians, the Yue-chis, the Khotanese, etc., who under the influence of ancient Iranian religion discovered in it elements with which they were already acquainted. As a philosophy it attracted the best Chinese intellects who could follow it to a considerable extent with the help of their own logic.

There is therefore no wonder that Buddhism began to prosper more in China after the introduction of the Mahāyāna. Although Mahāyāna originated much earlier in India, Kumārajīva was the first to preach it in China in a systematic way. He was the first to translate some of the most difficult texts of Mahāyāna philosophy. In fact, the greater portion of the texts translated by him into Chinese was of Mahāyāna inspiration—either dealing with the path of the Bodhisattvas (Bodhisattvayāna), its different stages and practices or with the philosophy of the Mādhyamika school. Hui-yuan, we have seen, was influenced not only by the religious aspect of Mahāyāna but also by its philosophy.

BODHIDHARMA IN CHINA

A great impetus was given to the propagation of the contemplative aspect of Mahāyāna by an Indian teacher whose personality has become almost mythical in the Far East. This was Bodhidharma, commonly known in China as *Ta-mo* (Dharma) and in Japan as *Daruma*. His portrait is very commonly found in those two countries. He is represented in it as a bearded person carrying a twig on his shoulder from which hangs one of his sandals. No other Indian monk attained such fame in China as Bodhidharma. His followers later on attributed many miraculous acts to him and that was the reason of his great popularity with all sections of the people, both young and old.

The Chinese accounts tell us that he was the third son of

an Indian king, most probably of the South (Kāñcī). He first went to the South Sea Islands (Indonesia) where he was initiated to the Dhyāna (contemplative) school of Buddhism. He attained such great success in this that he was given the robe and begging bowl of Śākyamuni which had come down through generations and he thus became a patriarch. He was the 28th in the line of succession from Buddha. He then embarked on a sea-going vessel which took him to South China.

He was first received by the Emperor Wu. The conversation which he had with the Emperor has been recorded in the Chinese accounts. "The Emperor said to him—From my accession to the throne, I have been incessantly building temples, transcribing sacred books and admitting new monks to take the vows. How much merit may I be supposed to have accumulated ? The reply was—None. The Emperor—And why no merit? The patriarch—All this is but the insignificant effect of an imperfect cause not complete in itself. It is the shadow that follows the substance, and is without real existence. The Emperor—Then what is true merit ? The patriarch—It consists in purity and enlightenment, depth and completeness, and in being wrapped in thought while surrounded by vacancy and stillness. Merit such as this cannot be sought by worldly means. The Emperor—Which is the most important of holy doctrines? The patriarch—Where all is emptiness nothing can be called holy. The Emperor—Who is it that thus replies to me? The patriarch—I do not know."

We can see from this reported conversation that Bodhidharma was speaking in the language of Nāgārjuna. But that language was unknown to the Chinese Emperor, whose mind could not be free from the vanity of taking credit for meritorious acts. Bodhidharma did not like to stay in the south. He went to North China which was then under the sway of the Wei rulers. He lived there in retirement in the monastery of *Shao lin sse* in Song-shan.

A number of miracles is attributed to him. While going to the north he broke a reed and used it as a raft for crossing the Blue River. At *Shao lin sse* he passed nine years cross-legged in one seat with his eyes fixed on a rock of *Shao lin sse*. We are further told that he was poisoned to death at *Shao lin sse* and was buried there. But a few years later while the Chinese envoys were coming back from India they met him in the Pamirs in his habitual dress with the sandal hanging from his shoulder.

Popular legends have driven the real history into the background and hence for his arrival in China we get at least four dates: 486, 520, 526, 527 and for his death 495, 527, 528, 535 and 536. In spite of this variance it is quite certain that Bodhidharma was in China in the second quarter of the 6th century. An almost contemporaneous account written in 534 tells us that he was seen praising the beauty of the famous monastery of *Yong ning sse*, which was built in 516 in Lo-yang, and saying that although he was then 150 years of age and that although he had travelled far and wide he had not seen the like of that temple.

But the greatest contribution of this half-mythical personage was the introduction of the contemplative form of Mahāyāna into China, where it is known as the school of *Ch'an* from Sanskrit *dhyāna* or meditation. This school had a long and prosperous career in China and was also introduced in Japan where it still flourishes under the name of *Zen*. It recommends to its followers to abandon all exterior objects and practices. Meditation or cultivation of one's own thought alone leads to the goal. The real nature of one's own thought is pure and when one attains it the reality reveals itself to him. One should therefore take away the mind completely from the grasp of the exterior objects. This can be done through the meditation of voidness. This we know is the path defined by the teachers of the Mādhyamika school of Nāgārjuna.

T'IEN-T'AI SCHOOL

The immediate followers of Bodhidharma in China were Hui-si and Chi-k'ai. While the former went on preaching the doctrines of his master the latter went much further and developed a new school of Buddhism in China called *T'ien-t'ai,* from the name of the place where Chi-k'ai retired, about 180 miles to the south-east of Hang-chou. Chi-k'ai attempted a syncretism of all the forms of Buddhism known till then. This has a unique importance. Lots of sacred texts had been translated till then. Different forms of the Buddhist religion had been brought to China by the most prominent Indian teachers but no system had been evolved in order to explain the unity behind this diversity.

Chi-k'ai was born in 531 in Ying-ch'uan. He joined the Buddhist order at the age of 17. He first followed the teachings of Bodhidharma and practised dhyāna. In his earlier days he was at Nanking and maintained a high reputation. When he decided to retire to a solitary place, the Emperor stood in his way as he did not like to part with his company. He then left Nanking against the wish of the Emperor and proceeded to T'ien-t'ai which was then an inaccessible valley in the remote corner of a hilly wilderness that had not been visited by anybody previously. He built a temple there and began to pass his days in contemplation. But the teachings of Bodhidharma did not satisfy him completely. His profound study of the sacred literature soon enabled him to evolve a new system which was capable of explaining all the apparent diversities and contradictions in the teachings of Buddha.

His considered opinion on the matter was: "The diversity of human conditions was extreme, the philosophical theories are multiple but the end is one. It is to get over the evils, to attain the truth and the ultimate good. Little matters by which way each of them arrives at it, it is enough if he can arrive at it. Those who do not understand it compare and discuss the teachings of various schools, those who understand it accept them all and assimilate them."

In order to make an orderly presentation of the teachings of Buddha as contained in the extensive literature which had grown up by then, he divided the teachings according to five periods :

1. *The first period.*—Just after his attainment of enlightenment Buddha passed 21 days under the Bodhi tree ; at that time he preached the law to the gods who had come down to pay respects to him. This teaching was the most sublime and contained the highest truth unintelligible to ordinary men. These teachings are contained in a class of texts called Avataṁsaka—*Hua yen.*

2. *The second period.*—During the first twelve years of his career as teacher Buddha met common disciples and for their benefit made the discourses now contained in the Āgamas (*A-han*) which constitute the Sūtrapiṭaka of the Hīnayāna.

3. *The third period.*—During the next eight years Buddha made discourses for the benefit of the ordinary disciples and had at the same time to discuss religious matters with them in order to remove the doubts which occurred to them under the influence of other systems. Hence Buddha had to bring in at times the problems relating to the more sublime truths of the domain of Mahāyāna. These mixed teachings are contained in a class of texts known as Vaipulya—*Fang teng.*

4. *The fourth period.*—The next twenty-two years of his life Buddha passed in meeting the attacks of other

philosophical schools and had to controvert their tenets by having recourse to the sublime truths of Mahāyāna. These teachings are contained in a class of texts known as Prajñāpāramitā—*Pan-jo*.

5. *The fifth period*—Buddha passed the last eight years of his life in making discourses bearing upon a higher sphere of religious life. These were about the path of the Bodhisattvas or the new aspirers after Buddhahood who wanted to work for the salvation of mankind. These teachings belonged to the domain of Mahāyāna and are contained in a class of literature known as Nirvāṇa—*Nie-p'an*.

This was in short the system evolved by Chi-k'ai. He was of the opinion that Mahāyāna contained the highest teachings of Buddha and that the apparent contradictions between this form of Buddhism and the Hīnayāna have to be explained by assuming that Buddha had to adapt himself to occasions according to the capacity of his disciples. This assumption was not new. The great teachers of India had all expressed this view and had according to it tried to explain the contradictions between Hīnayāna and Mahāyāna. But they did not have the same success. The syncretism which Chi-k'ai succeeded in introducing in China was not possible in India.

Chi-k'ai had been to Lu-shan. Hui-yuan was long dead but his work had not perished. We do not know what benefit Chi-k'ai derived from his stay in Lu-shan. He had been there probably to see how far the teachings of the Lu-shan school fitted in with his own system. Chi-k'ai worked tremendously, wrote a number of treatises in defence of his system and trained a large number of disciples who carried on the work after his death. He died towards the closing years of the sixth century.

The system of Chi-k'ai had a tremendous success in China. It was accepted by all the Buddhist communities and his classification of Buddhist literature was adopted by all later writers. It has come down to our times. The Buddhists of China since then began to study all the branches of the literature, both Hīnayāna and Mahāyāna, without feeling disturbed in the least. They clearly understood that each branch of the sacred texts has its own importance, and was not to be neglected. The teaching of the T'ien-t'ai school was also introduced in Japan and had great success there too. All the Japanese schools of Buddhism still follow the syncretism introduced by Chi-k'ai.

BUDDHISM UNDER THE T'ANG

From the beginning of the 7th century Buddhism was entering a new phase in China. Hui-yuan and Chi-k'ai had done for it what the earlier missionaries had not succeeded in doing. Buddhism was no more an exotic religion. It had taken deep roots in the Chinese soil. A period of assimilation had started. Buddhism was inspiring new creations of the Chinese mind. When the T'ang dynasty came in power and unified the whole of China after long centuries of internal strife, Buddhism entered upon the most glorious period of its history in China.

The Buddhists however did not have an easy sailing. The prestige which Buddhism was slowly attaining in China and the consideration shown towards it by the Emperors of China aroused the jealousy of the literati. The position of the literati was again gaining strength after the restoration of the Empire and so they could not remain idle. A vehement campaign was started against Buddhism and it was continued throughout the T'ang period. The leader of this campaign was Fu-yi (555-639) who exercised a great influence in the Imperial court. He submitted a vigorous anti-Buddhist memorial in 624 to the Emperor, couched in the following words :

"Buddhism infiltrated into China from Central Asia,

under a strange and barbarous form, and as such it was then less dangerous. But since the Han period the Indian texts began to be translated into Chinese. Their publicity began to adversely affect the faith of the Princes and filial piety began to degenerate. The people began to shave their heads and refused to bow their heads to the Princes and their ancestors. They began to roam and beg and became monks in order to evade the public duties. They studied the three *pāramitās* and six *gatis* and refused to pay respect to others on the pretext of strict observance of their religion and work for higher perfection. Ever since they began to honour this foreign sage (Buddha) the country became a prey to barbarian invasion. Real rulers disappeared, ministers became traitors, the Government became tyrannic and the sacrifices neglected. The result is that the monks and the nuns now count by tens of thousands. I request you to get them married so that the country may have a hundred thousand families. They will then bring up children to fill the ranks of your army."

The propaganda of the literati led to a temporary persecution but the Emperor soon realized his mistake. This persecution was bound to react within the country unfavourably and affect the foreign relations. The Turks had then accepted Buddhism. Buddhism was prosperous in various parts of Central Asia. Tibet which was then emerging out of its political obscurity and growing into a powerful state had accepted Buddhism as a state religion. Its relations with India were very intimate. The newly founded T'ang Empire could not neglect China's relations with all these neighbouring territories for the sake of its political integrity as well as its foreign trade which was the very basis of its prosperity. Buddhism with its wide international affiliations was the most effective means of maintaining it. Such was the policy of the great T'ang rulers and that shaped their attitude towards Buddhism. The propaganda of the literati in spite of all its vehemence did not have the desired effect on it.

The T'ang policy towards Buddhism was also actuated by the great success with which the famous pilgrim Hiuan-tsang brought India and China together and established contacts between the Indian rulers and the Chinese court. The frequent exchange of ambassadors between India and China in this period could not but impress the nobles and the functionaries favourably. It was therefore in the fitness of things that they should all extend their patronage to Buddhism which had served so well the interests of the Chinese nation. Monastery after monastery began to be built in the important cities of the country. Translators were encouraged to carry on their work and the Emperors themselves as well as the nobles of the court began to take a personal interest in the work of piety.

Hiuan-tsang returned to China after sixteen years' travel in 645. We have seen what great reception was accorded to him by the public. Although he had gone to India in violation of the imperial order, the Emperor pardoned him as soon as he came back and received him well. So long as Hiuan-tsang was alive the Emperor used to pass some time occasionally with him and listen to the stories of the foreign countries. He died in 664 and was given a state funeral. In his life-time he was called by the Buddhists of China "the present Śākyamuni".

The main account of his travels is contained in his *Si-yu-ki* or "Record of the Western World". Besides this, one of his disciples named Hui-li compiled his life which also contains an account of his peregrinations. Another disciple wrote the *She-kia fang che* or an "Account of the Land of Śākyamuni", which also was based on the *Si-yu-ki*. These works gave a vivid description of the Buddhist religion in Central Asia and India and created in China interest in Buddhism on such a wide scale as was not previously possible.

Hiuan-tsang followed the tradition of the T'ien-t'ai school. Although he was a staunch follower of the Mahāyāna and strictly adhered to its Yogācāra school, still the Hīnayāna was also quite important in his eyes. Among the works translated by him there are texts relating to both the forms of Buddhism. If he did not found any school he inspired the foundation of at least three of them.

NEW BUDDHIST SCHOOLS

The first was the school to which he personally adhered, viz. the Yogācāra or the Vijñānavāda. We have seen that it was founded in India in the 4th or the 5th century A. D. Hiuan-tsang studied the philosophy of this school for five years at Nālandā with Śīlabhadra who was the greatest exponent of that school in those days. Hiuan-tsang translated almost all the works of that school and also the commentaries of nine different teachers of the school, and added to it a commentary of his own. It was to a great extent a personal work of the pilgrim. These works were the basis on which a new school was founded in China under the name Fa-siang—*Dharmalakṣaṇa* or "the true nature of the objective world". The school is called in Japan *Hosso*. This school is a true interpreter of the idealist school of Buddhist philosophy. According to it the Vijñāna is the only reality—the world of phenomena is only a projection of this Vijñāna or consciousness. There are eight kinds of Vijñāna—the last is called Ālaya-vijñāna which is a sort of sub-consciousness and contains the seed of all the creations. The phenomena are all illusion—the consciousness alone is real. After Hiuan-tsang the principal exponent of this school was his disciple Kui-ki who is still regarded as the best exponent of this philosophy in the Far East.

Hiuan-tsang was the founder of another school known as *Kiu-she* (*-kośa*). The name is derived from the name of the

Indian work *Abhidharmakośa* which contains an exposition of the philosophy of the Sarvāstivāda school— a Hīnayāna school. The *Abhidharmakośa* is a work of Vasubandhu who was also the founder of the Vijñānavāda of the Mahāyāna. It is based on the seven metaphysical works of the Sarvāstivāda school. Hiuan-tsang translated most of these works into Chinese. The pilgrim wanted to popularize the ideas of this school because they were useful for a proper understanding of Vijñānavāda. In fact Vasubandhu himself meant his famous *Abhidharmakośa* to be a stepping stone to the Vijñānavāda. The philosophy of this school is a sort of materialism. True to the original teachings of Buddha, it holds that the self (Ātman) is not objectively real, it is an ephemeral combination of the five aggregates of existence (*skandha*). These aggregates are, however, real. They are composed of infinitely small atoms (paramāṇu) which alone are real. Their combinations are unreal and illusory. After Hiuan-tsang some of his disciples continued to preach the doctrines of this school. It was taken to Japan where it is known as *Kusha.*

Another school which was founded by a disciple of Hiuan-tsang named Tao-siuan was the *Liu* or the *Vinaya* school. In Japan it is known as *Riotsu.* It is not known how far Tao-siuan was influenced by his teacher in formulating the tenets of this school. It was not inconsistent with the attitude of the Buddhist scholars of China of that period. According to the true teachings of the T'ien-t'ai no branch of the sacred literature was without its own importance. Tao-siuan in the same strain taught that discipline was not to be neglected. It was of the greatest importance for the early preparation of the saintly life. Unless one passes through the life of strict monastic discipline he cannot form his character and never arrives at an advanced stage to practise the meditation with an amount of success. For the preparation of the early career Tao-siuan recommended the disciplinary code of the *Dharmaguptaka* school, also known as "the Vinaya of four divisions". The Vinaya of other schools had also been translated into Chinese but as they contained many other things besides the discipline and were very extensive, Tao-siuan selected the *Dharmaguptaka-vinaya* for the guidance of his followers.

These schools did not lose their importance after the death of their founders. They were followed during many years. The tradition of the Fa-siang school has not been lost in China. All the schools are still followed in Japan.

Buddhism continued to have a prosperous career in China up to the beginning of the 8th century. We have already mentioned the work of the Chinese monks who had been to India in this period. Yi-tsing who was the foremost among them tried to put greater emphasis on the scrupulous observance of the rules of conduct. He translated the biggest collection of disciplinary codes which was the Vinaya of the *Mūlasarvāstivāda* school. The number of other works translated in this period both by the Chinese and foreign monks was enormous.

MYSTIC BUDDHISM

But Buddhism soon entered into a new phase in China, till then altogether unknown in that country. It was the mystic phase. Buddhism was slowly changing in India. An esoteric Buddhism was growing under the influence of Brahmanism. It is generally known as Tantrayāna, but it included various forms of mysticism known as Vajrayāna, Kālacakrayāna, Sahajayāna, etc. Nālandā was no less a centre of this new form of Buddhism. It did away with all earlier practices and introduced the cult of many new gods and goddesses. The form of worship was also very mystic and involved some form of Yoga, use of mystic gestures and formulæ, contemplation on the mystic value of sound, etc.

This form of Buddhism was taken to China by Vajrabodhi, developed and extensively preached by his disciple, Amoghavajra. We have already spoken about these two teachers. All other teachers of this period and of the Song period belonged to this school and translated texts belonging to it. This school is known in Japan as *Shingon*. The primordial principle according to the teachings of this school is Mahāvairocana who is the same as the *Bhūtatathatā* of the philosophical schools—the Dharmakāya. The teachings of this school concern three mysteries—the body, the speech and the mind. It is found in all the beings either animate or inanimate. All aspects of nature are expressions of these three mysteries. These three mysteries in the human beings are the same as those in the Buddha. It is therefore possible to lead all beings to the state of Buddha. This march towards Buddhahood involves a system of mental evolution through the acquisition of merits. This system, however new it might appear, was a logical outcome of the Mādhyamika system of philosophy taught by Nāgārjuna.

This mystic Buddhism had a great success in the Far East. In China it influenced the Confucian philosophy of the Song period and in Japan, where it was introduced by Kobodaishi in the beginning of the 9th century, it is still esteemed as the best system of Buddhism on account of the deep philosophical insight inculcated by it.

But although the mystic Buddhism of Vajrabodhi indicated a new development which had its historical value both in India and China, it contributed to the rapid decline of Buddhism in both the countries. The historical Buddha had no place in it. The community had lost its importance because the religion had become highly individualistic—the fellow brethren had no part to play in the mental evolution of the follower of this faith. Under these circumstances the ever powerful Brahmanical systems which had by then developed a similar kind of mystic attitude easily assimilated the Buddhism of those days in India. India had nothing more to give to China. The creative genius of Buddhism through which the Indian internationalism manifested itself had reached its end.

During the latter part of the T'ang period and the first part of the Song period Chinese monks were still going to India, not with the purpose of study but in the simple discharge of pious missions—pilgrimage, collection of relics, erection of stūpas at Bodhgayā by the Imperial order and so forth. We no longer come across with a Hiuan-tsang or a Yi-tsing. Excepting a few translators, most of the Indians too who went to China in this period were ordinary monks, having no such definite object to fulfil in that country as their predecessors. The deeper aspect of the religion had been thrown into the background in China and formalism had come to the forefront. The renewed attacks of the literati soon succeeded in destroying much of the prestige which Buddhism enjoyed in the earlier periods. Besides, complete cessation of relations between India and China from the middle of the 11th century left Buddhism almost helpless in China. It soon ceased to be a living force in the national life of the country.

BUDDHISM UNDER THE MONGOLS

But before its final overthrow Buddhism won a new victory in China in the 13th century under the patronage of the Mongol rulers. It was the Lamaistic form of Buddhism introduced from Tibet. The military campaigns of Chinghiz Khan towards the end of the 12th century placed the Mongol power in an eminent position in Asia. One of his successors, the great Kublai extended the Mongol supremacy over the whole of China. The ascendency of Kublai in power in 1259 marks a new era in the history of Buddhism—a short period of glory just before its complete extinction.

Buddhism was in a difficult state in China in this period. The Taoists were growing to be dangerous adversaries of the Buddhist monks. They were misappropriating the properties of the monastic organizations and were turning their temples into sanctuaries of the Taoist sages. The Buddhists at first did not succeed in sending a good representation of their grievances to Chinghiz Khan who was then moving from place to place. The Taoists took advantage of this helpless state of the Buddhists for some time. But the situation changed during the reign of Manku Khan. On the 30th May, 1254, a great religious discussion was organized at Karakorum under the presidency of three representatives of Manku Khan—one a Christian, the second a Mahomedan and the third a Buddhist. The famous Friar William of Rubruck took part in this discussion and took the side of the Nestorians. They along with the Mahomedans succeeded in establishing the existence of one God. The Buddhists were silenced for the time being but did not give up their hopes at once.

In 1255 a new conference was held at Karakorum. Manku Khan himself attended it with his officials. The abbot of the temple of *Shao-lin* named Fu-yu represented the Buddhists. The Taoists were defeated and were ordered by an Imperial decree to return the Buddhist establishments occupied by them. But the Taoists did not act according to the order. Therefore the very next year (1256) another conference had to be called by Manku Khan. The most famous Buddhist monks came in numbers to attend this conference. But the Taoists did not turn up. The Khan took it to be a sign of their incapacity and recognized the superiority of Buddhism in these terms—"Just as the fingers come out of the palm of the hand, the Buddhist doctrine is likewise the palm, the other religions are like the fingers."

Tired of these theological discussions Manku Khan in 1258 entrusted his younger brother Kublai to take a final decision in the matter. Kublai called a great religious conference in 1258. It was attended by 300 Buddhist monks and 200 Taoists; 200 Confucian scholars served as arbiters. Among the Buddhists there was the abbot of the temple of *Shao-lin*, one Na-mo—a Rājaguru of the Western countries, and the famous Tibetan monk 'Phags-pa (1239-1280). The latter was the nephew of Sāskya Pandit of Tibet. Although he was only 19 years of age at that time, he played a decisive role in the conference. The Buddhists came out victorious through the eloquent exposition of the religion by 'Phags-pa. The Taoists were defeated and 17 of their leaders had to shave their heads and become Buddhist monks according to the engagement entered into. The Buddhists got back 237 religious establishments which they had lost. Kublai recognized the superiority of Buddhism and ordered the Taoist texts disparaging Buddhism to be burnt.

'Phags-pa was appointed the Kuo-she (Rājaguru) in 1260. He was the recognized head of the Buddhist Church in the vast empire of Kublai. Kublai established a special relation between Tibet and his dynasty through the Lamaist hierarchy and from this time the Tibetan monks began to take lead in all the Buddhist activities in China and Mongolia. 'Phags-pa devised an alphabetic system for all the languages in the Mongol Empire—Mongolian, Chinese, Tibetan, etc. It had a phonetic basis and was an adaptation of the Tibetan alphabet which was itself borrowed from India.

By the order of Kublai a new catalogue of the Buddhist literature was compiled in three languages—Chinese, Tibetan and Sanskrit. It was primarily a catalogue of the Chinese collection with references to texts in the Tibetan collection.

Kublai was probably entertaining the grandiose idea of

uniting the diverse elements in his vast empire giving it at the same time one culture, one script and one religion. This religion was no longer the earlier Buddhism which was long dead but the Lamaistic Buddhism of Tibet. India had no longer any place in this conception. Kublai's empire broke down just after his death. Buddhism in this new form after a short period of glory again lost all its chances in China.

Buddhism is practically a dying religion in China but its great work in all fields of Chinese life still survives. This work still bears testimony to the great effort made by two major countries of Asia, India and China, in building up a common civilization.

CHAPTER V

BUDDHIST LITERATURE IN CHINA

Buddhism possessed a vast literature but this literature has been preserved for us only outside the frontiers of India. The Pāli literature which is often wrongly supposed to be the only authentic canon of Buddhism has been preserved in Ceylon, Burma and Siam. No trace of it has been found on the Indian soil. A few Sanskrit texts belonging to the vast Sanskrit canon of Buddhism have been discovered from the ordinarily inaccessible valley of Nepal. The dilapidated Buddhist grottos of Afghanistan and the ruins of the Buddhist temples in the deserts of Central Asia have also yielded fragments of this Sanskrit canon. But this canon has been preserved in its entirety only in Tibet and China in large collections of old translations.

The Chinese Buddhist Tripiṭaka is mainly a literature translated from the Indian source. The latest Japanese edition of this collection includes 2184 texts in over 7000 chapters. Some of these texts are commentaries, exegetical texts and dictionaries compiled by Chinese Buddhist authors, but the greater bulk of it consists of translations of Indian texts, most of which are lost in their original form. These translations were made in China in course of the first millennium A. D. A few of them belong to the 13th century, the reign of the shortlived Mongol dynasty, but they were translations not of the Indian texts but of the Tibetan Buddhist texts.

The authors of these Chinese translations were at first the Buddhist monks who went to China from Central Asian countries such as Parthia, Sogdiana, Bactriana, Kucī, Khotan, etc. Although the translations made by these foreign monks were not satisfactory either from the Indian or from the

Chinese point of view, they helped considerably in attracting Chinese scholars to Buddhism. The Chinese Buddhist scholars soon felt the need of better and more authoritative translations of Indian texts. They sought the collaboration of those Indian scholars who had already begun to come to China in large numbers from the beginning of the 4th century A. D. A new era was opened by the translations made by Kumārajīva who was an adept both in Sanskrit and Chinese. Besides, he had deep insight into the subtle philosophy of Buddhism.

The second period in the history of translation is marked by an ever increasing part played by Chinese Buddhist scholars in the work. They not only collaborated with the Indian scholars in rendering the Buddhist texts but also translated the texts by themselves. They had begun to learn Sanskrit with the help of Indian scholars, and samples of Chinese-Sanskrit dictionaries which were used by them for the purpose have also come down to us.

The third and the most fruitful period in the history of translation is marked by the advent of Hiuan-tsang. He himself was a tireless worker in this direction and translated 75 works in about 1300 fasciculi. He seems to have been a Sanskrit scholar of a very high order and his knowledge of the Buddhist philosophy was profound. A large number of the translations made by him is from most abstruse philosophical texts. The Chinese translators who followed him were inspired by his ideal. They were all determined to make the translations intelligible to the Chinese Buddhists and to give at the same time the most correct idea of Buddhist doctrines.

Such colossal work could be possible not through individual efforts but through well-organized boards. We hear of regularly constituted boards of translators from the beginning of the T'ang period (A. D. 618). Prabhākaramitra, a

Buddhist scholar of Nālandā, who had gone to China was the first translator of this period. When he started his work of translation in A. D. 629 at Ch'ang-ngan, the high officials were instructed to give as much facility to him as possible.

The officials collected 19 talented scholars to help Prabhākara in his work. It was started in the monastery of Ta-hing-sse at Ch'ang-ngan. The Sha-men (Śramaṇa) Hiuan-wu, Seng-kia (Saṅgha) and others translated his words into Chinese. The master of the Tripiṭaka and Vinayadhara Kiu-to (Gupta) verified the translation. The Sha-men (Śramaṇa) Fa-lin, Hui-ming, Hui-che, Hui-tsing, and others wrote down the translation. The Sha-men Hui-sheng, Fa-ch'ang, Hui-lang, T'an-tsang, Che-kiai, Che-shou, Seng-pien, Seng-tsong, Tao-yu, Lin-kia, Wen-shuan and others copied the translation. The Emperor ordered the high officials to examine the final redaction and to supervise its execution. Thus was completed the translation of a work in 10 chapters. It was begun in the 3rd month of A. D. 629 and completed in the 4th month of the next year.

This account gives an idea of the complete apparatus of translation in the T'ang period. The principal translator need not have been a sound Chinese scholar. There were then in China Indian interpreters who were capable of rendering the Sanskrit explanations given by the Indian translators into Chinese. Such well constituted boards of translators helped in the production of good and authorized translations of Buddhist texts in a much shorter period than was possible before.

ANCIENT COLLECTIONS AND CATALOGUES

From the very outset both official and non-official organizations came into existence for making collections of the translations made. The available translations were catalogued from time to time and care was taken to preserve these translations for the benefit of posterity. In spite of this care, many of the early translations were lost. Although they are mentioned in the old catalogues their traces are no longer found in the official collections that have come down to us. A few of the lost translations have been discovered from Central Asia in course of the recent archæological explorations but many of them are still to be found out. Some of the old translations fell into neglect for the reason that they were not good and that more improved translations of the same texts had to be prepared in later times. Even in the present collections of Buddhist texts there is more than one translation of a number of texts. Some of the translations were lost for want of good communication between the various monastic organizations in the early period.

In the Chinese Buddhist literature there is mention of 46 different catalogues of the Buddhist translations. These catalogues meant as many different collections of translations made from time to time. Among these catalogues 24 were lost before A. D. 597. Three of the old catalogues were utilized in A. D. 597 when an official catalogue was prepared. Three more existed up to A. D. 730 when the first official catalogue of the T'ang period was compiled. The remaining 16 catalogues have come down to us and give us an idea of the collections.

The oldest catalogue of the Chinese Buddhist collection that exists was a private undertaking and was compiled by a Chinese Buddhist scholar named Seng-yu in the first quarter of the 6th century A. D. This catalogue mentions in all 2213 works, many of which are now lost. It was about that time that an official catalogue was also compiled by Pao-ch'ang. The Sui Emperor who was then reigning, we are told, was greatly devoted to Buddhism and made a large collection of Buddhist texts numbering about 5,400 volumes in the Hua-lin garden. Pao-ch'ang prepared a catalogue of this Imperial collection in A. D. 518 but this catalogue was subsequently lost.

Three more catalogues compiled in the 6th century have come down to us. The first of these was compiled by one Fa-king in A. D. 594. It mentions 2257 works in 5310 fasciculi. The traditional division of the canon into three collections, viz. Sūtra, Vinaya and Abhidharma, is adopted for the first time in this catalogue. The next catalogue was compiled in A. D. 597 by a monk named Fei Chang-fang by the Imperial order. It is one of the best catalogues that exists. The canon is divided into two main sections, Hīnayāna and Mahāyāna, each containing the three traditional classes: Sūtra, Vinaya and Abhidharma. The total number of works enregistered in the catalogue is 1076 in 3325 fasciculi. This catalogue for the first time attempts to give a connected history of Buddhism from the time of the birth of Buddha in the first few chapters. Towards the close of the century, the Sui Emperor Wen-ti passed an order for the compilation of a new catalogue. In pursuance of this order Yen-ts'ong and a few other Buddhist scholars of the monastery of Ta-hing-shan-sse of Ch'ang-ngan compiled the new catalogue in A. D. 602. This catalogue mentions 2109 distinct works in 5058 fasciculi. The authors followed a new plan and tried to produce a critical work. They, for the first time, tried to distinguish the genuine works from the spurious ones of which the number according to them was 209. They mention 402 works as missing.

A number of important catalogues compiled in the T'ang period has come down to us. Some of these catalogues are the surest guides that we still possess for our studies. The first of these was compiled in A. D. 664 by Tao-siuan, the famous disciple of Hiuan-tsang. The T'ang Emperor Kao-ts'ong ordered the monks of the Si-ming-sse monastery of Ch'ang-ngan to prepare a new and authoritative copy of the

Buddhist canon and Tao-siuan was entrusted with the work of cataloguing this collection. In the first section of the catalogue there is an account of the translators and their works. There is mention of 2487 works in 8476 fasciculi. In the second section we get a list of works that existed in his time. The number of the existing works is given as 799 in 3364 fasciculi, the total number of pages being 45626. A supplementary catalogue was prepared in A. D. 730. The author's name is doubtful. Three more catalogues were prepared in this period, one by Ts'ing-mai in A. D. 645, the second which is a shorter work and a supplement to the preceding one by Che-sheng in A. D. 730, and the third in A. D. 695 by Ming-ts'iuan by the Imperial order.

By far the best catalogue, entitled the *Ta t'ang k'ai yuan she kiao lu* was compiled in A. D. 730 by Che-sheng, a Buddhist scholar of the monastery of Si-ch'ong-fu at Ch'ang-ngan. It is the most critical and also the most comprehensive catalogue ever prepared. The author not only utilizes all the old catalogues but also examines them critically and classifies them scientifically. He enumerates 1124 complete works in 5048 fasciculi and separates from them 1531 works which were, according to him, either incomplete or spurious. In his time 1148 of the earlier translations had been already lost. In A. D. 794 a supplement to this catalogue was prepared by Yuan-chao. The same author compiled a new catalogue in 799 based almost on the same plan as that of Che-sheng. There is almost nothing in it that may be considered as original as the author reproduces the text of Che-sheng verbatim.

The last catalogue which is of some importance was compiled under the Mongols between A. D. 1264 and 1294 by the order of the Emperor Kublai. It is a comparative catalogue of the Chinese and the Tibetan Buddhist collections. A few more catalogues were compiled in later periods but they were of much less interest than the previous ones. The last

Chinese collection of the Buddhist Tripiṭaka was made under the Ming dynasty by the order of the Emperor T'ai-tsu. The Chinese catalogue of this collection was the basis of the first catalogue to be published in English in 1883 by the famous Japanese scholar Buniyo Nanjio.

The collections and the catalogues described above give some idea of the great efforts made by both official and non-official bodies in China to preserve the Buddhist translations in different periods. Although a number of translations has been lost still a fairly complete collection of Buddhist texts has been preserved on account of these efforts.

PRINTED EDITIONS OF THE CANON

Printing of the Buddhist canon was resorted to as soon as block-printing was sufficiently advanced. But for these old block-printed editions, the Chinese Buddhist collections might have been entirely lost to us. The first printed edition of the canon was prepared in the Song period. Emperor T'ai-tsong of the Song dynasty ordered some important personalities in A. D. 971 to go to Yi-chou (modern Ch'eng-tu) in Sse-chuan and to print the canon by means of wooden blocks. The order was executed in A. D. 972 and different editions of the canon were printed in gold and silver. The number of blocks made was 130,000 and they were presented to the Emperor when the work had been completed. Some texts belonging to this printed edition may still be found in Japan.

Two block-printed editions of the canon were pepared in the 11th and 12th centuries in Fu-kien. Both the editions were made by private institutions, one by the monks of the monastery of Tong-ch'an-sse and the other by the monks of the monastery of K'ai-yuan-sse. The first consisted of 564 works in 6087 chapters and was block-printed between A. D. 1080 and 1104. Some additions were made to this collection by an Imperial order when a reprint was made in A. D. 1172.

The second which also consisted of 564 works but in 6117 chapters was block-printed in the middle of the 12th century. Both the editions are still preserved in Japan. These are known as the Song editions of the Chinese Buddhist canon.

Another Song edition of the canon in 548 volumes consisting of about 5900 chapters was probably started in the middle of the 12th century and finished in the middle of the 13th century. It was most probably printed in Hu-chou. Two copies of this edition are preserved in Japan.

An edition of the canon was block-printed under the Mongol (Yuan) dynasty. The edition was prepared in Hang-chou in the monastery of Ta p'u-ning sse of Nan-shan. It is a reproduction of the last Song edition with some new additions. Copies of this edition also have been preserved in Japan.

Another block-printed edition was prepared in the beginning of the 14th century (A. D. 1301-1306) in Su-chou, but this edition was subsequently lost. An edition of the canon based on the Song edition was also printed in Corea in this period but it was later on destroyed. In 1251 another Corean edition was published and copies of this edition were preserved in Japan. The last Chinese edition to be published was printed in A. D. 1643, through the care of the monks of the T'ien-t'ai sect. This is what is still known as the Ming edition of which copies were preserved in Japan.

It is clear that these block-printed editions of the Chinese canon contributed to the preservation of the Buddhist literature of China. The modern editions of the canon published from Japan have mainly been based on the four editions, Song, Yuan, Ming and Corean. Unless copies of these editions had come down to us, it would have been utterly impossible to prepare a comprehensive edition of the canon. The latest Japanese edition known as the Taisho edition contains also texts discovered from other sources but its main sources are the old Chinese editions, copies of which had been preserved in Japan. It is likely that isolated texts may still be discovered in old Chinese monasteries after careful search.

HĪNAYĀNA LITERATURE—THE VINAYAPIṬAKA

According to a convention introduced very early in the Buddhist church, the literature came to be divided into two main classes—the Hīnayāna and the Mahāyāna. Although this classification is doctrinal, the two literatures are interwoven by many subtle links which are generally ignored. There is again no reason to think that the Hīnayāna literature is the older and more original collection of the Buddhist church while the Mahāyāna is a later growth. The development of both the branches belonged to a period which witnessed the highest development of Buddhism in India. The classification is therefore merely a conventional one and it was also adopted by the Chinese Buddhist scholars in classifying the Chinese translations of the canon.

The Vinayapiṭaka is mainly the code of monastic discipline. It however contains much more than that. It enumerates the offences which should not be committed by the monks and the nuns. It also records the incidents either real or fancied which led Buddha to prescribe suitable punishment for the commission of a particular offence by a monk or a nun. Sometimes in order to magnify the gravity of the offence committed, the past life of the guilty monk was narrated and it was pointed out that the same monk was guilty of the same offence in the previous life too. The Vinayapiṭaka contains also the rules and regulations for the management of the Buddhist community (Saṅgha), rules for the ordination of the monks, rules for the periodical confession of sins, for life during the rainy season, for housing and clothing, medicinal remedies, and procedure in case of schism in the church.

The Vinayapiṭaka is thus the most important work of the

Buddhist canon as it concerns the very foundation of the Buddhist church. Each of the important Buddhist communities of India therefore possessed a Vinayapiṭaka of its own. But many of these texts are now lost in their original and are found only in Chinese translations.

In Chinese translations there are five different Vinayapiṭakas, now lost in their original. The language in which they were originally composed is not known. It is however certain that some of them had been composed in Sanskrit whereas others were probably in local dialects. The Vinayapiṭakas preserved in Chinese are the following:

1. *The Vinayapiṭaka of the Mahāsāṅghika school* in 34 chapters. The manuscript of this Vinaya was discovered by the famous Chinese pilgrim Fa-hien in a monastery of Pāṭalīputra. The story of this discovery is thus given in the account of his travels: "Fa-hien's original object had been to search for the Vinaya. In the various kingdoms of North India, however, he had found one master transmitting orally (the rules) to another, but no written copies which he could transcribe. He had therefore travelled far and come on to Central India. Here, in the Mahāyāna monastery he found a copy of the Vinaya, containing the Mahāsāṅghika rules—those which were observed in the first Great Council while Buddha was still in the world. The original copy was handed down in the Jetavanavihāra." This manuscript was taken to China by Fa-hien and translated into Chinese by him in A. D. 424 in collaboration with an Indian Buddhist scholar named Buddhabhadra. The general plan of the work is similar to that of other Vinayapiṭakas but it is much richer than many of the works in anecdotal element throwing light on the social and economic history of Northern India.

2. *The Vinayapiṭaka of the Sarvāstivāda school* in 61 chapters. As the Vinaya is divided into 10 sections it is also known as the "Vinayapiṭaka in ten sections"—*She song liu.*

The original text was in Sanskrit. Certain portions of the original text have been discovered from Central Asia in course of archæological explorations. The text was translated into Chinese in A. D. 404 by Kumārajīva and Puṇyatrāta. Kumārajīva, we have seen, was a native of Kucī and educated in Kashmir. Puṇyatrāta was a Buddhist scholar of Kashmir who came to the Chinese capital about the closing years of the 4th century. Kashmir in this period was the greatest centre of the Sarvāstivāda school and it was the literature of this school that was most studied in the Buddhist monasteries of Central Asia.

3. *The Vinayapiṭaka of the Dharmaguptaka school* in 60 chapters. It is also known as the "Vinayapiṭaka in four sections"—*Sseu fen liu.* It was translated into Chinese by a Kashmirian Buddhist scholar named Buddhayaśas in the year 405 in collaboration with a Chinese scholar named Chu Fo-nien. Buddhayaśas had passed a considerable part of his active career in various parts of Central Asia and it was at the special request of Kumārajīva that he went to China in the beginning of the 5th century. The translation of the Dharmaguptaka Vinaya was commenced in A. D. 410 and completed in 413.

4. *The Vinayapiṭaka of the Mahiśāsaka school* in 30 chapters. The manuscript of this text was also procured by Fa-hien, from one of the monasteries of Ceylon during his sojourn in that country. Fa-hien however had no time to translate it into Chinese. So Buddhajīva was requested to do it. The latter, a Buddhist scholar of Kashmir, who came to China in A. D. 423, rendered the text into Chinese in the following year (A. D. 424.)

5. *The Vinayapiṭaka of the Mūlasarvāstivāda school.* It is the most extensive of all the Vinayapiṭakas either in Chinese or any other language. It was translated into Chinese by Yi-tsing, the famous Chinese pilgrim, who had come to

India in the 7th century A. D. The translation was made in the beginning of the 8th century. The *Dul-va* of the Tibetan Buddhist collection known as *Kanjur* is also a translation of the same work. The original work was in Sanskrit. Only some portions of this text have been discovered in India.

Besides these five complete Vinayapiṭakas, there are also Chinese translations of shorter texts belonging to the various Vinaya schools such as the *Prātimokṣa* or the Rules of ordination of the monks and the nuns, the commentaries on the Vinayas called *Vibhāṣā* and *Mātṛkā* and other miscellaneous texts. As a whole the Vinayapiṭaka in Chinese is the richest collection of the Vinaya literature that ever existed. The Pāli Vinayapiṭaka represents only one school but the Chinese collection represents five different schools and as such it affords us the greatest scope for the study of the ancient Vinaya literature.

A comparison of the Vinayapiṭakas in Chinese translation with the Pāli Vinayapiṭaka often brings forth new and important facts. The accounts given in the Chinese Vinayas are often more complete than those in the Pāli Vinaya and throw greater light on many aspects of the early Indian life and society. They also supply us with information on the doctrinal differences between the various Buddhist schools. In fact a study of the Chinese Vinayas is indispensable if we want to reconstruct the history of the early Buddhist church in India. The common points between the various Vinayas again take us back to the constitution of the primitive Buddhist order.

HĪNAYĀNA LITERATURE—THE SŪTRAPIṬAKA

The Pāli Suttapiṭaka (Sanskrit Sūtra-) is a collection of discourses attributed to Buddha himself. It is the main source of the Buddhist doctrines that are expounded in the innumerable dialogues contained in it. It is divided into five collections called Nikāya : Digha (Sanskrit Dīrgha), Majjhima (Sanskrit Madhyama), Saṁyutta, (Sanskrit Saṁyukta), Aṅguttara (Sanskrit Aṅguttara) and Khuddaka (Sanskrit Kṣudraka).

Corresponding to the Pāli Suttapiṭaka there is in Chinese translation a Sūtrapiṭaka which is now lost in its original. This original Sūtrapiṭaka was in Sanskrit and this is clearly proved by fragmentary remains of the original text discovered from Central Asia by archæologists. The close agreement of these fragments with the corresponding text in the Chinese translation shows that the original Sūtrapiṭaka from which the Chinese translation was made was in Sanskrit. This Sūtrapiṭaka most probably belonged to the Sarvāstivāda school which alone rivalled with the Pāli school in possessing a full-fledged Tripiṭaka.

The Chinese Sūtrapiṭaka unlike the Pāli, is divided into four Āgamas called Dīrgha, Madhyama, Saṁyukta and Ekottara, the last name corresponding to the Pāli Aṅguttara. There is nothing corresponding to the Pāli Khuddaka-nikāya in Chinese. The reason is not far to seek. The Pāli Khuddaka is not a collection like the first four Nikāyas. It is principally a collection of such heterogeneous texts as the Dhammapada, Udāna, Itivuttaka, Suttanipāta, Jātaka, etc. There are separate Chinese translations of the corresponding Sanskrit texts such as Udānavarga or Dharmapada, Jātaka, Arthavarga, etc.

Although the names of the first four collections of the Pāli and the Chinese Sūtrapiṭakas are the same, their contents are not exactly the same. There is no doubt a common foundation but in details they differ from each other to a considerable extent. Besides, the arrangement of the Sūtras in each of the four collections doesnot strictly follow the same order in the Pāli and the Chinese Sūtrapiṭakas. A comparative study of the two Sūtrapiṭakas alone can give us an idea of the Buddhist Sūtras that existed during the early days of the Buddhist community in India.

The Dīrghāgama was translated into Chinese by the Kashmirian monk Buddhayaśas in collaboration with the Chinese Buddhist scholar Chu Fo-nien in the beginning of the 5th century (412-413). It consists of 30 different Sūtras. The Madhyamāgama was translated in A. D. 397-398 by another Kashmirian scholar named Gautama Saṅghadeva. It consists of 222 short Sūtras. The Saṁyuktāgama was translated in A. D. 420-427 by Guṇabhadra who also had gone to China from Kashmir. The Ekottarāgama was translated by Dharmanandī in A. D. 384-385. It consists of 555 short Sūtras.

But although the complete Chinese translations of the four collections of the Sūtrapiṭaka belong to the end of the 4th and the beginning of the 5th centuries there are much earlier translations of a large number of texts belonging to one or other of the four āgamas. Sometimes there is more than one translation of the same text. The earlier translators from the middle of the 2nd century undertook to translate various texts of the Sūtrapiṭaka. As soon as the complete translations of the four āgamas became available no further need was felt to have separate translations of the individual texts and many of the earlier translations fell into neglect and were lost. But still nearly two hundred old translations of various āgama texts have come down to us. The earlier translations are in many cases abridgements meant to give an idea of the doctrines contained therein.

The Chinese Sūtrapiṭaka contains, besides the translations of the four āgamas, a large number of miscellaneous works such as the Sūtra on the Life of Buddha, the Jātakas, etc. The birth-stories of Buddha or the Jātakas were known in the Sanskrit collection as avadānas. A few collections of the avadānas were translated into Chinese very early. The famous collection of old verses which is known in Pāli as

Dhammapada was called Udānavarga in Sanskrit. There are three different Chinese translations of this text, two of which belong to the 3rd century and the third to the 4th century A. D. If we take all these texts into consideration the Chinese Sūtrapiṭaka represents a much bigger collection than the Pāli.

HĪNAYĀNA LITERATURE—THE ABHIDHARMAPIṬAKA

The Abhidharmapiṭaka in Pāli consists of seven works that are called: Dhammasaṅgani, Vibhaṅga, Kathāvatthu, Puggalapaññatti, Dhātukathā, Yamaka and Paṭṭhāna. The word Abhidhamma (Sanskrit Abhidharma) has the meaning of transcendental doctrine. The Abhidhammapiṭaka contains a scholastic exposition of the Buddhist philosophy. The third Abhidamma text, the Kathāvatthu is principally a book of controversy. It enumerates the doctrines of various Buddhist sects and the defence of the tenets of the school to which it belongs.

In the Chinese collection the Abhidharmapiṭaka is known as the collection of Śāstras. They are distinguished from the Sūtra because they are ascribed to authors of lesser importance. The Sūtra is supposed to be 'Buddhavacana' or the 'saying of Buddha'. The principal Abhidharma texts in the Chinese collection of Śāstras constitute the third piṭaka of the Sarvāstivāda school. These texts like the Vinaya and the Sūtra of that school were originally written in Sanskrit but unfortunately the originals are lost. The Chinese translations are now our only source.

The Sarvāstivāda school like the Pāli Tripiṭaka possessed seven Abhidharma texts: (1). *Jñānaprasthāna-śāstra* of Kātyayanīputra. (2). *Saṅgīti-paryāya* of Mahākauṣṭhila. (3). *Dhātukāyapāda* of Vasumitra (4). *Prajñāptisārapāda* of Mahāmaudgalyāyana. (5). *Dharmaskandha* of Śāriputra. (6). *Vijñānakāyapāda* of Devaśarman. (7). *Prakaraṇapāda* of Vasumitra. Of the seven texts, the first was translated by the

Kashmirian monk Gautama Saṅghadeva in collaboration with Chu Fo-nien in A. D. 383. The remaining six texts were translated by Hiuan-tsang between A. D. 651 and 660. The texts translated by the latter are less extensive than the first, the Jñānaprasthāna-śāstra, which seems to have been the principal work of the Sarvāstivāda Abhidharmapiṭaka.

The subject matter of both the Abhidharmas, the Pāli and the Chinese, is generally the same. But even a superficial comparison between the two collections shows that the latter is not a translation of the former. The Sarvāstivāda Abhidharma had an independent development.

Besides the seven Abhidharma texts of the Sarvāstivāda school, there is in Chinese translation a number of auxiliary texts of capital importance. The first of these is the *Abhidharma-mahāvibhāṣā-śāstra* which, according to the tradition, was compiled by 500 Arhats of the Sarvāstivāda school in the fourth Buddhist council that was held under the patronage of the Kushan emperor Kanishka. The work which is a commentary of the Jñānaprasthāna-śāstra mentioned above is in 200 chapters. It was translated between A. D. 656 and 659 by Hiuan-tsang. The original is lost. The second work which attained even a greater fame than the previous one is the *Abhidharmakośa-śāstra* which was composed in the 5th century A. D. by Vasubandhu. The Sarvāstivāda school had then divided itself into two camps, called the *Sautrāntika*, i. e. those who followed the authority of the Sūtrapiṭaka, and the *Vaibhāṣika*, i.e. those who followed the authority of the Vibhāṣā or the Mahāvibhāṣā, which we have just seen was the commentary of the Jñānaprasthāna-śāstra and was an epitome of the Abhidharma knowledge of the Sarvāstivāda school. Vasubandhu in this work upholds the position of the Sautrāntikas as against the Vaibhāṣikas. Vasubandhu criticizes the doctrines not only of the Vaibhāṣikas but also of all other schools that opposed the Sautrāntikas. The work was translated into Chinese by Hiuan-tsang in A. D. 651-654. The original is known to us only through a later Sanskrit commentary called Sphūṭārtha which was compiled by Yaśomitra. For the complete text and its commentaries by Vasubandhu himself the Chinese translations are our principal guide.

Among other texts, the Chinese Śāstra collection contains another important text known as the *Satyasiddhiśāstra*, or more correctly *Tattvasiddhiśāstra*. It was the work of Harivarman, a famous Sarvāstivāda teacher of Kashmir. But the views expressed in the work are different from those of the Sarvāstivāda school and it is just possible that Harivarman was a follower of some other Buddhist school so far as his views on the Buddhist philosophy were concerned. Harivarman's original work is now lost. The Chinese translation which has come down to us was made in the beginning of the 5th century by Kumārajīva. The work was held in high esteem in China, and an independent Chinese Buddhist school called *Satyasiddhi* or *Tattvasiddhi* based its doctrines on it.

There are a few other Śāstra texts in the Chinese collection such as the "Treatise on the eighteen Buddhist schools" by Vasumitra and works composed by Saṅgharakṣa, and a few others. The Sanskrit originals are all lost and the Chinese translations along with the Tibetan translations are our only guides.

It therefore seems clear from what has been said above that the Abhidharma-piṭaka as preserved in the Chinese translation is a much more comprehensive collection than the Pāli Abhidhamma-piṭaka and is indispensable for any study of the ancient philosophy of Buddhism. They supply us with useful materials even for the study of the later philosophical systems of Buddhism such as the Mādhyamika of Nāgārjuna and the Yogācāra-Vijñānavāda of Asaṅga.

MAHĀYĀNA LITERATURE—VINAYA, SŪTRA AND ŚĀSTRA

There is a large section of Mahāyāna literature in the Chinese canon. The translations of the Mahāyāna texts from Sanskrit are not less numerous than the Hīnayāna texts. In the classification of these texts the Chinese Buddhists adopted the same convention as for the Hīnayāna canon, and arbitrarily divided it into three classes—Sūtra, Vinaya and Śāstra. This classification is arbitrary because there is no trace of it in the Mahāyāna tradition of India. In Nepal where Mahāyāna has been a living form of Buddhism for many centuries, its literature is divided into nine classes called Vyākaraṇas. The principal texts belonging to these nine classes are the following: (1) *Aṣṭasāhasrikā Prajñāpāramitā*. (2) *Saddharmapuṇḍarīka*. (3) *Lalitavistāra*. (4) *Laṅkāvatāra*. (5) *Suvarṇaprabhāsa*. (6) *Gaṇḍavyūha*. (7) *Tathāgataguhyaka*. (8) *Samādhirāja*. (9) *Daśabhūmika*. The Chinese translations of these texts, as we shall see later on, are included in the Sūtrapiṭaka of the Mahāyāna. What is called the Mahāyāna Vinaya in Chinese is a misnomer. It is not a Vinayapiṭaka in the sense in which we have Vinayapiṭakas for the Hīnayāna schools: it consists of texts which might be very well included in other sections.

The Mahāyāna Vinayapiṭaka in Chinese consists of about 25 works, the principal among them being known either as Bodhisattva-caryā or as Bodhisattva-prātimokṣa. The most important of the former class is the *Bodhisattva-caryā-nirdeśa*. It was twice translated into Chinese. The first translation was made by Dharmakṣema, whom we have already mentioned, between A. D. 414 and 421. The second translation was made by Guṇavarman in A. D. 431. But the original text is not a Vinaya in the strict sense of the term. It is really a chapter of a famous Mahāyāna Śāstra work, the *Yogācārabhūmi-śāstra* which was the fundamental text of the Yogācāra system of philosophy. As the text deals with the special preparatory practices for those who want to follow the way of the Bodhisattva, the Mahāyāna ideal, it has been separately classed as a Vinaya text. There is another text known as the *Bodhisattva-prātimokṣa* or the "Rules of ordination for the Bodhisattva" in the Chinese translation. This also was twice translated into Chinese, the earlier translation being due to Dharmakṣema; it is an extract of the same Śāstra work. Kumārajīva translated a work entitled *Brahmajāla-sūtra* in A. D. 406. It is also classed as a Mahāyāna Vinaya work as it deals with the rules of ordination for the Bodhisattva. The original of this text cannot be clearly traced. Although the Chinese Buddhists in later times placed much emphasis on the Mahāyāna ideal, still for the purpose of ordination the Hīnayāna Vinaya code could not be dispensed with. In fact two ordinations were provided for, the first according to the Hīnayāna and the second according to the Mahāyāna codes just mentioned.

The Mahāyāna Sūtrapiṭaka, however, represents a more authentic collection of the Mahāyāna canon. The classification of the texts in the Chinese Tripiṭaka is purely a Chinese classification but almost all the texts belonging to the old Mahāyāna canon have been translated there. They are all supposed to be the words of Buddha (Buddha-vacana) and are considered as authoritative as the Sūtrapiṭaka of the Hīnayāna with this difference that while the latter represents the exoteric aspect of the teachings of Buddha, the former represents the esoteric aspect.

The Mahāyāna Sūtrapiṭaka as preserved in Chinese translation has five chief divisions, namely: (1) *Prajñāpāramitā*. (2) *Ratnakūṭa*. (3) *Mahāsannipāta*. (4) *Avataṁsaka* and (5) *Mahāparinirvāṇa*. This classification, as we have seen before, was the direct result of the T'ien-t'ai syncretism attempted in the 6th century A. D. It had no root in the Indian soil; the literature according to the ancient Indian tradition consisted of nine divisions (vyākaraṇa). Texts belonging to the various classes were being translated into Chinese from the 2nd century A. D. Some of the most popular texts such as the *Amitāyus-sūtra*, the *Vajracchedikā Prajñāpāramitā* were translated almost a dozen times.

(1). *Prajñāpāramitā*. This class consists of eight different texts of which the first six are only different redactions of the Prajñāpāramitā-sūtra, viz. the *Śatasāhasrikā Prajñāpāramitā*, the *Pañcaviṁśati-sāhasrikā*, the *Daśasāhasrikā*, the *Pañcaśatikā*, the *Saptaśatikā*, etc. All the texts were translated into Chinese between A. D. 222 and 659. The most extensive of all these works is the first—the Śatasāhasrikā, also called the *Mahāprajñāpāramitā-sūtra*, which is in 600 fasciculi and contains according to the traditional calculation 200,000 ślokas in verse or an equivalent number of syllables in prose. It was translated into Chinese by Hiuan-tsang in A. D. 659. The Sanskrit originals of some of the Prajñāpāramitā texts such as the Pañcaviṁśati-sāhasrikā and the Aṣṭasāhasrikā were discovered from Nepal, but for the complete collection we have to depend on the Chinese and Tibetan translations.

(2). *Ratnakūṭa*. The Ratnakūṭa is a collection of different texts of which the principal is called *Mahāratnakūṭa-sūtra* from which the name of the whole collection was derived. The Mahāratnakūṭa-sūtra is a collection of 49 different texts some of which were translated into Chinese in the 2nd and 3rd centuries A. D. Twenty-six texts belonging to this collection were translated in the T'ang period by Bodhiruci (A. D. 693-713). The famous *Amitāyus-sūtra* which is also known as the *Sukhāvatī-vyūha-sūtra* is a Ratnakūṭa text. It was translated into Chinese over 12 times, the earliest translation being dated A. D. 148. It was one of the most popular Buddhist texts in China and was the principal text of one of the Chinese Buddhist schools. The texts connected with the name of the future Buddha Maitreya also belong to this class. Some of the Ratnakūṭa texts have been made available in their original from the Nepalese collections and the Central Asian finds. But, for the complete collection, the Chinese translations are our only source.

(3). *Mahāsannipāta.* The principal text of this collection is called *Mahāvaipulya-mahāsannipāta-sūtra* which was translated into Chinese by Dharmakṣema in the beginning of the 5th century A. D. There is a number of other texts in this collection such as the *Candragarbha-sūtra*, *Sūryagarbha-sūtra*, *Kṣitigarbha-sūtra*, etc., but the most extensive and the most important is the Ratnakūṭa-sūtra. Its Sanskrit original is completely lost and the Chinese translation is our main source of information for this branch of the Mahāyāna literature.

(4). *Avataṁsaka.* The principal text of this collection is the *Buddhāvataṁsaka-mahāvaipulya-sūtra* in 60 chapters which was translated into Chinese in the beginning of the 5th century by the Kashmirian scholar Buddhabhadra. It was translated a second time in the 7th century by Śikṣānanda of Khotan. A most important text of Mahāyāna philosophy, the *Daśabhūmika-sūtra*, belongs to this class. It was translated a number of times into Chinese. The oldest of these translations belong to the 4th century A. D. The Sanskrit originals of some of these texts are now available, but the most complete collection is preserved only in Chinese.

(5). *Nirvāṇa.* The principal text of this class is the *Mahāparinirvāṇa-sūtra* in 40 fasciculi. It was translated into Chinese in A. D. 423 by Dharmakṣema. The remaining texts of this collection are either translations of extracts or supplementary portions of the same text. There is a Mahāparinirvāṇa-sūtra in the Āgama collection of the Hīnayāna canon, but the present text has nothing to do with that and is a purely Mahāyāna text.

Besides these five classes of texts, there is a miscellaneous collection of Mahāyāna sūtras in Chinese. This collection is one of the largest in Chinese and contains texts which could not be conveniently included in one or other of the five classes described above. Some of the important texts of this collection which are now available in their Sanskrit original are the *Saddharmapuṇḍarīka-sūtra*, *Suvarṇaprabhāsa-sūtra*, and *Lankāvatāra-sūtra*. But the great majority of the texts of this collection is lost in their original. This is why the Chinese translations are of the greatest importance to us for the study of the primitive Mahāyāna Buddhism, the diverse aspects of which, Indian or Ser-Indian, are still unknown to us.

The Abhidharmapiṭaka of the Mahāyāna or the collection of the Mahāyāna śāstras in Chinese is a unique collection as it contains texts that are of paramount interest for the study of the Buddhist philosophy. The Sanskrit originals of only a few of these texts are available; for the rest we have to depend mainly on the Chinese translations. The whole collection has been given the sanctity of the full-fledged piṭaka as the authors of the different texts belonging to it were great Indian personalities such as Nāgārjuna, Asaṅga, Vasubandhu, Aśvaghoṣa, Dharmapāla and others, all of whom had attained the high status of Bodhisattva. We shall here mention only the principal works in this collection.

The largest work of Nāgārjuna which is lost in original but preserved in Chinese translation is the *Mahāprajñāpāramitā-sūtra-śāstra* in 100 fasciculi. The original Sanskrit text, it is said, contained 100,000 ślokas in verse or a corresponding number of syllables in prose. It is a commentary of the Mahāprajñāpāramitā-sūtra which, we have seen, is the principal text of the first division of the Mahāyāna sūtra texts. The present śāstra text was translated into Chinese by Kumārajīva in A. D. 402-405. Amongst other works of Nāgārjuna, preserved in Chinese, mention may be made of the

Daśabhūmi-vibhāṣā-śāstra, a commentary of the Daśabhūmi-sūtra, also translated by Kumārajīva in A. D. 405. A few minor works of Nāgārjuna such as the *Nyāyadvāraka-tarka-śāstra*, the *Madhyāntānugama-śāstra*, and the *Dvādaśanikāya-śāstra* were translated into Chinese later. Nāgārjuna as is well known was the founder of a new system of Buddhist philosophy called the Mādhyamika. This philosophy was the direct outcome of his interpretation of the old Mahāyāna sūtras and hence his commentaries on the Mahāprajñāpāramitā-sūtra, Daśabhūmika-sūtra, etc. were the very foundations on which his new system was based. We have already seen in the last chapter what deep influence this system exercised on Chinese Buddhism.

The works of another great Mahāyāna teacher, Aśvaghoṣa, are also preserved in Chinese translations. Of these, two are the most important as Śāstra works—the *Sūtrālaṁkāra-śāstra* and the *Śraddhotpāda-śāstra*. In the latter work alone there is trace of a well-defined system of philosophy. It was translated into Chinese by Śikṣānanda in A. D. 695-700, while the *Sūtrālaṁkāra-śāstra* was translated by Kumārajīva in A. D. 430.

There are translations of a number of important śāstra works which are said to have been the works of the Bodhisattva Maitreya. It is not certain whether this Maitreya was a historical Mahāyāna teacher or the same as the legendary 'future Buddha'. The tradition says that these śāstras were communicated by Maitreya to Bodhisattva Asaṅga. This is the reason why these texts are generally considered as works of Asaṅga. The principal works of this group are: (1). *Yogācārabhūmi-śāstra* in 100 fasciculi. The Sanskrit text is said to have contained 40,000 ślokas in verse or a corresponding number of syllables in prose. The work was translated by Hiuan-tsang in A. D. 646-647. (2). *Mahāyāna-sūtrālaṁkāra-śāstra*—translated by Prabhākaramitra in A. D.

630-633. (3). *Mahāyāna-samparigraha-śāstra*—translated by Paramārtha in A. D. 563. (4). *Madhyāntānugama-śāstra*—translated by Gautama Prajñāruci in A. D. 543. These are the principal works which expounded the new system of philosophy called Yogācāra founded by Asaṅga. Unfortunately very few of the original works have come down to us. For a complete collection of the works of Asaṅga, the Chinese translation is our main source.

Vasubandhu who was the younger brother of Asaṅga was, in his early life, a follower of the Sautrāntika school of Hīnayāna. It was then that he composed his famous Abhidharmakośa which, we have already seen, is an important compendium of the Sarvāstivāda-abhidharma. Vasubandhu soon changed his allegiance and his convictions leaned towards Mahāyāna. He gradually formulated a new system of philosophy called the Vijñānavāda which is a further elaboration of the Yogācāra doctrines of Asaṅga. Although some of the original works of Vasubandhu have now been discovered from Nepal, the great majority of his works are now available only in Chinese translation. Some of the principal works lying in Chinese translation may be mentioned here: (1). *Vijñānamātratā-siddhi-śāstra*—translated by Hiuan-tsang in A. D. 559 along with the Sanskrit commentaries. (2). *Madhyānta-vibhaṅga-śāstra*—translated by Hiuan-tsang in A. D. 661. (3). *Tarka-śāstra*—translated by Paramārtha in A. D. 550. (4). *Viṁśikā-prakaraṇa*—translated by Hiuan-tsang in A. D. 661. The works of Vasubandhu and Asaṅga had a great influence on the famous Chinese pilgrim Hiuan-tsang and not only did he translate the chief works of these authors but also based on these works a new system of Chinese Buddhist philosophy which was highly esteemed in China long after his times.

The few Mahāyāna śāstra works described above are enough to show how rich is the Abhidharma-piṭaka of the

Mahāyāna as preserved in Chinese. Not only does it possess the largest number of Mahāyāna śāstra texts in any language, but it also contains the most important works of Mahāyāna philosophy which are otherwise lost to us. The few Sanskrit works extant are not enough to give an idea of the Mahāyāna philosophy. If we want properly to gauge the great contributions made by the most reputed Buddhist teachers like Nāgārjuna, Aśvaghoṣa, Āryadeva, Asaṅga and Vasubandhu to the development of Indian thought in general we have to go to the Chinese translations, which, in this respect also, are of invaluable help to us.

BUDDHIST MYSTIC LITERATURE

Certain forms of mystic Buddhism, generally represented by three schools called Vajrayāna, Sahajayāna and Kālacakrayāna, developed in India with the decadence of Buddhism that started in the 8th century A. D. That is the reason why the literatures of these schools are not so well represented in Chinese translation as in the Tibetan. There is a fairly large number of texts belonging to the Vajrayāna in Chinese but there is none belonging to the other schools. The interest of the Chinese Buddhists in these forms of mysticism was again very restricted. These late Buddhist schools in India had drawn considerably on the Brahmanical Tantras and that is why they could be best understood and followed in the light of that literature. The Brahmanical Tantra was completely unknown in China and although the Taoists had developed a highly mystic religion, still its technique did not much help in understanding the technique of the later Buddhist mysticism. The Chinese Buddhists naturally felt the ground much surer where Hiuan-tsang had left them.

Some of the Indian teachers who had gone to China in the later period tried to introduce the Vajrayāna works. The pioneers in this field were Vajrabodhi and Amoghavajra.

Both of them translated about 150 Vajrayāna treatises into Chinese from A. D. 719 to 774. Many of these works are *dhāraṇīs* or spells and *sādhanas* or methods of invocation of Mahāyāna gods and goddesses who were absolutely new-comers in a religion which originally did not possess a pantheon. Some translators of the Song period also translated a number of Vajrayāna texts into Chinese. Among them Fa-t'ien also called Fa-hien (Dharmadeva), a monk of Nālandā, translated about 118 small texts into Chinese between A.D. 973 and 1000. Some of the texts translated by him are pure Mahāyāna sūtras without any mystic element in them while the rest are dhāraṇīs and sādhanas. The last great translator of dhāraṇīs and sādhanas into Chinese was She-hu (Dānapāla ?), a monk of Uḍḍiyāna which was a great seat of mystic Buddhism in this period. He translated 111 works during the closing years of the 10th century. The originals of many of these works translated in the Song period are lost.

This short survey of the Buddhist literature, will, it may be hoped, give a general idea, however insufficient, of the service rendered by the Indian and Chinese scholars of ancient times. Their untiring work of collaboration during a period of about one thousand years has preserved for us a vast literature that has been lost to India. The history not only of Buddhism but also of Indian civilization in its various aspects cannot be properly studied without the help of this literature which China has so zealously preserved for posterity.

CHAPTER VI

INDIAN ART AND SCIENCES IN CHINA

MIGRATION OF INDIAN ART

Buddhism brought with it other elements of Indian culture to China besides philosophy and legend. China with her old heritage of a highly developed civilization could not remain contented only with a new creed from India. She had as much interest in other elements of Indian culture—such as art, astronomy, mathematics, medicine, etc. The influence of these aspects of Indian culture is still traceable in China.

When Buddhism was slowly infiltrating into Central Asia under the patronage of the Kushans, a hybrid Buddhist art was being evolved in North-Western India. It originated in the Indianized Greek *milieu* shortly before the Kushans entered India. Its highest development took place under the Kushans. The Hellenistic artists put themselves in the service of Buddhism, which was their religion by adoption. The art which they produced was mainly illustrative of this religion.

This art which was carried to Central Asia and China distinguishes itself by certain well-defined characteristics from the more developed Indian art which was flourishing in the interior of the country. It makes use of the Greek architectural motifs such as the Corinthian pillar, for floral designs it introduces the acanthus flower, and for drapery the Greek classical costumes as well as the Central Asian costumes and ornaments. In regard to composition it gives representations of scenes from the life of Buddha and also depicts the stories of his former birth. The image of Buddha is found here for the first time in India and in a large number. This art has been styled Indo-Greek or Graeco-Buddhist as its execution was Greek while its inspiration was Buddhistic. It flourished throughout the Kushan period and traces of it are found in various places in North-Western India up to the fifth century.

This art was gradually ousted by the more developed Indian art of the Kushan period which flourished specially at Mathura. It represented the orthodox art tradition of the country and was a direct development of the more ancient art of Sanchi and Bharhut. The Mathura school also produced a type of Buddha image which was not a copy of the Indo-Greek Buddha, but was distinctly its own creation. No characteristic of the Indo-Greek Buddha is found here. "The sculpture is in the round, or very high relief....the head is shaven, never covered with curls, the uṣṇīṣa wherever preserved is spiral, there is no ūrṇā and no moustache, the right hand is raised in abhaya-mudrā, the left is often clenched, and rests on the thigh in seated figures or in standing figures supports the folds of the robe, the elbow being always at some distance from the body, the breasts are curiously prominent, though the type is absolutely masculine and the shoulders very broad, the robe leaves the right shoulder bare, the drapery moulds the flesh very closely and is arranged in schematic folds, the seat is never lotus but always a lion throne (siṁhāsana) without miniature figures while in the case of standing figures there is often a seated lion between the feet, the gesture and features are expressive of enormous energy rather than of repose or sweetness." (Coomaraswamy). This art was not without the influence of the contemporary Indo-Greek art of the North-West, but its affiliation with the earlier Indian art was much closer, the Indo-Greek influence being only superficial.

The art of the Kushan period slowly gave rise to what is known as the Gupta art. This art flourished throughout the Gupta period and was replaced towards the 7th century by provincial arts which had more accentuated local characters. The Gupta art is the classical art of India and is a synthesis of all earlier elements. It has been defined by Coomaraswamy in the following terms : "The rich decorative resources of the Gupta art are to be understood in terms of its inheritance, indigenous, early Asiatic, Persian and Hellenistic. The Gupta style is unified and national. Plastically, the style is derived from that of Mathura in the Kuṣaṇa period, by refinement and definition, tendencies destined still later, in the natural course of events, to imply attenuation. Meanwhile Gupta sculpture, though less ponderous than the ancient types, is still distinguished by its volume; its energy proceeds from within the form and is static rather than kinetic." The technique has been perfected. It is now a sort of "language without conscious effort", and a medium of expression of the highest spiritual conception of the age. This development is visible not only in sculpture but also in painting. The Indian art has attained with it the classical phase of which the influence extended far beyond the frontiers of India. This phase is represented in the sculpture of all important centres of North India during the Gupta period and in painting in the famous frescoes of Ajanta.

We have seen that during the first period of Buddhist expansion outside India, it was the North-West, specially Gandhāra and Kashmir, which took the leading part. It is therefore quite natural that the missionaries of these two countries who went to Central Asia and China would carry with them the elements of the Indo-Greek art which was then, in their own country, the only medium of the plastic expression of their pious aspirations. When the whole of Buddhist India ranged itself behind the foreign missions, other styles of Buddhist art, Mathura, Gupta, etc. were also carried abroad along with Buddhism.

The artists and art elements from India thus migrated to

Central Asia and China along the same routes as followed by the merchants and missionaries. The vestiges of Indian art have been discovered by archæologists all along the Central Asian routes. In all the chief cultural outposts towards China, such as Bamiyan, Bactria, Khotan, Miran, Kuchar, Turfan, and Tun-huang they have discovered remains of Buddhist grottos, sculptures, paintings, etc. which bear testimony to the great effort made by Buddhist India to bind all the countries with lasting ties of cultural relationship.

Proceeding along the route leading towards Bactriana and Central Asia, we can discover the relics of the ancient art in the valley of Bamiyan. The grottos in the hills surrounding the valley are of the type of the Ajanta caves. They contain paintings in the walls and the ceilings. Superb pieces of sculpture were scooped out from the sides of the hills. In spite of the vandalism of the later invaders, what remains at Bamiyan gives us a clear idea of the art in its most flourishing days. The sculpture belongs to the Indo-Greek school. In the frescoes there is a good deal of Sassanian influence but still there are elements in it which remind us directly of the art of Ajanta. This is evident specially in the fresco representation of the *kinnaras* swimming in the sky. There are in the frescoes also the representations of solar and lunar symbols which are commonly found in the Buddhist and Manichæan art of Central Asia. This is generally supposed to be due to the influence of Sassanian art.

Proceeding along the route towards Bactriana we come to a place called Dukhtar-i-Nusirwan to the north of the Hindukush. The remains of Buddhist art discovered at this place are of the same type as those of Bamiyan. Bactriana itself suffered most at the hands of later invaders. Situated at the meeting place of highroads leading to India from the Persian Empire and Central Asia, it was in ancient times the greatest place of attraction for all foreigners. We have also seen what an important centre of Buddhism it was as late as the middle of the 7th century A. D. A few remains of this art have been discovered. It was certainly a great seat of the Buddhist art in ancient times. Hiuan-tsang tells us that the Navasaṅghārāma of Balkh was highly decorated. The chief image of Buddha in this monastery was artistically made of precious substances and its halls were adorned with costly rarities.

From Balkh to Khotan the road lay through hills which were difficult of access. The countries through which it passed was sparsely inhabited. Hence the work of art was also bound to be insignificant. Hiuan-tsang, however, tells us that in his days there were three Buddhist monasteries at Anderab, ten at Kunduz and four at Badakshan. The remains of these monasteries, if ever discovered, will surely unfold the traces of the same precious art as found in Bamiyan on the one hand and in Khotan on the other.

Along the southern route Khotan was the most prosperous seat of civilization in ancient times. Numerous archæological sites have been discovered in its neighbourhood, the principal among them being Yotkan, Rawak, Dandan Uilik and Khotan. The remains of sculpture found at Rawak belong to the Indo-Greek school of art. It is the Indo-Greek art not of the decadent type but at its best which flourished in India in the 1st and 2nd centuries of the Christian era. The frescoes and paintings discovered from Dandan Uilik either on silk or on wood reveal the different influences which the art of this region had received. A fresco which depicts the temptation of the monks reminds us at once of the art of Ajanta. Again, a Bodhisattva who is represented as a sort of Sassanian king with aquiline nose, black beard and a tiara on the head, dressed in a sort of yellow robe and heavy skin boots, bears clearly the Sassanian stamp. Besides, instances of sculpture inspired by the Græco-Buddhist school are not rare. In the later period Chinese, Tibetan and Uigur influences are also discovered in the art of this region.

Fa-hien in his description of Khotan speaks of a grand display of the Buddhist images in that country. He witnessed a procession of the images which directly reminds us of the Yātrā as seen in India even to our days (the Car festival of Jagannātha at Puri, the Matsyendrayātrā at Patan in Nepal, etc). Fa-hien gives the following description of the procession that was organized by the monks of the famous Gomati-vihāra and other monasteries of Khotan: "At a distance of three or four li from the city, they made a four-wheeled image car, more than thirty cubits high which looked like the great hall (of a monastery) moving along. The seven precious substances were grandly displayed about it, with silken streamers, and canopies hanging all round. The (chief) image stood in the middle of the car, with two Bodhisattvas in attendance, while *devas* were made to follow in waiting, all brilliantly carved in gold and silver, and hanging in the air. When the car was a hundred paces from the gate, the king put off his crown of state, changed his dress for a fresh suit and with bare feet, carrying in his hands flowers and incense, and with two rows of attending followers, went out at the gate to meet the image and with his head and face (bowed to the ground), he did homage at its feet, and then scattered the flowers and burnt the incense. When the image was entering the gate the queen and the brilliant ladies with her in the gallery above scattered far and wide all kinds of flowers, which floated about and fell promiscuously to the ground. In this way everything was done to promote the dignity of the occasion. The carriages of the monasteries were all different, and each one had its own day for procession. (The ceremony) began on the first day of the fourth month and ended on the fourteenth after which the king and queen returned to the palace."

This clearly shows that the Buddhist art in Khotan was in early times not merely confined to the halls of the monasteries, but also played a part in the national life of the people. The monasteries of Khotan in the time of Fa-hien exhibited the same artistic taste. He tells us that it took eighty years to build the king's new monastery. It was about 250 cubits (375 ft.) in height, rich in elegant carving and inlaid work, covered above with gold and silver, and finished throughout with a combination of all the precious substances. The Hall of Buddha near it was "of the utmost magnificence and beauty, the beams, pillars, venetianed doors and windows being all overlaid with gold-leaf. Besides this, the apartments for the monks are imposingly and elegantly decorated, beyond the power of words to express." Such a monastery was probably built after the model of the famous Kaṇiṣka-vihāra of Gandhāra which had aroused the wonder of all foreign travellers during the first few centuries of the Christian era. The number of monasteries in Khotan and its neighbourhood had risen to 100 in the time of Hiuan-tsang. Hiuan-tsang specially mentions a Buddha image of sandal-wood, 20ft. high, in a monastery in the neighbourhood of Khotan which was brought, according to an old tradition, from India.

At a place called Miran, on the southern route, situated to the south of Lob-nor similar remains of the art of an ancient period have been discovered. In the frescoes, influence of the art of Western Asia is preponderating. The art remains Buddhist, but its hybrid character is more accentuated than elsewhere in Central Asia.

In the northern part of Central Asia, Kashgar was, we have seen, a chief centre of Buddhism in early times. In the time of Hiuan-tsang Kashgar contained about a hundred Buddhist monasteries. The remains of art that were discovered at a place called Tumshuk near Kashgar, on the way towards Kuchar, gives an idea of the art that flourished in this region in ancient times. Buddhist images and bas-reliefs which were found in this place connect the art of this region directly with the Indo-Greek art of Taxila. The same types of Bodhisattvas and gods have been found at Taxila and Tumshuk. Probably the same Indo-Greek moulds were used in both the places.

On the northern route the richest art finds have come from the region of Kuchar and Karasahr. Three places near Kuchar have yielded the art relics—Kizil, Kumtura and Duldur-akur. A number of Buddhist grottos called Ming-oï (Grottos of Thousand Buddhas) were found in this region. The painting on the walls betray among other influences also an influence of Ajanta. There is also direct influence of the Indo-Greek art as well as that of the Indian art of the Kushan period traceable in this region. The remains of art discovered in the region of Karasahr are also of the same type. Sculpture like that of Tumshuk is closely connected with the art of the Indo-Greek school which flourished at Taxila in the 4th and 5th centuries A. D.

Hiuan-tsang gives a detailed description of the monasteries of Kuchar. He tells us that the images in some of the monasteries were beautiful, almost beyond human skill. Outside the gate of the capital he found two standing images of Buddha above ninety feet high, one on each side of the highway. These colossal images of Buddha remind us of the equally tall images of Buddha on the side of hills at Bamiyan. Procession of images (Yātrā) was in vogue also in Kuchar as in Khotan. "All the monasteries made processions with their images of Buddha, adorning these with pearls and silk embroideries. The images were borne on vehicles." The biggest monastery of Kuchar was called Āścarya-vihāra. It was, we are told, built in imitation of the great Kaṇiṣka-vihāra of Gandhāra. This monastery had "spacious halls and artistic images of Buddha." From this account it appears that Kuchar and Karasahr, whatever art influence they might have received from other sources, were for all practical purposes, like Khotan and its neighbourhood, a part of the great Buddhist India that had been built up in Central Asia.

Further, along the route towards China, Turfan and its neighbourhood (Idikut-sahri, Murtuk and Bazaklik) were in ancient times another seat of Buddhist culture which had received besides the composite element found elsewhere in Central Asia, a Chinese influence in its art and culture. There is also a direct influence of Indian art in this region. Bodhisattva and Buddha images are of the Indo-Greek school. Sometimes the direct influence of the Gupta art is also traceable. The representations of the nakṣatras in the painting show "in their Indian scarfs, the most successful synthesis of Indian suppleness, Greek elegance and Chinese prettiness". A detailed examination of the art relics discovered in this region shows that the Buddhist art which we saw at one end of the road at Bamiyan has not lost its traditions at the other end at Turfan in course of its migration through thousands of miles of deserts and hills. Buddhist inspiration is as strong as ever. It has in the mean time gathered other currents, which instead of weakening it have made it stronger and more impressive.

Thus while the Buddhist art reached the Chinese soil proper, it had strength enough to impose itself on the national art of the country for several centuries. It did not remain exotic but it grafted itself in such a way as to give birth to a new art in China which may be styled *Sino-Indian*. The ancient Chinese art existed in bronze, wood and jade. It began to be translated in stone only from the Han period. The oldest pieces of sculptures and bas-reliefs in stone hitherto discovered in China also go back to the Han period. Their workmanship clearly shows that the Chinese artists were not yet quite at home with this new material. The material was new, but the artists were experienced. They were perfect masters of their subjects as they were inheritors of the traditions of a developed and powerful art which ancient China had produced. With such traditions behind them it was easy for them to treat the Buddhist subjects with equal mastery and to make a marvellous synthesis of the art elements which they received from outside.

Buddhism gave a new vigour to the development of art in China. This art did not follow the Chinese classical traditions but represented, as we have said, a synthesis of strong Indian and Ser-Indian elements which gradually adapted themselves to the Chinese genius. There are therefore different stages in the evolution of Buddhist art in China.

The Chinese artists must have seen pieces of Buddhist sculpture carried to China by the first missionaries of Buddhism. The oldest Buddhist monastery of Lo-yang, the Po-ma-sse, must have been provided with such images. But the Chinese artists did not work for Buddhism before its position was thoroughly consolidated in China. Buddhism, we have seen, became a state religion in the Wei period (386-534). The Buddhist artistic activities commenced in China also in that period under the patronage of the Wei rulers. The Wei period was the golden period of the Buddhist art in China.

CENTRES OF BUDDHIST ART IN CHINA

There were three chief centres of Buddhist art in China—Tun-huang, Yun-kang and Long-men. Tun-huang is on the western frontier of China almost at the meeting place of the two great Central Asian routes. It was, we have seen, a great centre of Buddhist activities in early times. The art relics which Tun-huang has preserved follow both Chinese and Ser-Indian traditions. The construction of the grottos of Tun-huang started in the Wei period, but its art attained the greatest development a little later.

Yun-kang and Long-men were two earlier centres of Buddhist art in China proper. Yun-kang is situated in the neighbourhood of Ta-t'ong in Shan-si near the first capital of the Wei rulers. The grottos of Yun-kang were excavated between A.D. 398 and 493. The work of Long-men (near Lo-yang) was started after the transfer of the Wei capital to Lo-yang in 493. The work was continued throughout the Wei period and also later till the beginning of the T'ang period.

The part of the Buddhist missionaries in the development of this art cannot be ignored. We are told that work at Yun-kang was undertaken at the instance of a Buddhist monk who had come from Central Asia. His name was T'an-yao. He came to the Wei capital in Shan-si some time between A. D. 460 and 465, and settled in the monastery of T'ong yu sse where he soon assembled around him a number of Buddhist scholars and translated three texts into Chinese. One of these works was a collection of Buddhist stories which gave a special impetus to the Buddhist sculptors in China in their work.

T'an-yao proposed to the Wei Emperor to excavate the sides of the mountain ranges to the west of the capital and to convert them into Buddhist grottos. The work was done under the supervision of T'an-yao. A number of grottos was scooped out in the hills and also colossal images of Buddha varying in size from 60 to 70 ft. were carved out from the sides of the hills. The Chinese annalist tells us that the ornamentation was beautiful and far superior to what one could see. Besides, from a mass of uncertain documents Prof. Pelliot has restored the names of three Indian painters—Śākyabuddha, Buddhakīrti and Kumārabodhi who worked in various places in China in the same period. Their paintings were much esteemed and preserved in different monasteries.

The Chinese pilgrims who had gone to India were equally active in inspiring the artists in China. Fa-hien, we know, stayed for two years at Tāmralipti "writing out his Sūtras and drawing pictures of images." He must have brought his drawings to China along with his copies of the sacred texts in order to give Indian models to the artists of his own country. Among the treasures which Hiuan-tsang brought from India there were the following objects of art:

(i) One golden statue of Buddha with a glittering pedestal 3 ft. 3 inch. in height. The figure resembled the image of Buddha in the pose of turning the Wheel of Law at Benares.

(ii) A sandal-wood image of Buddha with a shining pedestal 3 ft. 5 inch. high. It was a copy of a famous image of Buddha which according to tradition was originally made by King Udayana of Kauśāmbī.

(iii) A figure of Buddha with a shining pedestal 2 ft. 9 inch. high after the model of the figure of the Lord when he descended on the jewelled ladder from the 33rd heaven to the country of Sāṅkāśya.

(iv) A silver figure of Buddha with a translucent pedestal 3 ft. 5 inch. high after a model at Nagarahāra.

(v) A sandal-wood figure of Buddha with a pedestal 1 ft. 3 inch. high after a model at Vaiśālī.

Hui-lun who came to India shortly after Hiuan-tsang, took with him a model of the Nālandā temple. Wang Hiuan-ts'ö came to India in the same period. His last visit to India was in 664-665. He had taken drawings of Buddhist images from India and, we are told, three out of ten chapters of his book contained such illustrations. He had also taken the copy of the image of Buddha at Bodhgayā which was deposited by him on his return in the Imperial palace. It served as the model of an image which was set up in the newly built Buddhist temple of Ki-ngai-sse in 665. Wang Hiuan-ts'ö supervised the work himself.

However scrappy these references may be, they show that the Buddhist artists in China were not working alone. The missionaries who had come to China as well as the Chinese pilgrims who had been to Central Asia and India were constantly helping them not only with instructions but also with drawings and models.

To come back to the question of the Buddhist art represented at Yun-kang, T'an-yao who supervised the work had gone from Central Asia. His exact origin is not known. He must have been himself an artist and had seen much of the work of the Indo-Greek school. Either he himself or some of his collaborators had knowledge of the art of Mathura of the Kushan period as well as of the art of the Gupta period. The sculpture of Yun-kang represents all these schools—Indo-Greek, Mathura and Gupta.

Yun-kang is about 30 li to the west of Ta-t'ong. The grottos excavated at this place are commonly known as the "grottos of P'ing-ch'eng". They are situated in the Wu-chou-shan mountain. They were formerly ten Buddhist temples. The work of construction was begun under the Emperor T'ai-tsong (414-415) and terminated under the Emperor Su-tsong (516-528). The entire construction thus took more than a century. The Buddhist sculptures are found largely on the inner walls. The principal temple, called Ling-yen sse, was constructed between A. D. 460 and 465 by the monk T'an-yao.

The work thus started in the 5th century was continued through the 6th and 7th centuries till the middle of the T'ang period. Twenty-eight caves in all have been explored revealing art of different periods. There are also minor caves in the neighbouring hills. Long-men is about 30 li to the south of Lo-yang in Ho-nan. There is a large number of grottos at this place which were constructed by the Wei rulers when they had transferred their capital to Lo-yang. The central grotto contains a colossal Buddha accompanied by the two disciples Ānanda and Kāśyapa and two Bodhisattvas. The statues are of enormous size. The walls contain bas-reliefs. "On one side is a procession of men with tall square caps and draped in flowing robes which wide open at the breast, reach to the ground; in front is the principal personage. The frieze on the other side represents a *cortège* of women whose costume is no less curious to behold. The person nearest to the entrance is especially noticeable." These bas-reliefs belong to the beginning of the T'ang period.

The Buddhist art of the Wei period is best represented in the grottos of Yun-kang and Long-men. It is best to describe the art of Yun-kang in the words of Chavannes who was the first to explore the region: "To thoroughly appreciate the fineness and elegance of the art of the Northern Wei, we shall best study those statues which are life-size. We shall see in them a gentleness of expression and a gracefulness of pose which other periods have not been able to render so successfully. Several of these statues are seated in a cross-legged posture in front of each other; this posture is no longer seen in the Buddhist carvings executed under the T'ang dynasty. It seems to me characteristic of the art of the Northern Wei, as besides, it has been noticed in the statuettes of Gandhāra, of which at least one had been carried to Turfan. We here have a proof that the artistic inspiration of the Northern Wei was derived from that of Gandhāra, that is to say, the art which sprung to birth in the region of Peshawar, north of the Indus, and which had been transmitted through Central Asia as far as Turfan."

But it has since then been recognized that the art of Yun-kang and Long-men is much more than what Chavannes held it to be. The sculpture is superior to the Indo-Greek in regard to the purity of line, sweetness of expression and elegance. In order to find so much of elegance and fineness one has to go to Ajanta; and to find a superior and more moving representation of God than the great Buddha of Long-men one has to refer to the Buddha of Sarnath or to the three-headed Siva of Elephanta.

The third great seat of Buddhist art in China was Tun-huang. Situated as it was in the meeting place of the Central Asian highways on the frontier of China, it had received almost all the Ser-Indian influences which we have observed in the art of Khotan, Kuchar and Turfan. But the Sino-Indian art of the Wei and the T'ang periods is also well represented at Tun-huang. Among the European archæologists, both Sir Aurel Stein and M. Paul Pelliot visited the ancient grottos in the hills of Tun-huang. Prof. Pelliot made a close study of the art of these grottos. The grottos which are situated in the foot-hills of the Nan-shan near Tun-huang are also known as the "Grottos of the Thousand Buddhas".

The construction of the grottos started in the 4th century. But the oldest dated grotto goes back to the Wei period. There are four different stages in the development of the art at Tun-huang: (i) The art of the Wei period—5th and 6th centuries A. D. (ii) The art of the early T'ang period—7th century. (iii) The art of the late T'ang period—from the middle of the 7th century to the 10th century. (iv) Restorations and additions carried on up to the middle of the 11th century.

A number of stūpas and images of Buddha in front of the grottos belong to the first period. They exhibit all the characteristics of the art of the Wei period. But the highest development of Tun-huang belongs to the T'ang period. The art of Tun-huang at its best "shows a progressive Chinese adaptation of the Gandhāra, Gupta and Iranian models. We can see, for example, a Samantabhadra which betrays very closely the Gupta influence : bare torso, slim figure, harmonious development of the hips, transparence of the floating scarf, treatment of the hand in the style of Ajanta. Not less Indian are a Padmapāṇi, a Mañjuśrī with a sword in hand, a Mañjuśrī with a book in hand, etc., found in the Stein Collection. In the sculptures of the Pelliot Collection this Indian Gupta type is already sinified, with the relative cramming of the face, replacing of the transparent clothing by lively painted stuff partly treated in the Chinese fashion. The same character is observed in the beautiful painting on silk in the British Museum representing Avalokiteśvara.... There is also evidence of the Græco-Roman type brought from India."

In the Pelliot Collection there is a picture of the paradise of Amitābha (Sukhāvatī), with a dancing Apsara, which reminds one of the style of Ajanta and the Japanese style of Yamato. On two sides of the principal scene there are beautiful marginal scenes representing the life of Bimbisāra and Ajātaśatru, treated in the Chinese fashion. There is also the Paradise of Maitreya, that of Bhaiṣajyaguru, that of Avalokiteśvara and that of Kṣitigarbha, surrounded by personages either Indian, Chinese, or Sassanian. Without going into further details it may be said that the art of Tun-huang represents the same composite elements as are found at Turfan. Among other influences the Indian influence still dominates the whole composition. In the later stage of the art, in the T'ang period, was introduced in it a dominant Chinese element in order to give the entire art a complete Sino-Indian character.

From the T'ang period a progressive natural transformation of the Buddhist art took place in China. Indian models were prized, but the artists had learnt to produce something which, while absorbing all the artistic traditions of the Wei period, was more Chinese in character. Indian artists continued to be esteemed in China up to the Yuan period. The story of an Indian artist named A-ni-ko is narrated by the Chinese sources. A-ni-ko was born in Nepal in A. D. 1243 and went to Tibet at an early age at the head of a band of sculptors and painters. 'Phags-pa, the Guru of Kublai Khan, ordered a golden pagoda to be built at the capital of Tibet. For that purpose he wanted to requisition the services of 100 select Nepalese artists. But only 24 artists were found. A-ni-ko, who was only 17 years old at that time, wanted to go but objections were made on account of his young age. He however replied : "I may be young in years but not so in mind." He was therefore allowed to go. When he reached the capital of Tibet 'Phags-pa was so highly impressed by the attainments of the young artist that the supervision of the entire work was entrusted to him. The construction of the pagoda was completed in two years. A-ni-ko then wanted to go back to his own country. But 'Phags-pa was so fond of him that he initiated him to monkhood and after some time sent him to the capital of China. On his arrival in China he presented himself to the Emperor Kublai. The Emperor enquired about his special attainments. The artist told him that he knew designing, modelling and metal casting. At the order of the Emperor he repaired many of the old statues in the palace, made a large number of statues for different monasteries within the empire and became widely known. No artist had attained the mastery he possessed. In 1274 he got from the Emperor supreme authority over the artists in metal in the empire. In 1275 A-ni-ko returned to the life of a layman, was appointed Controller of Imperial manufactures and honoured with many posthumous titles after his death. Traditions of Indian iconometry handed down by A-ni-ko were current in China for a long time.

PAINTING

How far Buddhism and Indian traditions helped in the development of Chinese painting is a matter that still remains to be studied. Traditions of art of the Wei period, we have seen, are closely connected with Indian traditions. There were Indian artists, both painters and sculptors, in this period in some parts of China. Works of some Indian painters of this and subsequent periods were much esteemed in China. We have already come across the names of three Indian painters—Śākyabuddha, Buddhakīrti and Kumārabodhi.

Chinese æsthetic traditions go back to the fifth century when Buddhism was well established in China. The oldest of these traditions strongly remind us of the Indian principles of æsthetics. Sie Ho, an artist who lived under the Ts'i dynasty of the south (479-501), is said to have formulated the following six great principles of painting for the first time :

(1) Mental revolution gives birth to the life motion.
(2) To bring out the anatomical structure with the help of the brush.
(3) To draw forms in conformity with nature.
(4) To make the colours correspond to the nature of the objects.
(5) To distribute the lines in their proper places.
(6) To propagate the forms by passing them on into the pictures.

These six principles do not seem to be different from the *ṣaḍaṅga* or the six essential things relating to painting as described in the ancient Indian literature. They are—*Rūpa* or form, *Pramāṇa*—proportion, *Bhāva*—idea or suggestion, *Lāvaṇya*, the finish, *Sādṛśya*—conformity with the object, and *Varṇikābhaṅga*—distribution of colours. The order is somewhat different but the principles are the same.

ARCHITECTURE

Buddhist architecture too in China must have undergone some Indian influence. In fact it is believed by some that the pagoda type of the temples with superimposed storeys was carried from India to the Far East. The vestiges of such constructions are still found in India and far away from the regions where the Chinese influence could infiltrate. Such constructions were known in various parts of Central Asia too. One of the oldest Buddhist temples of this type to be built in China was probably the Yong-ning sse at Lo-yang constructed in 516 under the Wei. It was an enormous Buddhist temple in nine storeys, more than 90 *chang* in height. The entire construction was in wood. The pillars were sculptured and gilded. It had bells hanging which had the shape of the water vases (kalaśa). On the top of the tower there was a golden mast. This was probably a temple in the Indian style. In fact, a special type of architecture was known in the Song period as the Indian style (called in Japan, Tenjikuyo) as distinguished from the T'ang style of architecture. It has been described as follows : "The Tenjikuyo renounces the two previous kinds of functional angle levers without giving up the far projecting eaves or supporting them through an additional outer array of posts. It permits the inner cross-beams to pass through the columns and continue below the eaves as supports in the shape of ordinary brackets....the posts end in a capital which carries a twofold purlin. The larger the building the farther do the eaves protrude in proportion, and the straight cantilever system consists of an equal number of successively protruding members....the stability of the structure, beyond a certain size, requires one or several outer tie-beams parallel to the eaves which bind together the straight cantilevers....these horizontal tie-beams....primarily fulfil an ornamental function without losing their structural significance."

This style of architecture was not officially recognized in China but was in private use. It was much in vogue in Shan-si, as Dr. Ecke has pointed out. It was, we know, a province where the Indian influence was much more dominant than elsewhere in China. Under these circumstances the Japanese tradition may be correct in tracing its origin to Indian style, but in the Song period it must have been much modified under the Chinese influence. Earlier Buddhist architecture of North China which was largely copied in Japan in the Nara period seems to have followed the Indian style more closely. The famous temple of Yong-ning sse built in 516 and many other temples of the period, with their superimposed series of roofs, their outstretched brackets from which hung the bells, their golden pinnacles, carved pillars, etc. belong to the first period of the Sino-Indian art.

MUSIC

While speaking of the traditions of Indian Fine Arts in Central Asia and China, we cannot ignore the influence of Indian music. The ancient Chinese were great musicians and music played a great role in their official cult. The court also admired foreign music. Orchestras from various countries used to visit the Chinese court occasionally where they received much appreciation. The ancient Chinese texts have preserved some interesting information on Indian music as practised in Central Asia and the Far East. The people of Kuchar were, we are told, fond of music and were skilled in wind and stringed musical instruments. It is said that the musicians of their country used to go to the fountains at the time of rainfall and translate the sound of falling waters into music. Indian music was carried to Kuchar along with Buddhism and there is evidence of families of Indian musicians having migrated to Kuchar in early times. The Chinese annals tell us that music was cultivated in their country in a *Brahmanical family* called Ts'ao, probably Jhā (=Upādhyāya), from father to son. The most remarkable representative of that family was Miao-ta who went to China in the period 550-577. In the sixth century Indian music, on account of his performance, became so popular in China that the Chinese Emperor Kao-tsu (581-595) tried to proscribe it by a decree, but without any effect. His successor Yang-ti was so fond of this music that he got a number of airs composed in this style by Po Ming-ta who was most probably a member of the Indo-Kuchean family mentioned above.

According to the Chinese evidence, these Indo-Kuchean musicians were so clever that they could reproduce an air on hearing it only once and with just a little practice. The Kuchean musical parties used to be accompanied by four dancers. One of their demonstrations was "the Song of Universal Peace" or "the Dance of Five Lions". Each lion was got up with 12 men and had a special colour. The demonstration required the assistance of 140 dancers.

Each year, on the invitation of these Chinese Emperors, musical parties from abroad used to go to China to play in the court. In 581, on the occasion of an Imperial banquet, musical parties went to China from various countries such as India, Kuchar, Bokhara, Samarcand, Kashgar and the country of the Turks. There were also musical parties from Japan and Cambodia. From the T'ang annals it appears that the ancient Cambodian orchestra was very much like the Indian. Ancient Cambodia or Fu-nan was, we have seen, an Indian colony and Indian musical parties must have found their way there too very early. The T'ang annals give a description of the Indian orchestra in the following words:

"The musicians use a cap of black cloth. They put on a silken white tunic, violet coloured breeches of brocade and a red mantle. The dancers are two in number. They have their hairs plaited and they put on a kaṣāya of *ch'ao-hia*, similar to the dress of the monks. They walk with shoes made of ropes and green hemp. For the music they use the gong (*t'ong ku*), the drums called *kie, mao-yuan*, and *tu-t'an*, the cornet of reed called *pi-li*, the transversal flute called *heng-ti*, the sphinx-headed lute called *k'ong-hou*, the guitar *p'i-pa* which has five cords, the cymbals and the conch."

The Indian music which was carried by the Kuchean musicians to China was long in favour in the Chinese court. We are informed by the Chinese annalists that a musician from Kuchar named Sujīva came to the Chinese court between 560 and 578. He could play well on the "guitar of the barbarians". In the music which he brought to China there were seven degrees in the gamut. He is also reported to have said that "his father who was famous in the west as a musician had learnt the music through a tradition transmitted through generations, that there were seven kinds of systems and that degrees in these seven systems, when compared, mysteriously *concorded*." The seven degrees mentioned are said to have been the following :—

1. *So-t'o-li*—even tone.
2. *Ki-che*—long tone.
3. *Sha-che* (Sanskrit Ṣaḍja)—simple and straight tone.
4. *Sha-hou-kia-lan* (Skt. Sahagrāma)—consonant tone.
5. *Sha-la*—consonant and harmonious tone.
6. *Pan-chen* (Skt. Pañcama)—fifth tone.
7. *Sse* (*hou*)-*li-she* (Skt. Ṛṣabha)—tone of the bull.

The seven degrees are evidently the seven notes (*svara*) of the gamut and their names, although they cannot be at present definitely identified for want of further information, seem to have been of Indian origin. The three names Ṣaḍja, Pañcama and Ṛṣabha clearly testify to that. So far as the seven systems referred to above are concerned, probably they mean the Jātis of the Indian texts on music. The Jātis were precursors of the Rāgas or musical airs, and if we take into consideration only the seven Śuddha or pure notes the number of Jātis also are seven. Two of the Sanskrit authorities on music, the *Bṛhaddeśi* and the *Saṅgītaratnākara* mention seven Śuddha Jātis which were based on the seven pure notes. The Chinese record when it mentions seven degrees of the gamut contemplates only the seven Śuddha notes.

Indian music had also been carried to Japan either from China or from the Indian colonies of Champa or Kambuja in the eighth century A. D. or a little earlier. According to the ancient Japanese traditions, two principal types of music called *Bodhisattva* and *Bairo* were taken from China to Japan by a Brahmin native of India named Bodhi. He came with a Chinese mission in 736 and was soon appointed a director of the Buddhist community at Nara. The music was a dance music and the name Bodhisattva shows that it was a religious piece of musical composition. In fact similar pieces of religious music of Indian origin are still known in Japan. They were carried there from China in the T'ang period.

Nothing definite has been as yet suggested about the identification of Bairo with any Indian piece of musical composition. However, the Japanese tradition says that "it is the work of one Han-ro-toku (Chinese, Pan-lang-to) and a music of India. It is executed in the army in order to ascertain the luck about death and life. While executing it seven times, if there is the sha-mo sound, it indicates that the army will be victorious over the enemy." It seems that the Indian name transcribed as Pan-lang-to is no other than Bharata, the Indian classical authority on music. The Chinese transscription of the name was based either on a Kambuja or a Champa pronunciation of the name. There are also parallels of such pronunciations coming from that region. Bairo which was an Indian air seems to be the classical Rāga called Bhairava (in Prakritic pronunciation, Bhairo). Bhairava personifies "the terrible" and as such according to Indian tradition it arouses an emotion of the same kind. As a god, Bhairava is only the terrible aspect of the supreme god of the Hindu pantheon—Śiva. *Sha-mo* is not, I believe, a sound. It is Sanskrit *Sama* (Hindi *Som*) which indicates the starting point on the instrument of percussion which keeps the beat (*tāla*). The musician comes back many times to the starting point (*som*) after expanding the Rāga at his will and then only is produced an effect which greatly contributes to the æsthetic development of the Rāga. To be able to maintain this *som* correctly presupposes an excellence in execution. To be able to do so correctly even after singing a Rāga seven times was certainly regarded as a proof of extraordinary skill and significant of success in all activities.

ASTRONOMY AND MATHEMATICS

Astronomy and astrology played a very important part in ancient Chinese culture as in India. It was believed in both countries that the planets influence and guide the destiny of men. There was a well-organized Imperial Bureau in China to prepare accurate calendars. In the T'ang period services of Indian astronomers were requisitioned on this Board for the purpose. There were in the 7th century three Indian astronomical schools at Ch'ang-ngan. They were known as Gautama, Kāśyapa and Kumāra. In 684 a member of the Gautama school named Lo presented a new calendar to the Empress Wu. The calendar was called *Kuang tse li* "the calendar of the bright house" and was in use for three years. Another member of this school named Si-ta (Siddhārtha) presented a new calendar in 718 to the Emperor. It was practically the translation of an Indian calendar. The *Kiu-che-li*, as it is called, or in Sanskrit *Navagraha-siddhānta* is still preserved in a collection of the T'ang period. It had greater success in China and was in use for four years. It contained a calculation of the moon's course and the eclipses. Since 721 the Buddhist monk Yi-hing adopted a new method of calculation evidently based on Indian sources which he had studied well. He undertook the compilation of a calendar named *Ta-yen-li*. Yi-hing died in 727 before the work could be completed. By the Imperial order the work was continued and completed in 729. The work was not without the influence of Indian astronomy as it introduced in the Indian fashion nine planets, the sun, the moon, the five planets and two new ones, the Rāhu and the Ketu, by which the Indian astronomers presented the ascending and the descending nodes of the moon.

In the annals of the Sui dynasty there is mention of the Chinese translation of a number of Hindu mathematical and astronomical works which have been long lost. These works were the following :

(i) *Po-lo-men t'ien wen king.*

(ii) *Po-lo-men kie-k'ie sien jen t'ien wen shuo*—the astronomical theories of the Brahmin Ṛṣi *Ki-k'ie.*

(iii) *Po-lo-men t'ien king.*

(iv) *Mo-teng-kie king huang tu*—a map of the sky in the Mātaṅgī-sūtra.

(v) *Po-lo-men suan fa*—the Hindu arithmetical rules.

(vi) *Po-lo-men suan king*—the Hindu arithmetical classics.

As these works are now lost it is difficult to say what their contents were and how far their theories were accepted by the Chinese scholars. But what has been said above clearly shows that in the Sui period and the T'ang period Indian astronomers were serving in the official astronomical bureau and that Indian astronomy and mathematics were esteemed in China.

Certain notions of western astronomy mixed up with

those of Indian astronomy had reached China in the T'ang period through Ser-Indian intermediaries, specially the Sogdians. Four Buddhist texts were translated in the T'ang period. One of them being due to the famous Amoghavajra, contains such notions. The names of the week days in these texts are given not in the Indian forms but in the Sogdian forms such as *mir* (Sunday), *max* (Monday), *wnxan* (Tuesday), *ṭir* (Wednesday), *wrmzt* (Thursday), *maxid* (Friday) and *kewan* (Saturday). But the names of Buddhist works in which they occur claim Indian origin. These works are : (i) *Fan t'ien huo lo kiu yao*—The *horā* of Brahma and the *navagraha.* (ii) *Ts'i yao sing ch'en pie hing fa*—the different influences of the seven stars and lunar mansions. (iii) *Ts'i yao jang tsai kiue*—Mantras for averting the evil influence of the seven planets. (iv) *Wen shu she li p'u sa ki chu sien so shuo ki hiong she je shan ngo su yao king*—Sūtra spoken by Bodhisattva Mañjuśrī and the sages on the auspicious and evil days and the good and evil planets and lunar mansions. This last was translated by Amoghavajra and was annotated by his disciple Yang King-fong in 764. The latter enumerates the seven planets by names in Sanskrit, Sogdian and Persian respectively and says : "The seven planets are the sun, the moon and five planets which preside over the destiny of men. Day by day they replace each other and at the end of seven days the cycle is completed. It then recommences. The planets are to be taken into account as each of them exercises either a favourable or unfavourable influence on this or that thing. If you do not remember the day of the week then ask a *Hu* (Sogdian), or a *Po-sse* (Persian) or the people of the five Indies who all know them."

MEDICINE

How far the Hindu medical system was known in China has still to be ascertained. A number of medical treatises some of which are of a purely Buddhist character, are found in the Chinese Buddhist collection. A treatise on the method of treatment of children's diseases by spell as well as by fumigation was translated in the 11th century from Sanskrit. The work is known as the *Rāvaṇakumāra-tantra*. Another small text on the treatment of pregnant women's diseases was translated in the same period. This seems to be a fragment of a well-known Āyurvedic compendium called *Kāśyapasaṁhitā*. But the Chinese Buddhist monks had felt interested in Indian medical systems probably much earlier. A Chinese noble named King-sheng who embraced Buddhism in the middle of the 5th century and had gone up to Khotan has left us a work which does not seem to be an exact translation from any Indian source but a compilation from different texts of the same origin. The work is called *Che ch'an ping pi yao fa* or the method of curing the diseases concerning meditation. It was translated in A. D. 455. The work gives a description of the nervous system within the body and deals with diseases of the heart and the nerves which generally arise from outside shock or disturbance in course of meditation.

Hindu medical books were widely known in Ser-India. Fragments of original texts on Āyurveda as well as their translations, either into ancient Khotanese or Kuchean, have been discovered by archæologists in the region of Khotan and Kuchar. King-sheng collected the text on the diseases concerning meditation while travelling in Central Asia. It is therefore quite possible that other medical treatises of Indian origin were also carried to China from the same source. The Chinese had their own medical system and they had taken every care to enrich it from time to time with materials received from outside.

In the T'ang period there was a craze amongst the Emperors and the nobles of the court to hunt for Indian thaumaturges (Tantrik Yogis), who were supposed to be in possession of secret methods of curing from the effects of old age. We have already seen that on two different occasions two Brahmins had been to the Chinese court for the purpose of giving long life to the Emperor. Although they had failed in their mission, a conviction in the efficacy of Indian drugs still persisted. Hiuan-chao, we know, was specially sent to India by the Emperor to collect rare Indian medicines.

CHAPTER VII

THE TWO CIVILIZATIONS—A SYNTHESIS

If two different people like the Chinese and the Indians, who lived in different climes, spoke different languages, and possessed different traditions of culture and religion, could meet on a common platform and work harmoniously for a common civilization, the reason was probably much more deep-rooted than we are generally used to believe. The cultural and social ideals of the two people had many things in common. It is possible to discover a community between the two amidst the great diversities of expressions. The same reliance on some heavenly order, the same force of tradition, and similar social ideals characterized the two civilizations in the past.

T'IEN AND VARUṆA

The central poi it in the ancient religious belief of China was the conception of *T'ien* "Heaven". The Heaven is the creator, the preserver as well as the destroyer of everything in the world. He is the august sovereign, full of majesty, who created and placed the people in their proper place. He is the guardian of the universal order. He controls the movement of the sun, the moon and the stars, the rotation of the seasons, and the ways of mankind. He sees everything and judges everything. He rules through a mandate which may be withdrawn in case those to whom it is entrusted do not preserve it according to his intentions. He is responsible for the security, prosperity and the good of mankind. Those who conform to his order never have to come to grief but those who violate it get destroyed. One of the old odes brings out his relations with man:

"May Heaven guard and keep you

In great security,
Make you staunch and hale,
What blessing not vouchsafed ?
Give you much in increase,
Send nothing but abundance.
May Heaven guard and keep you,
Cause your grain to prosper,
Send you nothing that is not good.
May you receive from Heaven a hundred boons,
May Heaven send down to you blessings so many
That the day is not long enough for them all."

There is a god like *T'ien* in the Hindu pantheon of ancient times—he is the Vedic Varuṇa. Varuṇa who corresponds to the Iranian Ahura Mazda, was the greatest Indo-Iranian god. In the Vedic hymns too he occupies the same position. The name meant "the Encompasser" and the god seems to have personified the entire shining heavens. He is conceived as the king of all, both gods and men—the universal monarch. He sends the dawns, makes the sun cross the sky and causes the rains. He is the upholder of both the physical and the moral orders. He is the great lord of the laws of nature. He established heaven and earth. He dwells in all the worlds. He is the guardian of the whole world and the supporter of the earth and the heaven. By Varuṇa's ordinances the moon and the stars move and shine. He regulates the seasons and the months. He is also the regulator of the waters that bring prosperity to the earth.

Varuṇa is also the moral governor. His anger is roused by sin, the infringement of his ordinances, which he severely punishes. He is a punisher of falsehood. He is an omniscient god and there is nothing in the world which he does not know. He is a constant witness of men's truth and falsehood. No creature can do, think, or devise anything without being noticed by him. So great and so powerful is the great god Varuṇa. Varuṇa's order is called *ṛta*. He is the chief guardian of this order. He does not allow anybody, either god or man, to infringe this order.

T'IEN-TSEU AND RĀJAN

According to old Chinese belief the Emperor was the sole trustee of the mandate of the Heaven and hence he was called—the Son of Heaven, *T'ien-tseu*. But the trustee could not afford to be an arbitrary ruler. The mandate which he received from the Heaven was not a perpetual mandate. It could be withdrawn the moment it was misused. We have seen that the Heaven was considered as the omniscient and all-powerful sovereign who could not brook the infringement of the universal order of which he was the sole guardian. So the Son of Heaven, the sovereign on earth by the heavenly mandate, had to know the heavenly intentions and follow strictly the heavenly order. Tradition records the fall of Emperors who had failed to understand these intentions and neglected the path of virtue.

Hence the Emperors are often reminded of their heavy duties. One of the ancient Emperors is reported to have said: "August is the Emperor above. Raise your aspirations above common level. I shall like your distinction and humility. When virtue shines on earth it is the glory of the Heaven. The Emperor who follows Him well gets abundance of good. Great is the mandate of the Heaven. It is not perpetual. It is not easy to keep it. In ancient times the Emperors had days of prosperity and happiness so long as they conformed to the intentions of the sovereign on high. Consequently I also fear the judgment of the Heaven day and night and thus conduct myself." Thus a prince who aspires after the position of a true sovereign must make himself perfect. He should fulfil his duties towards his parents, should know the Heaven and the people. The manifold duties of the Emperor, the Son of Heaven, are set forth in the Great Law which is said to have been promulgated by the Emperor Wu-wang in the 12th century B. C. As it has many points of similarity with the duties of the king (*rājadharma*) as set forth in the law-books (*dharmaśāstras*) it is better to give a full translation of the text. It is as follows :

> "Firstly, the five elements. The first is water, the second fire, the third wood, the fourth metal and the fifth earth. The nature of water is to drench, and to flow down, that of fire is to burn and rise high. The wood lends itself to be bent and shaped. The metal obeys the hand of the worker and assumes different shapes. The earth receives the seeds and yields harvest. Water drenches, flows down and produces salt. Fire burns, rises high and produces bitter taste. Wood, bent and shaped, produces bitter taste. Metal obeys, changes its forms and produces acid taste. Earth receives seeds, yields harvest and produces sweet taste.
>
> "Secondly, the five acts. The first is external bearing, the second speech, the third looks, the fourth hearing and the fifth reflection. The external bearing should be composed, the speech conforming to reason, the looks perspicacious, the ears extremely attentive and the mind meditative and penetrating. A well composed bearing is respectful, a speech conforming to reason is well regulated, a perspicacious look conduces to prudence, and application to hearing is the mother of good counsels, and a meditative and penetrating mind attains the highest wisdom.
>
> "Thirdly, the eight parts of administration. The first concerns the good (of the people), the second the commodities of life, the third sacrifices, the fourth public

works, the fifth education, the sixth criminal law, the seventh hospitality and the eighth military service.

"Fourthly, the five regulators of time. The first is the year, the second the month, the third the day, the fourth the twelve zodiacal signs and the stars and the fifth the time calculation or the calendar.

"Fifthly, the highest perfection befitting an Emperor. Oh, Prince, by setting example of the highest perfection you will get the five blessings which you must divide among your numerous subjects. Your numerous subjects will imitate your sublime perfection and will help you to preserve it. When your numerous subjects do not create unrest and your ministers do not enter into a conspiracy against you it is the effect of the highest perfection of which you will set the example.

"Do not oppress the weak that has neither brothers nor children. Do not fear those who hold a high rank. Among the officers who are talented and who administer the affairs well, excite the desire to advance always in the path of virtue and your state will be flourishing. Men entrusted to govern are virtuous when they are affluent. If you do not know the means of enabling them to maintain good harmony in their families which are also yours, they will commit crimes. If you shower favours on those who do not love the virtue you will have to repent for having vicious men in your service.

"No partiality, no injustice, administer justice like a sovereign. No special and irregular affection, follow the principles which the sovereign teaches us by example. No special and unruly aversion, let us follow the way that is indicated by the sovereign by his example. Let us, all together, advance toward sublime perfection of which the sovereign is the example. Let us reach, all together, this sublime perfection. The exposition of the sublime virtues of the Emperor, when developed, become the law of customs, the most perfect teaching.

"Sixthly, the three virtues. The first is uprightness and equity, the second firmness in the government and the third softness in the government. It is necessary to govern the quiet and peace loving men with an equitable uprightness, those who resist and refuse to obey with firmness and those who are docile and obedient with softness. It is necessary to govern with firmness those who stagnate in indolence and with softness those who distinguish themselves by their talents and good disposition.

"Seventhly, the examination of doubtful things. It is necessary to select and appoint soothsayers to ascertain the truth, some by means of the tortoise shell and some by means of the reeds. When you have doubts on an important affair, discuss it yourself, discuss it with your ministers and officers, consult the people and have the tortoise and the reeds consulted. If your undertaking is approved by yourself, by the tortoise, by the reeds, by your ministers and officers and by the people unanimously it will succeed.

"Eighthly, the different effects. These are rain, fair weather, heat, cold and wind as well as the periods. While all the five things come in sufficient quantity and each of them in time, all the plants prosper. If one of them comes too abundantly or fails to come it is calamity. There are beneficent effects also. The seriousness of the Emperor causes rain at the proper time, his good administration causes serenity of the sky, his prudence causes heat, his mental application causes cold, and his great wisdom causes the wind. There are also unfortunate effects. The inconsiderateness of the Emperor makes the rain last long, his errors the serenity of the sky, his indolence the heat, his hastiness cold and his stupidity wind. Let therefore the Emperor examine them every year, let the high nobles examine them every month and let the officers examine them every day. If nothing untoward happens then you will see that the grains have ripened, that the administration is intelligent, that the talented men are honoured and the families enjoy peace and happiness.

"The people are like the constellations (the Emperor and his ministers are like the sun and the moon). Some constellations like the wind, some the rain. The sun and the moon accomplish their revolutions and thus bring the winter and the summer. The moon goes round the constellations and brings the wind and the rain.

"Ninthly, the five blessings. The first is longevity, the second health, the third health and peace of mind, the fourth the love of virtue and the fifth a complete life. The six evils are: the first, a life shortened by misfortune, the second illness, the third sorrow, the fourth poverty, the fifth perversity and the sixth weakness (of character)."

Kingship was also largely regarded as a divine institution by the Hindus in ancient times. The kings in the Vedic hymns associate themselves with the acts of the great god Varuṇa and consider themselves as the true representatives of Varuṇa on earth on whom the gods bestow their principal energies. Varuṇa is the *rājan*, king, *samrāj*, universal monarch and the *kṣatra*, the possessor of sovereign power on high. So also is the king on earth. He is the rājan, samrāj, kṣatriya. Varuṇa is the lord of *ṛta* or *dharma*—the cosmic law. The king on earth is also the protector of this law. Assumption of royalty was accompanied by a series of sacrifices beginning with *abhiṣeka* or consecration and ending with the *aśvamedha* or the full consummation of the royal power. These sacrifices alone could establish complete unity between the gods and the kings and this unity was essential as authority was supposed to come from the divine guardian of the cosmic order. As the kings considered themselves the counterparts of the gods on earth, a moral sanction was necessary for their acts and this sanction could be procured by offering sacrifices to the gods. It is again through the sacrifices alone that the divine intentions could be properly understood.

The position and the duties of the king are more fully described in the law-books (*dharmaśāstras*) as well as in the Great Epic (*Mahābhārata*). The picture of the king as drawn in this literature is in every respect similar to that of the "Son of Heaven". It is said that the king is a divinely appointed person. He combines in himself the essence of the presiding deities of the eight quarters of the earth, viz., Varuṇa, Indra, Vāyu, Yama, Sūrya, Agni, Candra and Kubera. He is not an ordinary man but the great god in the form of human being.

But this divinely ordained king cannot afford to be an arbitrary ruler. Acquisition of qualities, similar to those mentioned in the Chinese "Great Law", is the *sine qua non* of his assumption of royalty. He must be an embodiment of fatherly love, protection and care. He is the model for his people who rise with him or fall with him. "As is the king so is the people." Even the nature of the age is determined by the king's personal conduct. It is categorically said: "Let a man be purified in heart, let his folks and ministers reverence his acts and he is a king, the best of kings." He is responsible for the happiness of his kingdom. He must learn to control himself, overcome love and anger, and subdue his passions. The virtues of the king that became proverbial in the Epic and the Law-books are wisdom, breeding, self-respect, knowledge, courage, generosity, gratitude, and uprightness. The people suffer if the king is sinful and they enjoy prosperity if he is virtuous. He remains the custodian of the divine trust so long as he follows the path of virtue.

ANCESTOR WORSHIP AND PITṚIYAJÑA

The manes occupied a large place in the Chinese religion of early times. Next to the Heaven, their influence was considered as the most important in shaping the future of posterity. Sacrifices were offered to them periodically as it was by pleasing the departed ancestors that their children could expect to attain prosperity, longevity, happiness, peace, etc. Their way was considered as the straight road that was to be followed by their children. This is clearly stated in the old texts: "In the temples the musical instruments resound forcefully and harmoniously. The ancestors hear their sounds. They come down and bring with them all the blessings. They receive the offering through the intermediary of the personage that represents them. Through the mouth of the master of the ceremony they say: you will have a long life, you will have an endless life." At the end of the sacrifice, the sacrificer exclaims as if under a divine inspiration: "The representative of our ancestors has eaten and drunk. Wealth and happiness will be showered on us. Misfortune will never visit us."

Much about this sacrifice to the manes is said in the ancient odes preserved in the She-king. These odes are often characterized by a simplicity and elegance that reminds us of the hymns of the Rig-Veda. One example from the fine translation of Arthur Waley will be sufficient to give an idea of this type of poetry. To take the Ode No. 204 addressed to the ancestors—

> "Ah, the glorious ancestors—
> Endless their blessings,
> Boundless their gifts are extended;
> To you too, they needs must reach.

We have brought them clear wine;
They will give victory.
Here too is soup well seasoned,
Well prepared, well mixed.
Because we come in silence,
Setting all quarrels aside,
They make safe for us a ripe old age,
We shall reach the withered cheek, we shall go on and on.
With our leather-bound naves, our bronze clad yokes,
With eight bells a-jangle
We come to make offering.
The charge put upon us is vast and mighty,
From heaven dropped our prosperity,
Good harvests, great abundance.
They come, they accept,
They send down blessings numberless."

Thus it was not merely for long life and prosperity that sacrifices had to be offered to the ancestors. Good harvests also depended on their kindness. That is why they had to be offered all the best things available—the first fruits, good food and drink, the best animal for sacrifice and so on. The details of the sacrifice are also available from the odes. Thus we are told that one person while sacrificing to his ancestors presented cucumbers, the hairs, the blood and the fat of an ox that was killed for the occasion. He offered perfumed wine as libation. The hairs of the animal were offered to prove that the animal was pure . Its blood was offered to show that the animal had been really killed. The libations of scented wine were given so that its smell could attract the ancestors to the sacrificial place. The fat was burnt for the same purpose.

The Pitṛis, the departed ancestors, occupied the same important place in the life of the Hindu as in the life of the

Chinese. Sacrifice to the manes (pitṛiyajña) was the most important duty of the householder. No social and religious ceremony would be complete without an offering to the manes. In the Vedic hymns the Pitṛis are regarded as the companions of the gods. They live in the highest heaven and revel with the gods. They receive oblations along with the gods as their food. Sacrifice is offered to them with the hope that they would intercede for and protect their votaries. They have the power to injure their descendants for any sin committed against them and hence their favour is implored. They are capable of giving wealth, offspring and long life to their sons who follow their way. The way of the Pitṛis (pitṛiyāna) is regarded as more important than the way of the gods (devayāna).

The sacrifice to the manes figure even more prominently in the Hindu social and religious life of later times. It gradually became more elaborate. It had to be performed regularly not only in the appointed season of the year but also at the time of the important social ceremonies such as investiture with sacred thread, marriage, etc. It was considered that without imploring their favour none of these family duties could be properly fulfilled. In spite of considerable changes in the religious ideas the importance attached to the Pitṛiyajña in ancient times is still maintained in the Hindu life of today.

SOCIAL AND POLITICAL IDEALS OF CONFUCIUS

The name of Confucius, Chinese K'ong Fu-tseu, stands very high in the history of China. He stands for all that is noble, rational and beneficial in the ancient civilization of the country. He was born in 551 and died in 479 B. C. and was entrusted with many important administrative functions in the State during his lifetime. He was the first to systematize and codify the ancient social and political ideals for the benefit of posterity. He was not a mystic and a pacifist like his famous contemporary Lao-tseu. He formulated no new philosophy of his own. He was a staunch follower of the ancient tradition and a strong believer in the T'ien, in the utility of the sacrifices to the Heaven as well as to the manes, in the necessity of divination with the tortoise shell and the reeds as a means of ascertaining the will of the Heaven and in such other things.

The family is regarded according to this system as a sort of microcosm, the State being the macrocosm. As the Emperor, or the Son of Heaven, has for his duties the maintenance of order in the State and the welfare of the subjects, so also the head of the family has his duties towards the members of the family as well as neighbours. As the members of the family have to obey the head of the family so also the head of the family owes loyalty to the Emperor. The principles enunciated in the Great Law were applicable to both. Confucius laid great emphasis on the duties relating to filial piety and these were the very basis of his political philosophy. The State as well as the family were governed and united by this doctrine. Confucius says: "The law of filial piety is to serve your parents as Heaven. Of all beings man is the noblest. Thanks to his parents he is born as a complete being. He should also die as a complete being if he wants to be a pious son. He should neither mutilate nor stultify his body. Filial piety demands that the son should not go far from his father. Even if he goes his parents should be informed of it. He should go with their consent. So long as the parents are alive they should be consulted in every undertaking. During their lifetime the parents should be served according to the rites. When they are dead they should be buried according to the rites. Then offerings should be made to them according to the rites. They should be obeyed during their lifetime and they should be imitated after their death." Celibacy accordingly was a sin as it interrupted the duties of filial piety. In the larger family, the State, the Emperor was to act as a father to his subjects and the subjects owed to him the same duties of filial piety.

The social and political ideals as set forth in the Hindu law-books, *dharmaśāstras,* bear close resemblance to what was advocated by Confucius and his followers. The relations of the king with his subjects, those of the head of the family with other members and the neighbours, those of the father with the children, etc. are defined almost in an identical language.

TAOISM AND INDIAN THOUGHT

We have seen that according to the ancient Chinese belief it was of the utmost importance for the king and the people to ascertain the intentions of the T'ien (Heaven) and to work according to them for the preservation of the Heavenly order. The intentions of the Heaven were ascertained objectively by divination with tortoise shell and reeds at the time of the sacrifice. This was the traditional method. A subjective approach seems to have been discovered much earlier and it was further developed by a philosopher named Lao-tseu.

Lao-tseu was an elder contemporary of Confucius and lived between 570 and 490 B. C. His personal history is not much known. He was most probably a librarian in the court of the Chou Emperors and it is said that while engaged in the study of the ancient archives there, he discovered his new philosophy. He has himself told us that his philosophy was not his own creation and that it was embedded in the old tradition. His credit was merely to discover it.

The word *Tao* has been differently understood. It is admitted by all that the word cannot be properly rendered into a foreign language. In the old texts it means : 'way',

'way of virtue', 'principles of wisdom', 'the way of perfection', and so forth. *T'ien-tao* meant 'the way of the Heaven'. It thus came to be considered as the unique principle behind the appearance of things. It is both transcendent and immanent. That is the reason for which it lends itself to be realized subjectively. Lao-tseu believed that it could be realized by religiosity, fervour and mystic union with the principle.

Lao-tseu's philosophy is contained in a famous book entitled *Tao-tö-king.* Tao is defined in it as the eternal universal principle. It is said that it cannot be expressed or defined in language and that "if a name has been given to it, it is as a symbol, if not of its unfathomable essence, at least of the way in which it manifests itself on earth." The text further says :

"This principle which is enunciated is not that which always existed. The being that may be named is not that which always existed. Before all times, there was an ineffable and unnamable being. When he was still unnamable he conceived the heaven and the earth. He then became namable and gave birth to all beings. Man's knowledge of the universal principle depends on the state of his mind. The mind which is habitually free from passions knows its mysterious essence. The mind which is habitually full of passion knows only its effects."

The disciples of Lao-tseu while explaining the passage say that before all times there was a being who was self-existent, eternal, infinite, complete and omnipresent. It is impossible to name him and speak of him because human words apply to perceptible beings. But the primordial being was at the beginning, as after, essentially imperceptible to the senses. Before the origin of the world there was nothing beyond him. His essence alone existed at the beginning. This essence possessed two immanent properties—the *yin*, that is the state of concentration and *yang*, that is expansion. Their exteriorization gave birth to the two perceptible forms of the heaven and the earth. The principle thus assumed a name. The state of *yin*, the state of concentration and repose, is the real state of the principle. The state of *yang*, the state of expansion and action or the state of manifestation in perceptible beings, is its condition in time, a condition which is illusory.

To these two conditions of the principle correspond in the mental faculty of man the two states of repose and activity. As long as the mind is productive of ideas it is full of images. It is then moved by passions and recognizes only the effects of the principle. But when the cogitation of the mind stops and the mind becomes void and calm, it then becomes a pure and unstained mirror in which the ineffable and the unnamable essence of the principle reflects itself.

This principle is farther defined in the *Tao-tö-king* as the "true nature". The superior kind of wisdom consists in knowing this true nature of self. It can be attained by imposing one's own will on himself and in mastering his passions. It can be realized by renouncing all forms of conventional knowledge and worldly activities. In the words of Lao-tseu, a true sage "acts without acting, is busy without being busy, tastes without tasting, sees with the same eye the great and the small, much and little." These words of Lao-tseu are capable of only one interpretation. Man ought to realize the universal principle or the true nature of his self. This principle which is identical with the true nature cannot be defined by words, it has to be realized. Realization is possible only when the passions have been mastered, the worldly ideas and images have been removed from the mind and a perfect calm has been attained. The mind goes back to its real nature when it is completely clean and void.

This cannot be attained through conventional knowledge. When it is attained, the mind undergoes a complete change. The man then moves in the world but not as others do. As he is then free from passions, he acts but he is not moved by any of his actions; he looks at others but sees in them only one universal principle. He does not then distinguish this man from that man.

There is a practical side of this mysticism. The method by which the transcendental state can be reached is indicated by Lao-tseu in the following words : "Close your mouth and nostrils and you will run to the end of your days without any decay. To talk too much and to indulge in too many anxieties is to waste yourself and to shorten your life. To concentrate the rays of intelligence on the intelligence and not to allow the mental functions to disturb your body is to cover (or to protect) the body so that it may endure long." This method is set forth much more elaborately by his disciple Chuang-tseu (380-320 B. C.?) in the following words: "One should retire to river banks or solitary places and abstain from doing anything just as those who really love nature and like to enjoy leisure do. To take in breath in a measured way, to evacuate the air contained in the lungs and to refresh it by fresh air lengthens one's life."

There is no doubt a close similarity between this conception of Tao and that of the Upanishadic Brahman. Like Tao, Brahman is also conceived as the unique reality behind the universe. He is eternal, omniscient and omnipresent. He is both transcendent and immanent. He is the cosmic *ātman* while the individual *ātman* or self is one with him. It is not possible to describe this Brahman in language. It is not possible to know him with our senses. It is only by purifying our mind, by *tapas* or by religiosity and fervour that we can realize him. The whole science of *yoga* was evolved as an expedient of this realization. It required complete concentration, expulsion from the mind of all impressions of the exterior world either through breath control or meditation in secluded places. Realization of the Brahman meant the establishment of perfect unity between the cosmic and the individual *ātman*. This could be possible in a mind completely free from the grasp of the objective world. This realization also meant a going back or return to the original principle (*kāraṇa*). Further, in the Yoga texts it is clearly stated that *Prakṛti* or the creative principle has two movements, outward and inward, and when its inward movement reaches completion, liberation is attained. The outward movement leads to the creation of illusory objects which bind down the mind to the objective world. These two movements are similar to the conceptions of the *yin* and the *yang*, the states of concentration and expansion inherent in the Tao.

The analogy can be carried even farther. But what has been said above makes it quite clear that the philosophy of Lao-tseu and the Upanishadic philosophy had some striking similarities. It is impossible to maintain that Tao was a borrowed conception. There is no evidence of any contact between India and China before the 1st century B.C. The ancient Taoism was by then a fully developed philosophy. Besides, we have seen that the conception of Tao was a logical development of some of the old Chinese religious ideas.

The similarity was due to a natural and inevitable development of similar religious ideas of a more distant past. As in China so also in India the old religion gave rise to ritualism (*karma*) on the one hand and philosophy (*jñāna*) on the other. In China the former was developed in the hands of the literati headed by Confucius who upheld the traditional and elaborate sacrifice to the T'ien and the manes, the divination, etc. The latter, the philosophical aspect, was developed by Lao-tseu and his followers. Lao-tseu had probably his predecessors. They advocated a subjective approach for the realization of the divine will. In India too the traditionalism was advocated and developed by the makers of the Law-books (*dharmaśāstras*) while the philosophical approach defined for the first time in the Upanishads was further developed in the various systems of later times.

A SYNTHESIS

The schools of Buddhist philosophy established in China in the T'ang period were not without effect on the Chinese mind. The popularity which some of these schools attained through the Chinese commentators and interpreters was not insignificant. The war that the Confucian literati waged against the Buddhists in the T'ang period is a sufficient proof of this. The Taoists led a different sort of campaign against Buddhism. They performed forgeries to prove that Buddhism was nothing but a form of Taoism transplanted to India and that Buddha was none but a later incarnation of Lao-tseu, the founder of Taoism. The Taoists thereby counted on gaining a higher prestige than Buddhism in the country and on destroying the very foundation of Buddhism in China. The Taoist blackmailing of Buddhism commenced much earlier in a book entitled *Hua hu king* written by a Taoist priest, Wang Fou, in the 4th century. The book was further developed and given wide publicity in the T'ang period when it had to be proscribed by an Imperial decree. The book contains a description of the supposed conversion of the barbarians by Lao-tseu. In one place we are told that Lao-tseu incarnated himself in India as Buddha, the son of Māyā and converted the people of the country to his new doctrine. Buddhism therefore would be the same religion as Taoism which was first promulgated in China by Lao-tseu.

But it is not by blackmailing that Buddhism could be ousted from the Chinese soil. With the rise of a rationalistic school of philosophy it died almost a natural death. This new philosophy assimilated those elements of Buddhism that could be of use in making a new synthesis. Chu-hi who flourished in the 12th century was the greatest exponent of this new system of philosophy. This new movement was started in the 11th century and its pioneers made use of Indian mathematical and cosmological notions that had reached them through Buddhism.

One of the pioneers of the new rationalistic movement, Chou-tseu (A. D. 1017-1073), declared for the first time that the ancient teachers had no sense and that the old cosmological notions that centred round the two principles, the heaven and the earth or the *yin* and the *yang*, were insufficient. According to him it was necessary to suppose the existence of something else beyond these two principles for explaining the origin of the universe. This something was the T'ai-ki or the great principle as suggested by Lao-tseu. Chou-tseu was therefore of the opinion that there is a unity above the duality of the heaven and the earth which is the sole cause of evolution. The highest limit of this evolution is man and it is in man only that matter becomes endowed with intelligence. The intelligence of all human beings again is not equal. There are degrees of intelligence according to the degrees of evolution. The most intelligent men are the wisest like Confucius. Perfection consists in going back to nature as much as possible. In order to do this one should practise laws of morality as enunciated by Confucius such as humanity, propriety, rite, judgement, loyalty, etc.

Another great philosopher of this new school was Shao-tseu (A. D. 1011-1077). He had a greater leaning towards Taoism than his predecessor, but he had also a high regard for Confucius. His philosophy did not differ in its general principles from the philosophy of Chou-tseu. He was of opinion that man along with the Heaven and the Earth is one with all beings at all times. This is because the universal norm is one. The norm of the Heaven and the Earth is shared by all alike. There is only a difference in degree of perfection attained by each individual.

The greatest exponent of the new philosophy was Chu-hi (A. D. 1130-1200). He maintained, contrary to the views of the ancient philosophers, that there is no God, no sovereign, no judge, no providence. The whole universe is composed of two co-eternal principles. These are the *li* and the *k'i*, i.e. the norm and the matter, which though distinct in nature are inseparable from each other. The norm is also called *T'ai-ki*, because it is the directing force and *Wu-ki* because it is an imperceptible, subtle force. It is further described as one, infinite, eternal, immutable, unalterable, homogeneous, fatal, unconscious and unintelligent. It is under the impulsion of this norm that the matter (*k'i*) evolves alternately as *yang* (progression) and *yin* (regression). Let us translate Chu-hi's own words :

At the beginning the heaven and the earth were a mass of matter in the process of evolution rotating like a grindstone. Its rotating movement accelerated more and more ; the heavy portions condensed in the centre formed the earth, while the lighter portions drawn towards the periphery formed the sky, the sun, the moon and the stars which continued to rotate. The earth is in the centre of the universe and not in the bottom as some think it to be. The sky is therefore a whirlpool of matter, extremely rarefied in the regions near the centre, more and more condensed towards the periphery. The last layer is a solid crust, the skeleton of the universe, like the shell of the egg. There are not nine concentric skies as some think—they are nine concentric vaults of the celestial spiral.

The heaven is the azure sky that revolves over our heads. In this azure there is no sovereign of the heaven who governs this world. There is nobody there to count the sins of human beings. On the other hand we should not say that the world is without a master, as the (unconscious and fatal) norm governs it.

The norm is not outside the matter which it moves into action. It does not and cannot exist separately. While the norm remains immobile, it produces the manifestations or the beings in this world. Seen in relation to the central immobile norm these manifestations are not properly speaking successive. They are rather simultaneous like the points on a periphery. These are the translations of the force into action, passage from the non-perceptible to the perceptible and the corresponding reappearances. The multiple parts of the norm of the individuals are one like the shoots of the universal norm and not really separate. The unique norm has as many terminations as individuals. The particular norms are like divisions, loans. It is like the moon which reflects in thousands of water pots although it remains one all the time.

Man is made of the norm and the matter. This matter is twofold, the *p'ai* which is the solid issue of the sperm and the *hun* which is the airy issue of the heaven and the earth. The norm is not substantially united with the matter. It floats on the surface without coagulating with the matter. It is an extension and not a portion of the universal norm. The conjunction of these two makes man and their separation unmakes him. The norm then goes back and the matter is dissociated. The *hun* goes up and loses itself sooner or later in the celestial matter. The *p'ai* goes down and loses itself sooner or later in the terrestrial matter. It is like the fire that is extinguished. The smoke goes up to the sky and disappears. The ashes that remain are soon scattered. To say that soul survives death is a Buddhist error. There is no metempsychosis. Every time that a man is born his elements are derived anew from the two great reservoirs, the norm and the matter.

As it is of man so it is of the fruit which is first green, then ripe, over-ripe and at last decomposed matter. A green fruit can last but a ripe fruit cannot. When a man has lived till the end of his days and dies contented, his matter being over-ripe gets decomposed. Everything is then finished. This is the law of the wise men of old times.

When a man dies before his time, his *p'ai* being too green cannot dissolve so soon. Similarly for those who have much nourished their *hun*, as the monks do by meditation, the *hun* being too strong cannot dissolve too soon. In such cases, the *hun*, the *p'ai*, or both can survive for some time, can gain a prestige, can take revenge and so forth. They may be favourable if offerings are given to them. These offerings prolong their survival but without them they die out.

We should not say that nothing exists of the dead. Something of them survives in their descendants. So long as they have descendants they themselves are not nothing. What is given by them to their descendants survives. The descendants are like slips of the ancestors who are destroyed. They make offerings to express their gratitude for the act of generation by which their ancestors had got the life for them. The act is past, the ancestor is no more but the life and gratitude remain....As it is for the generations of human beings so it is for the waves of the sea. Each wave is complete in itself. The first is not the second, the second is not the third. But they are all modalities of the same water. So also of man. My existence is only a modality of the universal norm and of the matter of the earth and the heaven. My ancestor was also a modality of the same elements. He is no more but the elements remain. I am one with him by the community of the constituents, the norm and the matter.

Chu-hi must have been influenced by Buddhist thought as expounded by the T'ien-t'ai school. As is well known Buddhism believes in universal and eternal causality. This causality is independent of space and time. The chain is infinite, one effect becoming the cause of the other effects and so on. The essence of the universe is eternal and the ephemeral beings are only momentary small waves in the unique permanence. The waves of the ocean neither add nor take away from its water. The same is true of the transitory phenomena. There are two causes, material and efficient. From a unique material cause innumerable efficient causes create innumerable beings that are distinct in appearance. All beings appearing distinct which fill up the world have all been formed of the common material cause, each of them having a special efficient cause. In the world of the living efficient cause is the *karman*. Chu-hi succeeded in making a perfect synthesis of the old philosophical ideas of China and the new ones from India which, conveyed through Buddhism, had proved more attractive and rationalistic to a section of the people.

CHAPTER VIII

CHINA AND INDIA

Cultural relations between India and China seem to have been mostly a one-way traffic. That is why no serious attempt has ever been made to discover any Chinese influence on Indian life and thought. In fact, the impact of Indian cultural influence on China has been so heavy that the possibility of any Chinese influence on India has not occurred to anybody. Besides, from the Han to the Song period the number of Chinese scholars that came to India was much less than the number of Indian scholars that went to China.

It is always difficult to trace the influence of any foreign idea on ancient Indian thought. The ancient texts do not as a rule indicate the provenance of an idea even if it be borrowed. India, faithful to her time-honoured tradition, had no interest in the history of an idea. Her real interest was in the idea itself and in how far it could contribute to the advancement of her own cultural ideals. When an assimilation seemed possible the synthesis became so perfect that no trace of its foreign origin could be discovered.

It is however possible to trace certain Chinese influences on Indian life and thought at the very first sight. In material culture we had borrowed a number of Chinese things since very early times. Trade relations with China were as old as the time of Chang Kien. Chang Kien speaks of these relations by the Burma road and refers to Chinese commodities imported from South-Western China by Indian merchants. Hiuan-tsang, we have already seen, speaks of the introduction of peaches and pears in India from China in the Kushan period. Vermilion, I have suggested, probably came from China. Porcelain industry known in later periods in certain parts of India seems to have been introduced from China. It is well known that some varieties of silk (cīnāṁśuka) came from China. Besides, plantation of tea and *leechee* was also introduced from China in comparatively later times.

What is however more important is the Chinese influence on certain types of literary compositions and mystic cults. Strictly speaking we never developed the tradition of writing history or historical annals in ancient times. There is reference to Itihāsa in old texts but we do not know what sort of composition it really was. In some of the Purāṇas we get the list of ruling dynasties and the names of kings but there is no attempt to record the political events of any particular reign or give a chronological picture of the succession of rulers. It cannot be considered as a historical annal in the real sense of the term. Albiruni states that the Shahi rulers who claimed descent from the ancient Kushans possessed dynastic annals which were written on silk. These annals were preserved in the fort of Nagarkot but were destroyed during the Muslim invasion. These are probably the same records which Hiuan-tsang refers to as ni-lo-pi-t'u (nīlapītaṁ) which contained official annals and State papers. The colour "blue and yellow" evidently speaks of the colour of the silk on which the records were inscribed. It is needless to say that the custom of keeping such records on silk is Chinese. The Kushans had very intimate relations with China and it is quite likely that they introduced the practice of keeping State annals from that country.

Since early medieval times some of the Hindu States in India started appointing official annalists to keep historical records of the reigns of their rulers. This is first noticed in Kashmir and Nepal. The *Rājataraṅgiṇī* and its supplement are systematic annals of the kingdom of Kashmir. The Vaṁśāvalīs of Nepal go back to about the 9th century. The treatment of historical data is more accurate in these Vaṁśāvalīs than in the Kashmir chronicles as they indicate the dates of the reigns and the events occurring during a particular reign. In the East the Ahoms introduced the practice of writing such annals which are called Buranjis. The practice of writing dynastic annals is so new to Indian tradition that one is tempted to attribute it to Chinese influence. In China alone this tradition was developed since very early times. In India it was followed mostly in the outlying kingdoms which were in close contact with China for several centuries.

The Indian Buddhist world used to take real interest in China and the Chinese. The Chinese records tell us that a king named Śrī-Gupta had built a monastery at Bodhgayā for the use of the Chinese monks. We do not know who this Śrī-Gupta was but he might have been connected with the early rulers of the Gupta dynasty. Hiuan-tsang was held in high esteem even long after his departure from India. A story reported by a Japanese Buddhist traveller in India in the 9th century says: "In large number of Buddhist temples in Middle India, Hiuan-tsang was represented in paintings with his hemp shoes, spoon and chop-sticks mounted on multicoloured clouds. The monks paid respect to the image on every fast day."

In the Brahmanical mystic literature, the Tantras, Mahā-cīna ("the Great China") occupies a very important place as being the seat of a special type of mystic cult called Cīnācāra or the practice of China. The object of this cult is a goddess called Mahācīna-tārā. The cult was held to be so important that a great sage like Vasiṣṭha is made to travel to China to get his initiation to this cult. It is said that he got his initiation to this new form of mysticism from Buddha whom he found there practising the cult in the company of women. However mythological the account might appear, it seems to contain some historical truth. Its implication may be better understood from a comparison of later Taoism with certain forms of Indian mysticism.

Attempts to trace the philosophy of Lao-tseu to Indian sources have not achieved any positive result. Historical relations between China and India started much later than the times of Lao-tseu or even the time when the famous Taoist classic *Tao tö king* appeared in its completed form. But the resemblance of Taoism with the ancient Indian philosophy was so striking that the Indian scholars who first went to China could not but be impressed by it. They found something of their own in the Taoist philosophy. The first Buddhist missionaries in China were sheltered in the Taoist temples and got mixed up with the Taoist priests. It is not unlikely that some of these priests on their return to India would make use of their knowledge of Taoism in developing their own philosophy. Kumārajīva who was a follower of Mahāyāna and a great exponent of the philosophy of Nāgārjuna is reported to have written a commentary of the *Tao tö king*. Some of his Chinese disciples made deliberate attempts at a synthesis of the Mādhyamika philosophy of Nāgārjuna and the Taoist philosophy.

In later times, specially in the T'ang period, India seems to have taken some interest in Taoism. Towards the middle of the 7th century, a king of Eastern India (Kāmarūpa, Assam) named Kumāra also called Bhāskaravarman who was a follower of the Brahmanical faith, spoke of his keen interest in Lao-tseu and his philosophy to two Chinese envoys in India—Li Yi-piao and Wang Hiuan-ts'ö. He asked the latter for a portait of Lao-tseu and requested the former to send him a Sanskrit translation of the *Tao tö king*.

The request was communicated by the Chinese envoy to the Emperor and the latter immediately promulgated an edict by which Hiuan-tsang was entrusted with the work of the Sanskrit translation of the text in collaboration with Taoist scholars. The text was discussed and scrutinized during several days. The Taoist teachers were mixing up Buddhist technical terms as found in the Abhidharma and Mādhyamika texts with Taoist terms but Hiuan-tsang was against it. He was of opinion that to use Buddhist terms in translating Taoist terms would lead to a misunderstanding of both the philosophies.

There was some difficulty in translating the word Tao. Hiuan-tsang proposed to translate the word as mo-k'ie—*mārga* "the way"—but the Taoists would translate it as p'u-ti—*bodhi* "illumination". After a long discussion Hiuan-tsang succeeded in convincing his Taoist opponents that a correct translation of the word would be *mārga* "the way". The Sanskrit translation was then completed without further hindrance.

There is however no information as to whether the translation was sent to the Indian king. The translation was completed in 647. Wang Hiuan-ts'ö, we know, led three more missions to India, the first in 647 and the last two in 657 and 664. So occasions were not wanting for presenting the translation to king Bhāskaravarman. There are reasons to believe that the translation reached India and was introduced in the circle of Buddhist mystics who utilized it in their own way to develop a new school.

This school of Buddhism is called Sahajayāna. Whereas some of its tenets can be traced back to the fundamental Mahāyāna philosophy, there are others which seem to be quite exotic. The literature of this school does not seem to be very old. It flourished mostly between the 7th and the 12th centuries and its oldest text the Hevajratantra may go back to the 7th century. The fundamental metaphysical doctrine of the school is called *Sahaja* or "the doctrine of Sahaja". Sahaja literally means "nature" and hence "the true nature" and it is not used in that sense in any other early Indian philosophy. The Sahaja is defined in the standard texts of the school thus: "The whole creation is bound by this Sahaja nature. It is neither positive nor negative. It has the character of emptiness. It cannot be defined in words. It is something to be realized by self." The method of realization involves Yoga—meditation, breathing exercises, postures, etc., and also a number of mystic practices in the company of women.

It is needless to go into a detailed comparison between the Taoist and the Buddhist Sahajayāna practices here. Such a comparison will show a perfect agreement between the ideologies of the two schools. Hiuan-tsang's translation of the word Tao as *mārga* was only a literal translation. It did not convey the metaphysical implications of the word and so a new and more appropriate translation was *Sahaja*. The author of the translation has been forgotten but he was without doubt an Indian Buddhist mystic.

A Vaiṣṇavite sect of Eastern India called *Sahajiyā* is in fact a later development of the Sahajayāna school of Buddhism. It originated most probably in the 11th century. Its adherence to Vaiṣṇavism is only superficial. Its mystic practices have much in common with the Buddhist mysticism of later times. It retains the doctrine of Sahaja, sets forth methods for its realization which are similar to the Buddhist and Taoist methods and uses technical terms which are similar to those used by the later Taoists and the Buddhist mystics.

Later Taoism therefore was known in India and was extensively utilized by the Indian mystics, whether Buddhist, Brahmanical, or Vaiṣṇavite, in developing their doctrines. Both in India and China their practice was confined to secret societies.

APPENDIX III

BIOGRAPHICAL NOTES ON INDIAN SCHOLARS WHO WORKED IN CHINA

[References at the end of each note are to the two volumes of my *Le Canon Bouddhique en Chine*. Each biographical notice has been fully dealt with in that book. These are the names of only those who translated Indian texts into Chinese. We get also hundreds of names of other Indians who went to China as simple missionaries. Those names do not occur in this list.]

AJITASENA—a Buddhist scholar of Northern India mentioned in Chinese sources as *A-che-ta-sien*. He had gone up to Kuchar which was then the seat of the Chinese administration in Central Asia. He translated there three works in the beginning of the 8th century, the translations presented to the Chinese Court in A. D. 732.—II. p. 567.

AMOGHAVAJRA—the name given in Chinese as *A-mu-k'iu-po-chö-lo* but he was commonly known in China under the Chinese name Pu-k'ong. He was born in a Brahmanical family which had gone from Northern India to Ceylon. He was taken to Further India by his uncle when he was only ten years of age. He was converted to Buddhism by Vajrabodhi at the age of 15. He went to China with his teacher. They reached Lo-yang in A. D. 724 and resided in the temple of *Kuang fu sse* where he worked till A. D. 731. He then went back to Ceylon at the request of his teacher to search for Sanskrit texts. He started in 736 and reached Ceylon the next year. He stayed in the Dantavihāra of Ceylon till 746 when he went back to China with the official mission sent by the king of Ceylon to the Chinese court. Since his return he worked in various places in China—Lo-yang, Ho-si, Leang-chou, etc. till his death in A. D. 774. He was a great exponent of the Vajrayāna mysticism. 119 of his translations exist.—II, 568.

ATIGUPTA—in Chinese *A-ti-k'iu-to*, a Buddhist scholar of Central India, reached the Chinese capital in A. D. 652 after travelling by the Central Asian route, stayed in the *Ts'eu ngen sse*, translated between A. D. 653 and 654 one work in the *Hui-je sse* and the *King-hing sse*. He was assisted by two monks of Mahābodhi named Saṅghānandamokṣa and Kāśyapa who were then in China.—II, 499.

ĀDISENA (?)—the name given in Chinese as *A-mi-chen-na*, provisionally restituted as Ādisena. He was also known as Ratnacinta. He was a Buddhist monk of Kashmir, and originally belonged to a royal family of Kṣatriya origin, a specialist in Vinaya. He reached Lo-yang in A. D. 693, was accommodated in *T'ien-koan sse*, translated 7 works from Sanskrit between A. D. 693 and 706. He founded a monastery named *T'ien-chu sse* "the monastery of India". Died in A. D. 721.—II, 522.

BODHIRUCI—*P'u-ti-liu-che*, the name translated in Chinese sometimes as *Tao lie*, sometimes as *Kiao hi*. He was a Buddhist teacher of Northern India, went to China by the Central Asian route reaching Lo-yang in 508. He was appointed head of the Buddhist community of seven hundred monks who knew Sanskrit. The famous monastery of *Yong ning sse* was built in 516. Bodhiruci shifted to that place and worked there till 534. He went to the new capital at Ye where he worked till 536. He translated 39 texts into Chinese.—II, 252.

BODHIRUCI (II)—in Chinese *P'u-ti-liu-che*, also known as Dharmaruci–*T'an-mo-liu-che*. The former is translated into Chinese as *Fa hi* and the latter as *Kio ngai*. He originally belonged to a Brahmin family of South India, was converted to Buddhism by a Mahāyāna teacher named Yaśaghoṣa. He most probably accompanied the official mission sent by the Chālukya king in 692 to China. He reached China in 693 by the sea route. He lived both in the north and the south and was highly honoured by the Emperor. He died in China in 727 at an advanced age. He worked tremendously, translating 53 works among which the Mahāratnakūṭa-sūtra alone consisted of 120 chapters. He had among his assistants a number of Indian scholars then living in China such as the Buddhist monk Canda, the Brahman layman Li-wu-ch'a (Romodana?), Īśvara—a prince of Eastern India, the Buddhist monk Dharma of North India and Prajñāgupta of South India.—II, 540.

BODHISENA—the name given in Chinese as *P'u-t'i-sien*. He had most probably gone from India. He compiled one work in A. D. 824.—II, 628.

BODHIVARDHANA (?)—The name is given in Chinese as *P'u-ti-teng*; *teng* means to "add, increase. . . ." The name may therefore be restored as Bodhivardhana. He came to South China from India most probably by the sea route during the Sui period. He was in Kuang-chou in A. D. 593 and translated one work into Chinese.—II, 462.

BUDDHABHADRA—Chinese *Fo-t'o-po-t'o-lo*; translated as *Kiao hien*. He claimed descent from the Śākya family of Kapilavastu. His family was probably long settled in Nagarahāra. He studied the Buddhist literature in Kashmir. He accompanied Che-yen, who had come to India with Fa-hien, to China and reached South China in the beginning of the 5th century. He stayed most of the time at Nan-king and had been to Lu-shan for some time at the invitation of Hui-yuan. He died in China in A. D. 429. He translated 15 works, the most extensive of which was the *Avataṁsaka-sūtra* in 50 chapters.—I, 341.

BUDDHAJĪVA—in Chinese *Fo-to-she* translated as *Kiao she*. He was a teacher of Vinaya in Kashmir, and a follower of the Mahiśāsaka school. He translated three works of the same school in Chinese between A. D. 423 and 424.—I, 363.

BUDDHAŚĀNTA—in Chinese *Fo-to-shen-to,* translated as *Kiao ting.* He was a Buddhist monk of North India, came to China in 520 and at first resided in the *Po ma sse* at Lo-yang and then in *Kin hua sse* at Ye. He was in China till A. D. 539 and translated 9 works into Chinese.—I, 251.

BUDDHATRĀTA—in Chinese *Fo-to-to-lo* translated as *Kio kiu.* He was a Buddhist monk of Kapiśā, who went to China probably towards the end of the 7th century and resided in the monastery of *Po ma sse* at Lo-yang. He translated one work into Chinese.—II, 512.

BUDDHAPĀLA—in Chinese *Fo-to-p'o-li,* name translated as *Kio hu.* He was a Buddhist monk of Kapiśā. He had heard that Mañjuśrī resided at Wu-t'ai shan in North China and hence he undertook a pilgrimage to that mountain reaching there in A. D. 676. It is said that the Bodhisattva appeared to him. He then came to Lo-yang where he resided in the *Si ming sse* and translated one work into Chinese. This translation was made in A. D. 683. He then went back to Wu-t'ai shan and never returned from that place.—II, 513.

BUDDHAVARMAN—in Chinese *Fou-t'o-po-mo* or *Fo-t'o-po-mo,* the name translated into Chinese as *Kio k'ai.* He originally belonged probably to Kashmir and had specialized in Vibhāṣā. He went to Western China shortly before A. D. 433. He translated the *Mahāvibhāṣā-śāstra* in 60 chapters between A. D. 437 and 439.—I, 223.

BUDDHAYAŚAS—in Chinese *Fo-to-ye-she,* the name translated as *Kio ming.* He originally belonged to a Brahmanical family of Kashmir, converted to Buddhism when he was only 13 years of age. He left the country when he was 27 years of age and travelled in different parts of Central Asia. He at last went to Ch'ang-ngan on an invitation from Kumārajīva. He translated 4 works into Chinese including the *Dīrghāgama* and the *Dharmaguptaka-vinaya* between 410 and 413 A. D. He subsequently returned to Kashmir.—I, 200.

BHAGAVADDHARMA (?)—the name is given in Chinese as *Kia-fan-ta-mo* and translated as *Tsui fa* "Venerable-law". He was a Buddhist monk of Western India. He translated one work into Chinese in the T'ang period.—II, 498.

CHE KI SIANG—this is the Chinese name; it was probably the translation of some Sanskrit name like Jñānaśrī(?). He was a Buddhist monk of Western India and went to China in A. D. 1053 with a number of Sanskrit manuscripts. He translated two texts into Chinese.—II, 607.

CHEN CHE—this is also the Chinese form of the name; it seems to be the translation of some Sanskrit name like Satyajñāna (?). He was an Indian monk who went to China in the Mongol period (1280-1368) and translated one work. —II, 612.

DĀNAPĀLA (?)—the name is given in Chinese as *She hu* "gift protector". He was a Buddhist scholar of Uḍḍiyāna in North India. He went to China in 980 and translated 111 works into Chinese.—II, 597.

DEVAPRAJÑA—he was probably an Indian monk but a native of Khotan. His name is given in Chinese in various ways but it is translated as *T'ien che* "heaven wisdom". He was a follower of the dhyāna or contemplative form of Buddhism. He went to China in A. D. 689 and worked till 691. He translated 7 works into Chinese.—II, 514.

DIVĀKARA—his name is given in Chinese as *Ti-po-ho-lo* and translated as *Je chao* "rising sun". He was a Buddhist monk of Central India and went to China in A. D. 676 and worked till 685. He lived in the monasteries of *T'ai yuan sse* and *Hong fu sse.* He translated 19 texts.—II, 504.

DHARMABODHI—the name is given in Chinese as *T'an-mo-p'u-ti* and translated as *Fa kiao.* He translated one text into Chinese under the Eastern Wei dynasty (534-550) at Ye.—I, 269.

DHARMACANDRA—the name is transliterated into Chinese as *Ta-mo-chan-nie-lo* and translated as *Fa yue* "the law moon". He was a Buddhist monk of Eastern India and most probably passed some time in Nālandā. He first went to Kucī in Central Asia. From there he went to Ch'ang-ngan in 732 and was presented to the court. He stayed in China till 739 and then left China for going back to his own country. He came to Khotan where he fell ill and died in A. D. 743. He translated one text into Chinese.—II, 565.

DHARMADEVA—better known under his two Chinese names *Fa t'ien* and *Fa hien*. He was a Buddhist monk of Nālandā and went to China in 973. He remained in China till his death in 1001 and translated 118 texts into Chinese.—II, 585.

DHARMADHĪ(?) —the name is transliterated into Chinese as *T'an mo che* and translated as *Fa hui* "law wisdom". He went to China between 357 and 384 and translated three texts into Chinese in collaboration with other monks.—I, 154.

DHARMAGUPTA—the name is transliterated into Chinese as *Ta-mo-kiu-to* and translated as *Fa mi* "secret of the law". He was a native of the kingdom of Lāṭa in Western India. He had his education in Kanoj and passed some time in the kingdom of Ṭakka and Kapiśā and then started for China by the Central Asian route. He reached Ch'ang-ngan in A. D. 590. He died in Lo-yang in 619. He translated 10 texts into Chinese.—II, 464.

DHARMAKĀLA—the name transliterated into Chinese as *T'an-ko-kia-lo* and translated as *Fa she* "law time". He originally belonged to a noble family of Central India, adopted Buddhism and specialized in the Abhidharma. He reached Lo-yang in A. D. 222 and remained in China till his death. He died shortly after A. D. 250. He translated one Vinaya work, the Prātimokṣa of Mahāsāṅghika school into Chinese.—I, 73.

DHARMAKṢEMA—the name is transliterated into Chinese as *T'an mo ch'an* or *T'an wu ch'an* and translated as *Fa feng* "law prosperity". He belonged to Central India. He was a follower of Mahāyāna Buddhism and at first went to Kashmir which was then a great seat of Buddhist learning. He then went to China by the Central Asian route reaching Leang-chou in the beginning of the 5th century. He was forced to remain at Ku-tsang which was then the capital of an independent kingdom. He translated 25 texts into Chinese. While attempting to go back to Khotan in 433 without the permission of the local chief he was murdered in the desert.—I, 212.

DHARMAKṚTAYAŚAS—the name transcribed in Chinese as *T'an mo kia-to-ye-sho* and translated as *Fa sheng ch'eng* "law born fame". He was a monk of Central India who went to Nan-king by the sea route reaching there in 481. He worked till 485 and translated one work.—I, 407.

DHARMAMATI—given in Chinese transliteration as *T'an-mo-mo-ti* and in translation as *Fa yi*. On the invitation of Fa-hien he resided in *Wa kuan sse* at Nan-king and translated two texts in A. D. 490.—I, 409.

DHARMAMITRA—the name given in Chinese transliteration as *T'an-mo-mi-to* and in translation as *Fa siu* "law flourishing". He was a Buddhist monk of Kashmir who at first travelled in different places in Central Asia and then went to China in A. D. 424. He went to Nan-king where he resided in the *Che huan sse* (Jetavanavihāra). He subsequently went to North China where he died in 442. While in the south he translated 12 texts into Chinese.—I, 388.

DHARMANANDĪ—the name is given in Chinese transliteration as *T'an-mo-nan-ti* and in translation as *Fa hi* "law joy". He was a monk of the Tukhāra country and probably of Indian origin. He went to Ch'ang-ngan in A. D. 384 and translated 5 texts into Chinese.—I, 157.

DHARMAPRIYA—the name given in Chinese transliteration as *T'an-mo-pi* and in translation as *Fa ngai* "law love". He was at first in Ch'ang-ngan where in 382 he translated one work. He then went to Nan-king where he translated another work in A. D. 400.—I, 156, 340.

DHARMARAKṢA—the name given in Chinese transliteration as *T'an-mo-lo-ch'a.* He is better known by his Chinese name Chu Fa-hu. He was of Indo-Scythian origin and born in Tun-huang. He first travelled in various places in Central Asia, learning the languages and studying the Buddhist literature. He at first translated a number of texts at Tun-huang and then went to Ch'ang-ngan where he worked from A. D. 284 to 313. He translated in all 211 texts.—I, 83.

DHARMARAKṢA(II)—he is known as *Fa-hu* "law protector". He was a Buddhist monk of Magadha and was most probably at Nālandā. He went to China in A. D. 1004 with a number of Sanskrit manuscripts. He died in China in 1058. He translated 12 texts into Chinese.—II, 605.

DHARMARATNA (?)—one of the two first Indian monks to go to China. His name is given as *Chu Fa-lan, Chu* being the indicative of his Indian origin. The name has been provisionally restored as Dharmaratna. He reached Lo-yang probably in A. D. 67 and translated 6 texts in collaboration with his compatriot, Kāśyapa Mātaṅga. He died at Lo-yang.—I, 3.

DHARMARATNA (?)—the name is given in transliteration as *T'an-wu-lan* and in translation as *Fa-cheng* "law correct". He translated 110 texts in the period A. D. 381-395. Only 29 of these works remain.—I, 322.

DHARMARUCI—the name is given in transliteration as *T'an-wu-liu-che* and in translation as *Fa hi* and *Fa lo* "law joy, liking". He was a Buddhist monk of South India. He reached Lo-yang in the beginning of the 6th century and translated three works between A. D. 501 and 507.—I, 246.

DHARMASENA—nothing is known about him excepting that he translated one work in the T'ang period.—II, 628.

DHARMAYAŚAS—the name is given in transliteration as *T'an-mo-ye-she* and in translation as *Fa ming* or *Fa-ch'eng* "law glory". He was a Buddhist monk of Kashmir and a disciple of Puṇyatrāta who had also gone to China. Dharmayaśas went to China in the period 397-401. He was in Ch'ang-ngan from 405 to 414 when he translated three works into Chinese. He went back probably to Kashmir after A. D. 424.—I, 174.

DHYĀNABHADRA—his name is given in Chinese translation as *Che k'ong*. He was a Buddhist monk of Central India and went first to China. From China he went to Corea in 1326 and died there in 1363 (?). He translated two works.—II, 637.

GAUTAMA DHARMAJÑĀNA—the name is given in transliteration as *Kiu-t'an Ta-mo-shö-na* and in translation as *Fa che* "law intelligence". He was the son of Gautama Prajñāruci who also had gone to China and translated Buddhist texts between A. D. 538 and 543. It is not known exactly when he had gone to China. He is said to have acted as a provincial governor under the Chou rulers between A. D. 557 and 581. He was well treated by the Sui emperor when the latter rose to power in 581. He then translated one work into Chinese in A. D. 582.—II, 439.

GAUTAMA PRAJÑĀRUCI—the name is given in transcription as *Kiu-t'an Pan-jo-liu-che* and in translation as *Che-hi* "law joy". He was a Brahmin of Benares converted to Buddhism. He reached Lo-yang in 516. He worked till 543 and translated 20 works into Chinese. He was the father of the former, Gautama Dharmajñāna who had probably accompanied his father to China.—I, 261.

GAUTAMA SANGHADEVA—his name is given in Chinese transliteration as *Kiu-t'an Seng-kia-ti-po* and in translation as *Chong t'ien* "community god". He was a Buddhist monk of Kashmir and a great scholar of Abhidharma. He went to China reaching Ch'ang-ngan about 384. He remained in the North till 391; then he went to South China. He first went to Lu-shan and reached Nanking in 397. He translated 8 works into Chinese.—I, 161 and 335.

GĪTAMITRA—his name is given in transcription as *Ki-to-mi* and in translation as *Ko yu* "music friend". He was in China between A. D. 397 an 418 and translated 25 works into Chinese.—I, 349.

GUṆAVARMAN—the name is given in Chinese transliteration as *K'iu-na-pa-mo* and in translation as *Kong tö k'ai* "merit armour". He originally belonged to the royal family of Kashmir. After adopting Buddhism he first went to Ceylon and then to Java. He was then induced by the Chinese monks to proceed to China. In A. D. 431 he reached Nanking where he resided in the *Che huan sse* (Jetavanavihāra). He died there the same year at the age of 65. He translated 11 works.—I, 370.

GUṆAVṚDDHI—the name is given in transcription as *K'iu-na-pi-ti* and in translation as *Ngan sin* or *Tö sin* "merit increase". He was a Buddhist monk of Central India. He went to China in 479 and settled in Nan-king where he died in A. D. 502. He translated 3 works between 479 and 492. —I, 410.

GUṆABHADRA—the name is given in Chinese transliteration as *Kiu-no-po-to-lo* and in translation as *Kong tö hien* "merit good". He was a Buddhist monk of Central India and had specialized in Abhidharma. He first went to Ceylon and thence proceeded to China by the sea route reaching Canton in A. D. 435. He remained at Nan-king till his death in 468 and translated 76 texts into Chinese.—I, 378.

GUṆASATYA (?)—The name is given in Chinese translation as *Kong tö che* "merit sincere". He went to

China in the period A. D. 454-465. He translated two works in 462.—I, 398.

GUPTA—his name is given in Chinese transliteration as *K'iu-to*. Nothing precisely is known about him. He went to China in the T'ang period and translated one work shortly before A. D. 865.—II, 632.

ĪŚVARA—his name is given in Chinese transcription as *Yi-ye-po-lo* and in translation as *Tseu tsai* "self existing". He went to China in 426 and compiled one work in Chinese. —I, 370.

JINAGUPTA—he was a Buddhist monk of the kingdom of K'ien-t'o-lo (Gandhāra). He originally belonged to a noble family and then adopted Buddhism. He went to China in A. D. 557 by the Central Asian route. He reached Ch'ang-ngan in 559 where he worked till 572 and translated 4 works into Chinese. He was then compelled to leave China on account of political troubles and go to Central Asia. There he lived amongst the Turks till 582. On the establishment of political order in China he went back to Ch'ang-ngan where he worked till his death in 605 or a little later. This time he translated 39 texts.—I, 276; II, 446.

JINAYAŚAS—his name is given in Chinese transcription as *Shö-na-ye-she* and in translation as *Sheng ming*. He was a Buddhist monk of Magadha who went to China towards the middle of the 6th century. He translated 6 texts between A. D. 564 and 572.—I, 274.

JÑĀNABHADRA—the name is given in transcription as *Jang-na-p'o-t'o-lo* and in translation as *Che hien*. He was a Buddhist monk of Padma (?) country in India. He went to China in the middle of the 6th century and lived in the *P'o kia sse* at Ch'ang-ngan. He translated one work in A. D. 558.—I, 273.

JÑĀNABHADRA (II)—the name is given in transcription as *Jo-na-p'o-to-lo* and in translation as *Che hien*. He was a Buddhist monk of Ho-ling (Java) and probably of Indian origin. He did not go to China but translated one text for a Chinese pilgrim in A. D. 664. The translation was taken to China.—II, 503.

KĀLAYAŚAS—the name is given in transcription as *Kiang-liang-ye-she* and in translation as *She-ch'eng.* He was a specialist in Abhidharma. He went to China in A. D. 424 and translated two works into Chinese. He died in China shortly after A. D. 444 at the age of 60.—I, 391.

KĀLARUCI—the name is given in transcription as *Kiang-liang-liu-che* and in translation as *Chen hi.* He translated one work into Chinese in A. D. 281.—I, 114.

KĀLODAKA—the name is given in transcription as *Kia-liu-to-kia* and in translation as *She shui.* He translated one work in A. D. 392.—I, 334.

KĀŚYAPA MĀTAṄGA—he was one of the two Buddhist monks who went to China in A. D. 65. The other was Dharmaratna. He translated five works in collaboration with the latter.—I, 3.

KEKAYA (?)—the name is given in transcription as *Ki-ki-ye* and in translation as *Ho she.* He translated 5 works in 472 at Pei t'ai, the capital of the Wei in Shan-si.—I, 244.

KIN TSONG-CHE—an Indian monk whose Indian name is not known. It was probably Suvarṇadhara (?). He translated two works into Chinese in A. D. 1113.—II, 608.

KUMĀRABODHI—the name is given in transcription as *Ku-mo-lo-fo-ti* and in translation as *T'ong-kio.* He was the Rājaguru of the king of Turfan and went to China in A. D. 382. He translated one work into Chinese.—I, 156.

KUMĀRAJĪVA—born of Indian father and Kuchean mother; educated in Kashmir; a scholar of great reputation in Central Asia and China. He reached Ch'ang-ngan in A. D. 401 and worked there till 412. He died in China most probably in 413. He translated 106 works into Chinese.—I, 178.

LI-WU-CH'AN—he was a Brahmin of Lampāka in North India. The Indian form of the name was probably Romodana. He went to China in A. D. 700 or a little earlier. He translated one work into Chinese the same year.—II, 521.

LIU-YEN—The Indian form of his name is not known. It was probably Vinayātapa (?). He was an Indian who had gone to China probably in the second quarter of the 3rd century. He translated 4 works into Chinese in A. D. 230. —I, 302.

LOKAKṢEMA—an Indo-Scythian monk. His name is given in transcription as *Lu-kia-ch'an.* He went to Lo-yang shortly after A. D. 148. He translated 23 works into Chinese in the 3rd quarter of the 2nd century A. D.—I, 38.

MAHĀYĀNA—the name is given in Chinese translation as *Ta-sheng.* He translated 2 works between A. D. 483 and 493.—I, 407.

MANDRASENA—the name is given in Chinese transcription as *Man-to-lo-sien* and in translation as *Jo-sheng.* He went to China in A. D. 503 and translated 3 works into Chinese.—I, 414.

MITRAŚAMA (?)—the name is given in transcription as *Mi-to-shan* and in translation as *Tsi yu* "quiet friend". He translated one work into Chinese in A. D. 705.—II, 521.

MAITREYABHADRA—the name is given in Chinese translation as *Ts'eu hien.* He was a Buddhist monk of Magadha. He was the Rājaguru of an Emperor of the K'i-tan dynasty (A. D. 911-1125). He translated 5 works into Chinese probably towards the end of the 11th century.—II, 608.

MOKṢALA—his name is given in transcription as *Wu-cha-lo.* He was probably an Indian monk who went from Khotan to China towards the end of the 3rd century. He translated one work in A.D. 291.—I, 119.

NANDĪ—his name is given in Chinese transcription as *Nan-ti* and in translation as *Hi* "joy". He was a Buddhist layman who had gone to China and translated 3 works into Chinese in A. D. 419.—I, 352.

NANDĪ (II)—his name is given in Chinese translation as *Fu sheng* "joy produce". He had another name *Pu-ju-wu-ta-ye* (Puṇyamodaya). He was a Buddhist monk of Central India. He left the country at an early age, went first to Tokharestan and then to Ceylon. He went to China by the sea route and reached the capital in 655 with a large collection of Sanskrit MSS. He went to the South Sea Islands in 656 at the Imperial order to collect medicinal herbs. He returned to China in 663 when he translated 3 works into Chinese.—II, 500.

NARENDRAYAŚAS—his name is given in Chinese transcription as *Na-lien-t'o-li-ye-she* and in translation as *Tsun ch'eng*. He was a Buddhist monk of Uḍḍiyāna in North India. After leaving India he travelled in different places in Central Asia and at last went to China in 556. He translated 7 works between 556 and 568 and 8 works between 582 and 585. He died in China in A. D. 589.—I, 270 and II, 442.

NĀRĀYAṆA—his name is given in transcription as *Jo-lo-yen*. He translated one work into Chinese at Ch'ang-ngan under the Western Ts'in dynasty (265-316).—I, 148 .

PARĀMITI (?)—the name is given in Chinese transcription as *Pan-la-mi-ti* and in translation as *Ki leang* "extreme measure". He went to China by the sea route reaching Canton in A. D. 705. The same year he translated one work into Chinese. He was assisted by Meghaśikha, a Buddhist monk of Uḍḍiyāna who was then in China.—II, 551.

PARAMĀRTHA—the name is given in Chinese transcription as *Po-lo-mo-t'o* and in translation as *Chen ti*. He had another name, Guṇaratna. He was a Buddhist monk of Ujjayinī. He travelled by the sea route reaching China in 546. He went to Nan-king in A. D. 548. He translated 70 works into Chinese. He tried to go back to India in 563 but in vain. He died in China in 569 at the age of 71.—I, 418.

PRABHĀKARAMITRA—the name is given in Chinese transcription as *Po-lo-p'o-kia-lo-mi-to-lo* and in translation as *Kuang che.* He was born in a noble family of Central India and converted to Buddhism at an early age. He was educated at Nālandā and later on became a teacher of great repute in that institution. Subsequently he left the country with a number of disciples to carry the message of Buddha to the foreign lands. He went to Tibet (?) and Central Asia. He reached Ch'ang-ngan in 627. He translated 3 texts into Chinese. He died in China in 633 at the age of 69. —II, 468.

PRĀJÑA—the name is given in transcription as *Pan-jo* and in translation as *Che hui.* He was a Buddhist monk of Kapiśā who was educated in the Buddhist lore in Kashmir. He passed some time also at Nālandā. He went to China by the sea route reaching there in 781. He then went to the north and settled down at Ch'ang-ngan in 810. He translated 8 works into Chinese.—II, 582.

PRAJÑĀBALA—the name is given partly in transcription and partly in translation as *Pan-jo-li.* He was a Buddhist monk of Kashmir. He translated one work probably in the T'ang period.—II, 628.

PRAJÑĀCAKRA—the name is given in transcription as *Pan-jo-chö-kie-lo* and in translation as *Che hui lun.* He translated 4 works between A. D. 847 and 860.—II, 629.

PRAGUṆAVIŚVĀSA(?)—the name is given in transcription as *Po-lo-kiu-na-mi-shö-sha.* He was a Buddhist monk of the Vajrāsana at Bodhgayā. He compiled one work in Chinese.—II, 629.

PI-TI-MO-TO—the original form of his name is not known. He translated one work under the Ts'in (A.D. 384-417).

PUṆYATRĀTA—his name is given in transcription as

Fo-jo-to-lo and in translation as *Kong tö hua*. He was a Buddhist scholar of Kashmir. He went to China in the beginning of the 5th century and translated one work in A. D. 404 in collaboration with Kumārajīva.—I, 176.

RATNAMATI—the name is given in transcription as *Lö-na-mo-ti* and in translation as *Pao yi*. He went to Lo-yang in A. D. 508 and translated 8 works in collaboration with Bodhiruci and Buddhaśānta.—I, 248.

SANGHABHADRA–the name is given in transcription as *Seng-kia-po-to-lo* and in translation as *Chong-hien*. He was a specialist in Vinaya. He went to China by the sea route and translated one work into Chinese in A.D. 488.—I, 408.

SANGHABHARA—the name is given in transcription as *Seng-kia-p'o-lo* and in translation as *Seng-yang*. He was a Buddhist monk of the Hindu kingdom of Fu-nan (Kambuja) and a specialist in Abhidharma. He went to China in the beginning of the 6th century and translated 11 works. He died in China in A. D. 524 at the age of 65.—I, 415.

SANGHAGHŪTI—the name is given in transcription as *Seng-kia-po-ch'eng* and in translation as *Chong-hien*. He was a Buddhist scholar of Kashmir who went to China in A. D. 381 and translated 3 works into Chinese in 383.—I, 160.

SANGHAVARMAN—the name is given in transcription as *Seng-kia-po-mo* and in translation as *Chong-k'ai*. He was an Indian monk who went to China in A.D. 433. He translated five works between 433 and 435.—I, 375.

SVARA (?)—the name is given in transcription as *Su-fo-lo*. He translated one work in the T'ang period.—II, 632.

ŚUBHĀKARASIMHA—the name is given in transcription as *Shu-p'o-kie-lo-seng-ho* and in translation as *Shen wu wei*. He was a Buddhist monk of the Śākya family. He reached Ch'ang-ngan in 716 by the Central Asian route. He translated 5 works between 716 and 724. He remained in China till his death in 740 at the age of 99.—II, 562.

SUBHŪTI—the name is given in transcription as *Siu-p'u-ti* and in translation as *Shen-kien.* He translated one work in the period A. D. 557-559.—I, 431.

SŪRYAKĪRTI—the name is given in translation as *Je-ch'eng.* He translated 7 works in the Song period.—II, 609.

SUVARṆAKŪṬA (?)—the name is given in Chinese as *Kin-kiu-ch'a.* He translated one work in the T'ang period. —II, 631.

T'AN-YAO—his original name is not known. He was probably of Indian origin and went to the capital of the Wei in Shan-si where he translated 3 works and directed the work of the Buddhist temples at Ta-t'ong fu between 460 and 465.—I, 242.

T'IEN-SI-TSAI—the original name is not known. He was a Buddhist monk of Kashmir who went to China in 980. He died in China in A.D. 999. He translated 18 works.—II, 595.

UPAŚŪNYA—the name is given in transcription as *Yue-p'o-shö-na.* He was a Buddhist monk of Ujjayinī who went to North China in A. D. 538-539. He went to Khotan on an Imperial mission in 548. He went to the south in 565. In both the capitals of China he translated in all 6 works.—I, 265, 431.

VAJRABODHI—the name is given in transcription as *P'o-je-lo-p'u-ti* and in translation as *King kang che.* He was at first the preceptor of the king of Kañchī. He was educated at Nālandā. He first went to Ceylon and then to China in 710. He was in China till his death in 732. He won a great reputation in China by preaching a mystic form of Buddhism. He translated 11 works.—II, 554.

VIGHNA — the name is given in translation as *Chang nei* "obstacle" and in transcription as *Wei-ki-nan.* He reached the Chinese capital in A. D. 224. He translated two works into Chinese.—I, 300.

VIMALĀKṢA—a Buddhist monk of Kashmir. His name is given in transcription as *Pi-mo-lo-ch'a* and in translation as *Wu ke yen.* He travelled by the Central Asian route and went to China in the beginning of the 5th century. He was a great collaborator of Kumārajīva. After the death of the latter he went to the south where he died. He translated two works into Chinese.—I, 338.

VIMOKṢASENA—the name is given in transcription as *Pi-mu-ch'e sien.* He belonged to the Śākya race and was the son of the king of Uḍḍiyāna. He went to China with Gautama Prajñāruci and translated one work in 541.—I, 267.

VINĪTARUCI—the name is given in transcription as *Pi-ni-to-liu-che* and in translation as *Mie hi.* He was a Buddhist monk of Uḍḍiyāna. He reached the Chinese capital in A. D. 582 and translated 2 works into Chinese.—II, 441.

YAŚOGUPTA—the name is given in transcription as *Ye-shekiu-to* and in translation as *Ch'eng tsang.* He was most likely an Indian monk who went to China in the period A. D. 561-578. He was a collaborator of Jinayaśas. He translated 3 works into Chinese.—I, 275.

BIBLIOGRAPHY

(*Mention is made only of the principal books and articles that have been consulted.*)

Bagchi P. C.—Le Canon Bouddhique en Chine, les traducteurs et les traductions; Tomes I, II.

Bagchi P. C.—India and China, *Bulletin of the Greater India Society*, 1926.

Beal—Life of Hiuan tsang by Hwui li.

Couvreur—Chou king, texte Chinois avec traduction.

Coomaraswamy A.—History of Indian and Indonesian Art.

Chavannes E.—Les Religieux éminents qui allèrent chercher la loi dans les pays d'occident.

Chavannes E.—Le voyage de Song-yun dans l'Udyāna et le Gandhāra, *B.E.F.E.O.*, 1903.

Chavannes E.—Les voyageurs chinois, *Guide Madrolle*, Chine du Sud.

Chavannes E.—Les Inscriptions Chinoises de Bodhgayā, *Revue de l'Histoire des Religions*, 1896.

Chavannes & Lévi—L'itinéraire d'Ou-k'ong, *J. As.*, 1895;

Chavannes & Pelliot—Un traité manichéen retrouvé en Chine, *J. As.*, 1913.

Demiéville—Sur les éditions imprimées des canons chinois. *B.E.F.E.O.*, 1924.

Ecke & Demiéville—The Twin Pagodas of Zayton.

Edkins—Chinese Buddhism.

Fujishima—Le Bouddhisme Japonais, l'histoire des XII sectes bouddhiques.

Grousset R.—Histoire de l'Extrême-Orient; vols. I, II.

Hackin J.—Guide-Catalogue du Musée Guimet, les Collections Bouddhiques.

Legge—Travels of Fa-hien.

Lévi S.—Les missions de Wang Hiuan-ts'e dans l'Inde, *J. As.*, 1900.

Lévi S.—Le Tokharien B., langue de Koutcha, *J. As.*, 1913.
Nanjio B.—A Catalogue of the Chinese translation of the Buddhist Tripiṭaka.
Pelliot P.—Deux itinéraires de Chine en Inde, *B.E.F.E.O.*, 1904.
Pelliot P.—Trois ans dans la Haute Asie, *Asie Française*, 1910.
Pelliot P.—Mou-tseu ou les doutes levés, *T'oung Pao* XIX.
Pelliot P.—Autour d'une traduction Sanscrite du Tao-tö-king, *T'oung Pao* XI, (1912).
Pelliot P.—Influences Iraniennes en Asie Centrale et en Extrême-Orient, *Rev. Hist. des Religions*, 1912.
Pelliot P.—Quelques Artistes des Six Dynasties et des T'ang, *T'oung Pao*, 1923.
Pelliot P.—Une bibliothèque mediévale retrouvée au Kansou, *B.E.F.E.O.*, 1908.
Stein, Sir Aurel—Innermost Asia as a Factor in History—*The Geographical Journal*, May-June, 1925.
Takakusu—Records of the Buddhist Religion (account of Yi-tsing).
Waley A.—The Book of Songs (translations from She king).
Wieger—Textes Historiques : Tomes I, II.
Wieger—Les Pères du système Taoiste.
Wieger—Histoire des Croyances religieuses et des opinions philosophiques en Chine.
Watters—On Yuan Chwang, 2 vols.

INDEX

Abhidharma, 36, 201.
Abhidharmakosa, of Vasubandhu, 113, 143.
Abhidharmakosa-vyakhya, 83f. n.
Abhidharmapitaka, of the Hinayana School, 134f.
Afghanistan, 3.
Agnidesa (Karasahr), Buddhism in, 15, 48, 62.
Ahoms, 199.
Ajanta, 161.
Ajatasatru, 161.
Albiruni, 11, 198.
Alexander, the result of the campaigns of, 1.
Amitabha, 99, 101, 161.
Amitayus-sutra, the, 139.
Amoghavajra, 53-4, 115, 144, 171.
Amrtodana, uncle of Buddha, 44, 52.
Ananda, 159.
Ancestor-worship, in China, 182f; in India, 183-4.
A-ni-ko, an Indian artist, 162.
Annam, ancient kingdom of, 22.
Architecture, influence of Indian on Chinese, 164.
Art, Buddhist, during the Wei dynasty of China, 96, 160; during the Gupta period, 147f.; importance of, 148-9; at Bamiyan, 149; at Ajanta, 149-150; at Khotan, 150; influence of Ajanta at Karasahr, 153; migration of, to China, 146-7; Indo-Greek, 146-7; Mathura School of, 147; centres of ancient, 155; in Turfan, 154; during the T'ang period in China, 160.
Asanga, a Buddhist philosopher, 102, 136; author of *Sastra* works, 142; founder of the Yogacara school of philosophy, 143.
Asoka, efforts of to spread Buddhism, 1-2; his son Kunala, 13.
Assam, 16, 17.
Astronomy, 167-171.
Asvaghosa, a Mahayana teacher, 142.
Avalokitesvara, 101.
Avatamsaka, the, 140.
Ayodhya, 42.

Bactria, Bactriana, 2, 3, 11, 12, 15.
Bairo, a type of music, 168.
Balhika, 11 (see Bactria).
Bamiyan, importance of the position of for the spread of Buddhism, 10, 45.
Bandhudatta, a Buddhist philosopher, 33.
Barmak, 11 f.n.
Barygaza, 25.
Bhairava, an Indian raga, 168-9.
Bharata, an authority on Indian music, 168.
Bharukaccha (Broach), 25.
Bhaskaravarman, King of Kamarupa, 17-18, 70.
Bimbisara, 161.
Bodhi, an Indian musician in Japan, 168.
Bodhidharma, spread of Mahayana Buddhism by, 103f.
Bodhiruci, 51-2, 98, 139.
Bodhisattva, 8; name of a type of music, 168.
Bodhisattva-carya-nirdesa, 137.
Bodhisattva-pratimoksa, 138.
Bodhisattvas, 101.
Bodhisattvayana, 101.
Brahma, a Buddhist monk, 51.
Brahmajalasutra, the, of Kumarajiva, 138.
Brhaddesi, the, a work on music, 168.

Kublai, 116; recognition given to Buddhism by, 118; religious conference held by, 118, 125, 162.
Kuci, its history and importance, 14, 15; its role in the spread of Buddhism, 32-3; relations between and Kashmir, 37-8, 40, 42, 47, 48.
Kui-ki, a disciple of Hiuan-tsang, 112.
Kui-pao, a Buddhist monk, 86.
Kumara, King of Kamarupa, 200, 201. See also under Bhaskaravarman.
Kumara, an astronomical school, 169.
Kumarabodhi, an Indian painter, 156.
Kumarajiva, a Kuchean Buddhist, 33; efforts of to spread Buddhism in China, 34, 35, 37, 38, 44, 45, 98, 100, 103; his literary abilities, 121; his translation of the *Vinaya-pitaka*, 130, 136, 138; his translation of the *Mahaprajnaparamita-sutra*, 141; the *Dasabhumi-vibhasa-sastra*, 142; the *Sutralamkara-sastra*, 142; his commentary on the Taoist work *Tao to king*, 200.
Kumarayana, 33.
Kunala, son of Asoka, 13.
Kunming (Yunnanfu), 17.
Kushans, invasion of India by the, 3; extent of the empire of, 3; role of the, in the spread of Indian culture, 4; spread of Buddhism under the, 9; their conquest of Chinese territory, 58, 198.
Lankavatara-sutra, the, 141.
Lao-tseu, 185-6.
Leang-chou, 34.
Lin-kia, 122.
Liu Ngan, Prince, 7. (See Huai-nan-tseu.)
Li Yi-piao, a Chinese ambassador in Harsha's court, 74, 200.
Lo, a Chinese astronomer, 169.
Long-men, a centre of Buddhist art, 155, 156, 158, 160.
Lo-yang, 48, 53, 60.
Lu-shan, 36, 45, 99.

Macedonia, spread of Buddhism to, 2.
Madhyadesa, 41.
Madhyamika, a Mahayana school of Buddhism, 102, 142, 200, 201.
Madhyantanugama-sastra, the translation of by Gautama Prajnaruci, 143.
Madhyanta-vibhanga-sastra, the translation of by Hiuan-tsang, 143.
Mahabharata, reference to China in the, 7.
Mahacina-tara, a goddess, 199.
Mahakausthila, 134.
Mahamaudgalyayana, 134.
Mahaparinirvana-sutra, the, of the Hinayana School, 140; translation of by Dharmaksema, 140.
Mahaprajnaparamita-sutra, the, 53; translation of by Hiuan-tsang, 139: of Nagarjuna, 141.
Mahasanghika, 129.
Mahasanghika-vinaya, the translation of Fa-hien, 62.
Mahasannipata, 140.
Mahavaipulya-mahasannipata-sutra, the translation of by Dharmaksema, 140.
Mahavanavihara, a Buddhist monastery, 46.
Mahayana, 42, 84, 85; development of in India, 101, 108; literature pertaining to, 137f.; *Sutrapitaka* of the, 138; miscellaneous collection of *sutras* pertaining to, 141; importance of the Chinese translations for the study of, 141.
Mahayana-deva, name of Hiuan-tsang, 80.